A HISTORY OF SOCIAL THOUGHT

A HISTORY OF SOCIAL THOUGHT

BY

EMORY S. BOGARDUS

GYAN

ISBN : 978-81-212-1766-8(HB)

First Published, 1922

Published, 2018

Published by

Gyan Publishing House
5, Ansari Road
Daryaganj, New Delhi-110002
Phone: 011-47034999, 9811692060
www.gyanbooks.com
E-mail: books@gyanbooks.com

Printed at: G. Print Process, Delhi.

DEDICATED TO MY STUDENTS
WHO ARE TRANSFORMING THEIR SOCIAL THOUGHT
INTO HELPFUL LIVING

CONTENTS

PREFACE

This book is written for the world of students. In it any seriously-minded person should find a fundamental background for understanding the central theme of human progress, a substantial basis for attacking the most important problems of the day, and a call to renew his faith in the soundness of human aspirations.

Inasmuch as this treatise is written for students, it is not intended to be the last word on the subject, but simply a first word. The theme of each chapter is in itself a subject for further investigation. In fact, the student with an alert mind will find in each chapter many subjects concerning which he will want to learn more. If the discussions in this book stimulate the student to make inquiries on his own initiative, they will have accomplished more than the author could have expected.

EMORY S. BOGARDUS.

University of Southern California.
June 1, 1921.

A HISTORY OF SOCIAL THOUGHT

CHAPTER I

THE NATURE OF SOCIAL THOUGHT

Man faces a world of social problems. As a result he is perplexed beyond description; his thinking often ends in confusion. Inasmuch as the average citizen, for the first time in the world's history, is beginning to attack social problems, he is entitled to all the aid that can be made available. Upon the success of the average person in mastering the intricacies of social thinking, the cause of democracy depends.

A large proportion of the analyses of social questions has been academic. These discussions have often terminated in quibbles or erudite generalizations. Insofar as social theories have been correct they have unfortunately been reserved for the theorists alone. The people themselves have not understood the nature of social thought; they have not benefited; and hence, they have held social thought in contempt. Sound social thought needs to be democratized, that is, to be made available for all people.

In thinking about social problems, the so-called practical person has proceeded in his own way. He has had personal experience—and that to him has been sufficient. He has been motivated by a sense of injustice, and stung into fervid thought by circumstances which seemed to him unfair; he has concocted a make-shift remedy, or impulsively accepted a ready-made program. Perhaps he has urged a single cause for all social ills and prescribed a single remedy for all social diseases. Usually, he has been very limited in his observations, untrained in making proper inductions, and hence, narrow and intolerant in his conclusions. He has been entirely baffled, or else he has felt cock-sure.

The practicalist is often a poor theorist. He may be even the most dangerous type of theorist. He has scoffed at theory and then fallen into the pit of incorrect theory. He has failed to see, for example, that a good bridge does not project itself across a chasm, but that a correct bridge-building theory is essential. With social practicalists and theorists calling each other names, instead of cooperating and unselfishly giving the world of people the benefit of their combined points of view, the world has floundered and its social problems have piled up, mountains high.

Another difficulty in the pathway of sound social thinking is found in an absence of proper backgrounds. People are prone to offer solutions for social questions without first equipping themselves with a knowledge of foundational elements. Moreover, they are often unwilling to acquaint themselves with these necessary factors. It is only by accident, however, that current social movements can be understood unless the historical sequences of social cause and effect are perceived. Nearly all social problems are essentially the outcroppings of tendencies which have had a long human history. A current social maladjustment is generally indicative of a long line of antecedent factors. A knowledge of societary fundamentals is essential to sound thinking about present-day evils. A history of social thought furnishes a minimum social background for the understanding of current social processes and problems.

Social thought, as distinguished from individual thought, treats of the welfare of one's associates and of groups. It may be very simple, merely observational, the result of daily experience, or it may be a scientific study of social processes. Sociology as an organized science has developed only during the past few decades. Inasmuch as sociology has simply begun its work of formulating the principles of societary progress, a large proportion of the thinking that has thus far been done in human history about the welfare of *socii* or associates is either individual or social, rather than sociological. A history of social thought, therefore, includes the larger social field as well as the more specific one of recent development, namely, the sociological. The time is hardly ripe for a history of distinctly sociological thought.

Social thought, as here used, is a synthesis of the observations of individuals about the welfare of other individuals, considered as individuals or as groups. The focus of social thought is not the welfare of the ego but of the alter, not of the self but of others, not of the individual but of the class, group, organization, or process. Social thought draws from the thought-life of persons who have done unselfish thinking and who have focalized their attention upon the nature and principles of associative activities. It tests group progress by the degree in which human personalities secure constructive, co-operative expression. It measures the individual in his relationships to the social whole, whether that unit be the family, school, church, state, or the world society. It rates the individual in terms of a functioning unit in group life. It evaluates the group both in regard to the quality of the personalities which it produces in its membership, and to the loyalty which it manifests as a unit of a larger group, even of human society itself.

Social thought is both concrete and abstract. Concrete thinking rarely goes deep. It asks few questions, raises few doubts, and perceives few connections. Abstract thinking seeks causal explanations, classifies concretenesses, penetrates relationships, and proposes well-balanced procedures, The distinction, however, is largely one of degree. Concrete thinking is characteristic of every normal person, but abstract perceptions are uncommon. The ability to do abstract thinking, to get at the deeper meanings of phenomena, to penetrate the mysteries of life, is rare. Concrete thinking constitutes the major sector of the thought-life of every person, nearly all the time.

Here and there, however, in human history we find individuals who have been freed or who have freed themselves from the daily struggle for a living, from the race to make money, or from the selfish enticements of life-long loafing, and have joined the world of scholars, seeking to know the truth, the truth which makes men and women free—free to develop useful personalities in a vast, changing complex of human living. When man, having leisure to think abstractly, has set himself to the task of thought research, his mind has ventured along at least five pathways.

(1) Man has given considerable attention to his relation to the universe. Primitive man conceived of a personal universe, peopled with spirits. Throughout human history man has been a religious being, trying to solve the problems of a universe ruled by spirits and gods or by one supreme God. This type of thought has produced polytheisms, monotheisms, theocracies. It has formulated theological creeds and led to bitter eccle-

siastical controversies. It has created fears, hopes, faiths, social ideals, and sacrificial standards.

(2) Irrespective of religious needs, man has endeavored to discover proper relations to his universe. He has philosophized. He has tried to reduce to terms of thought this baffling, intangible, universal environment. He has searched for a specific ground for explaining the universe. He has sought unity in change and monism in multiplicity. He has proclaimed that change itself is Lord of the universe, or perhaps he has found solace in a creative evolution. At any rate, he has sought ultimate meanings in as unbiased an interpretation of the universe as is humanly possible.

(3) From the far-flung horizons of religious and philosophic theory, man has turned his thought in an opposite direction — he has directed his thought upon itself. He has maneuvered his thought processes introspectively. He has puzzled over the structure and functions of his own mind. These series of studies have led on the one hand to treatises such as the *Critique of Pure Reason,* and on the other hand to the current expressions of behavioristic psychology or of psychoanalysis.

(4) Man has sought to fathom the material secrets of the earth. Since the Industrial Revolution in England, inquiring minds have focussed tremendous energies upon attempts to master the physical elements. Rocks and strata of rocks have been caused to yield a wealth of ores, and subter-

ranean caverns have been made to pour forth reservoirs of gas and oil. Modern transportation has been made possible by the use of steam, gasoline, electricity. Mechanical inventions have followed one another in unanticipated fashion, paying awe-inspiring tribute to the genius of man. Abstract thinking has given man a marvelous degree of control over the material side of life.

(5) Recently, the problem of man's adjustment and responsibility to his fellowmen is being accorded a worthy hearing at the bar of scientific thought. For millenniums man has pondered hard over his relations and obligations to his God and to his universe, over the nature of his mind and spirit, over ways and means of acquiring individual success through a manipulation of the material resources of the earth. Incomprehensible as it may seem, it is true, however, that man has neglected almost wholly, until recently, the very heart of all successful living, namely, his relations and obligations to his fellow men and to society. Social thought, the center of all sound thinking, has been ignored. Consequently, the world, beneath its load of social ills, has slipped backward nearly as often as it has advanced.

In the present age, however, the world is making unprecedented demands upon social thought, long before social thought is adequately prepared for its gigantic tasks. Religion is seeking re-vitalization through socialized thinking. In its modern endeavor to win the world, Christianity is making tremendous demands upon applied sociology.

After many vain searches among false theories and impersonal ends, philosophy is seeking to find itself in a social universe. Psychology, likewise, is no longer individual, structural, and formal; it is now trying to interpret itself in terms of human behavior. Group processes are being searched for the origins of stimuli that will explain individual conduct.

Economic thought, too, has reached a stage where it is endeavoring to re-define its concepts in the light of sociological knowledge. The material resources of the earth as well as industrial and business enterprises, in fact all economic values, are being measured, and re-valued in terms of their societary significance. The meaning of industrial democracy is being sought in sociological terms.

In the distinctively associative life enormous demands are being made upon sociology. It is invited to formulate the criteria by which the worth of an educational system may be determined. Groups are trying to provide for the use of the leisure time of their members by methods that are socially valuable. Many attempts are being made for restoring to the family its fundamental prerogatives as a social institution.

The history of social thought rises out of the beginnings of human life on earth and with jagged edges extends along the full sweep of the changing historical horizon. It finds expression through some of the world's best minds. Our quest will bring us in contact with the most vital moments of the world's most valuable thinkers.

Chapter II

Earliest Social Thought

Primitive people were inquisitive. They thought about what happened and they sought explanations. Their attention was centered on the tangible phenomena of life. Their imagination worked out fantastic and superstitious interpretations. They reasoned about the daily occurrences of life in concrete, graphic, and personal terms.

Primitive people everywhere, apparently, sensed in a piecemeal and microscopic way the meaning of social relationships. Archeological records disclose crude and simple, but nevertheless genuine social implications. Early mythologies recognize the importance of social bonds. Out of the dim dawn of tribal life there appeared a rough-hewn sense of social property. The proverbs of primitive people include implications, if not definite statements, of social responsibility.

Primitive people lived simple group lives. If the paternal relationship was not always known or recognized, the maternal relationship functioned for at least a few years. The loose family ties harbored a degree of social responsibility. Wherever ancestor worship developed, the family group assumed large proportions and manifested strong social characteristics. The clan, or *gens,* betokened social fealty.

Communal property testified to communal thinking. The existence of common hunting grounds and tribal flocks was indicative of folk thought. Group dances, feasts, building enterprises, celebrations delineated the social spirit. Warfare produced bursts of tribal loyalty. An examination of the folkways reveals indistinct but incipient notions of societal welfare. Such a treatise as Sumner's *Folkways* chronicles a vast amount of elemental folk thinking.

Folk thinking permeated primitive religions. The earliest forms of religion presupposed societies of spirits or gods. The conduct of the individual was regulated by his ideas concerning the ways in which he had pleased or offended the spirits or gods. An infant was born into a society peopled with human and spirit beings. The latter were often more numerous than the former; they frequently were more feared; and hence were more powerful. The living people, the departed spirits, and the gods in a hierarchal order constituted an effective society for the exercise of many vigorous forms of social control.

If pestilence came, it was because the gods had been offended by some human being. As a result of the offense of one individual, the whole tribe was considered to be liable to punishment. Consequently, the tribe in turn would punish the offending member and through the use of force and fear would exert a tremendous power over the conduct and thought of individuals.

Primitive people were dominated by custom. They were subject to the autocracy of the past. They were hopelessly caught between ancestral ascendance and current fears. They threaded their way, mentally, through tantalizingly uncertain and narrow apertures. They learned the meaning of obedience, but obedience to a harsh and rigorous past and a fickle and disconcerting future. Leadership was drastic and capricious; followership was frantic and tremulous.

Some of the incipient social concepts of primitive peoples have been preserved in the form of proverbs, maxims, fables, and myths. Many of the subtler social relationships of life were recognized by early man. His limited thinking drifted into simple formulae. His vocabulary was scanty; his ideas were few. He spoke in conventional sayings. "Primitive man spoke in proverbs."

Many folkthoughts, or primitive conceptions of social obligations, have been preserved. The early proverbs of man reveal the beginnings of social thought. Equally valuable and similar materials are found in the sayings of the tribes which today are in a state of arrested development. A few illustrations of embryonic social thought will be given here.[1]

The first examples will be selected from the folk-thoughts of the Africans of the Guinea Coast. The proverb, Ashes fly back in the face of him who throws them, recognizes that evil deeds return upon the doer, or as moderns declare, Curses come home to roost. In the saying, Cowries are men, primitive man roughly but succinctly stated the theory of the economic determination of human history. It is cowries, or money, which molds human thought, determines human evaluations and attitudes, gives social power, and "makes the man." An age-long conception, indicative of a low sense of social feeling, but possessing great force in society, is revealed in the dictum, Full-belly child says to hungry-belly child, "Keep good cheer." Throughout human history, the fortunate glutton has always recommended patience and tranquility to the unfortunate, hard-working brother. An eminent American financier of the multi-millionaire class expressed pity for telephone girls who undergo hard labor, but declared that their harsh conditions were what the good Lord had made for them. But how far has this well-groomed citizen of our century advanced beyond the "full-belly" social philosophy of savage man?

In the observation, A fool of Ika and an idiot of Iluka meet together to make friends, the African has noted that friends are persons of similar types, of similar minds, of similar prejudices, and that "birds of a feather flock together." Whether conscious or unconscious, association occurs among persons of a kind, among fools of Ika and idiots of Iluka.

Romantic love, evidently, has always been fickle, for the African has discovered that "quick loving a woman means quick not loving a woman." If this naïve but shrewd reflection concerning love-making were taken at its real worth at the present time, it would be crystallized into a federal marriage law requiring that a license to marry should be obtained at least fifteen or thirty days before the marriage could be celebrated.

A rather keen sense of social injustice is expressed in the monologue: "The ground-pig said: 'I do not feel so angry with the man who killed me as with the man who dashed me on the ground afterward.'" Here the injustice of striking an individual when he is down is depicted. Even primitive man has a sense of sympathy for the defeated and helpless.

"Three elders cannot all fail to pronounce the word *ekulu* (antelope); one may say *ekúlu;* another *ekulú;* but the third will say, *ékulu* (which is correct)." In other words, several heads are better than one; or, in a multitude of counsellors there is safety. It was this simple social precept which a highly individualistic man like Roosevelt used frequently to the advantage of himself and the nation. When a perplexing problem would confront President Roosevelt, he was wont to invite to the White

House persons whose beliefs were contrary to his own in order to secure their opinions. He acted independently, but after taking counsel with several "elders."

In *Thinking Black,* Daniel Crawford has presented phases of the colored man's philosophy.[2] While much is individual, more is social philosophy. Custom imitation prevails. The social philosophy of the African Negro is summarized in the rule: Follow your leader. Social precedent, not principle, is the guide to conduct. If you are a follower, follow patiently; if you are a leader, lead drastically. "If thou art an anvil, be patient . . . but if thou art a hammer, strike hard."

The African understands the social psychology of language. He watches the eyes more carefully than the voice. To him the human eye speaks all languages under the sun. Mr. Crawford says that the wary eye of the African "can easily fish news out of the two deep liquid pools of your eye-balls." If your eye says one thing and your tongue another, then the African "will plump for the verdict of the eye."

The aphorism, There is no pocket in a shroud, warns the individual against the possibility of taking his material goods into the next world. To share with other persons is rated a higher act than to store from others. He is richest who shares most. Among the Africans with whom Mr. Crawford worked, the word for criminal was not applied to the person who had stolen property or who had taken life, but to the one who eats alone. "The high crime and misdemeanor of the town is to dine alone;" the criminal above other criminals is "Mr. Eat-Alone." He who refuses to share his food with those who are less fortunate than himself is an arch-devil. Such a vice is common among beasts; it is beneath the dignity of man—according to the African. When several primitives were taken to London and shown the wealthy and the poor sections of that city, they were dumbfounded. They were ütterly unable to understand how any persons with the slightest spark of human nature in them could endure to live to themselves in wealth when in the same city there were the wretched and prostrated multitudes of Whitechapel and the other cheerless slums.

"What baby lion ever trembled at his father's roaring?" A few mornings ago, I heard an angry parent yelling at his son, but the disobedient child kept on in his own way. I wondered how far this father had advanced in parental influence and discipline beyond the stage represented by the African seer who drew his social images from a lion-frequented environment. "If a tree has grown up crooked, it is because no one straightened it when young." This statement postulates social responsibility for juvenile delinquency and even for adult crime. The underlying principle is the same as that in the Hebraic injunction: Train up a child in the way he should go; and when he is old, he will not depart from it. The principle has received current recognition in the doctrine of contributory negligence of parents. The modern observation full of socially dangerous implications, that parents are blind to the weaknesses of their children, has its African counterpart: The beetle is a beauty in the eyes of its mother. A gleam of light is thrown upon the current discussions concerning social parasitism by the African's assertion: The parasite has no roots.

The Australian Blackfellow who goes upon a journey, sometimes takes a handful of mother earth with him. In this way he testifies to his loyalty to home, and provides against the rise of lonesomeness which he will experience during tribal hunts. His act crudely represents the essence of the concept of patriotism. A sense of justice is common to primitive Australians. Among the Whayook of Australia a man who has wounded a fellow tribesman is required to present himself to the injured in order to receive a similar wound.[3] Among the Wumbais, a person who is absent when a relative dies must not speak on his return to camp to anyone until he has had spears thrown at him.[4] Spencer and Gillen report that the Australian primitive regards any offense as wiped out by a suitable proffer of atonement.[5]

The Filipino declares: A piece of green wood will burn if placed near the fire. In other words, temptation is a subtle element that ultimately may destroy even persons who are supposedly temptation-proof. In the proverb, Boastfulness drives away wisdom, the Filipino has pointed out that the desire to make a strong impression upon associates hinders intellectual progress. The chief danger of luxury is stated in the saying: He who is raised in ease, is usually destitute. The leading result of being financially fortunate is summarized thus: Easy earning means quick spending. The evils of hypercriticism are bluntly phrased: The fault-finder has the biggest faults. The law of social compensation is stated as follows: You laugh today; I laugh tomorrow. The organic nature of society is implied in the truism: The pain of a finger is the suffering of the whole body. The need for independent thinking is urged in the declaration: Whoever believes everything said, has no mind of his own. On the other hand, the ego-centric mind receives solemn warning in the dictum: He who despises counsel is on the way to misfortune. The value of a social spirit is proclaimed as follows: Kindness is a great capital; and again: Good deeds are more precious than gold or silver. A gentle hint of social importance is given in the formula: Kindness is with kindness to be paid, not with gold or silver. In these and related proverbs the earliest social thought of the Filipino mind is indicated.

Let us now examine a few ancient Japanese

axioms. (1) The mouth of the mass melts gold. This proverb refers to the fundamental force of public opinion. (2) The world is like a looking-glass; if you smile, others also smile. Here is depicted the elemental character of unconscious imitation. (3) What the ruler wants, the ruled also wants. In other words, what the upper classes desire, the lower classes long for; or, as Tarde has said: "The superior are imitated by the inferior." (4) Three men get together and have knowledge equivalent to that of Monju (a famous Buddhist thinker). The African, Filipino, and English equivalents of this adage have already been given. All races, apparently, have early observed the safety which comes from taking counsel. (5) The net of Heaven is rough, but will never miss one victim. Our equivalent, of Graeco-Latin origin, is: The mills of the gods grind slowly, but exceedingly small. Evil brings its own rewards sooner or later. The law of retribution cannot be overcome, even by social manipulations. (6) If one dog barks a falsehood, ten thousand others spread it as a truth. In these words, gossip is condemned, and the humanity-wide tendency of hearsay evidence to gain social force is pictured. (7) The tongue is but three inches long, but it can kill a man six feet high. Again, the vicious nature of gossip is shown. Further, the severest punishment is not always physical; it may come from the human tongue. (8) A man takes a drink; then the drink takes the man. In this dramatic description, the drinking of intoxicating liquors is effectively indicted. (9) Applause is the root of abuse. Even the Japanese have recognized the force of opinion in influencing the individual, and of favorable opinion in unduly expanding the ego. A unique characteristic of many Japanese proverbs is the fundamental and deep-moving knowledge of social psychology which they show. Judged by their proverbs, the Japanese possess an unusual understanding of human nature.

Bulgarian proverbs disclose social thought. The "full-belly" philosophy of the African, or the pig-trough philosophy that has been analyzed by T. N. Carver, has its Bulgarian counterpart: The satiated man cannot believe the hungry man. The South Slavs are noted for their weddings which often continue for three days. When these festivities are over, the bride enters upon a more or less monotonous round of bearing and rearing children. These social conditions are aptly described:

Dum! Dum! for three days;
Oh dear! Oh dear! for all days.

Patience is enjoined in the Bulgarian adage: Endure, O horse, until the time of green grass. Hope that rises in the heart of man is paid homely but genuine tribute in the rural Slavic proverb: The hungry hen dreams of millet.

The Danes have many sayings which emphasize social dependence. The individual is instructed:

Act so in the valley that you need not fear those that stand on the hill. The shrewd man is socially dangerous, for: Cunning has little honor. Gossip is shown as a swift messenger in the axiom: A man's character reaches town before his person. The most serious result of cheating others is the effect upon the cheater, or: He is most cheated who cheats himself. The common character of sin is recognized in the Danish proverb: He must be pure who would blame another. Custom is a powerful agency of control. The Danes command: Follow the customs, or fly the country.

The Portuguese have a social saying to the effect: He buys very dear who begs. The unscientific nature of love is indicated in the Portuguese declaration: Love has no law. The frequent antithesis between money lending and friend making is succinctly phrased: Money lent, an enemy made.

A few Arabian proverbs state social ideas. The laws of human association and imitation can be found in the following axiom: A wise man associating with the vicious becomes an idiot; a dog traveling with good men becomes a rational being. The strength which comes from unity is forcibly phrased: Three if they unite against a town will ruin it. The transforming power of love is recognized: Love can make any place agreeable. An idealistic social standard is set for the individual in the aphorism: It is more noble to pardon than to punish. On the other hand, mercy may be misplaced: Mercy to the criminal may be cruelty to the people. The individual must beware of being an ingrate; he must not permit his selfish desires to crush out the spirit of gratitude: A tree that affords thee shade, do not order it cut down. The omnipresence of envy is understood: Envy assails the noblest; the winds howl around the highest peaks. The anti-social tendency of a vicious habit is well described: A hand accustomed to take is far from giving. Perhaps the Malthusian advocate will find solace in the simple dictum: If the sailors become too numerous, the boat will sink. He who pleases everybody has done so at the expense of his own character, or as the Arabs say: He deserves no man's good will of whom all men speak well.

From Ceylon comes the philanthropic request: When you eat, think of the poor. The Cingalese, however, recognize the importance of maintaining the scientific attitude in charity, for they have a saying: He who gives alms must do it with discretion. The blighting influence of wealth is stated in the Cingalese axiom: A covetous man has two sources of iniquity—how to amass money, and how to use it.

Among Mexican proverbs, social ideas are not missing. The reader will catch the social significance of the following: (1) A howling cat is not a good hunter; (2) Everybody can climb up the limbs of the fallen tree; (3) A rich widow cries with one eye and rings the wedding bells with the other; (4) The tongue slow, the eyes quick; (5) From January to January the bankers have all the money.

The illustrations which have been given from several racial sources will suffice to show the nature of the earliest social thought of primitive peoples. By way of comparison, a few social proverbs which are common among English, Scotch, French, and German speaking peoples, and which are of various origins, will be given. It will be unnecessary to comment upon the social thought which is stated or implied in these proverbs.

That is not lost which a friend gets.
The shortest road is where the company's good.
A man is known by the company he keeps.
Do unto others as you would have others do to you.
A man who would have friends must show himself friendly.
One bad example spoils many precepts.
Honesty is the best policy.
One good turn deserves another.
Birds of a feather flock together.
As the twig is bent, the tree is inclined.
People who live in glass houses mustn't throw stones.
Bare is the gift without the giver.
What is not good for the swarm is not good for the bee.

He laughs best who laughs last.

To make a happy couple, the husband must be deaf and the wife blind.

Charity gives itself rich; covetousness hoards itself poor.

The nature of the primitive social thought that has been preserved through proverbs and sayings justifies the following observations. (1) Primitive social thought was exceedingly simple, crude, and undeveloped. (2) It was uncorrelated and unsystematic. (3) A classification of the total number of known proverbs of any primitive people into individual and social types shows that not more than ten per cent are social. Primitive thinking was done in terms of the welfare of the individual himself. The social thought was commonly of individualistic origin. A social idea was originally not suggested for its own sake or disinterestedly, but for the reason that its observance would enable individuals to live together more harmoniously and prosperously. (4) Social proverbs employ figures of speech. Similes from nature are frequent; physical analogies are not uncommon. Many of these figures disclose a rural or bucolic mind. (5) Frequently, the social proverbs of the various races pertain to family and community relationships. The sense of social responsibility does not penetrate as a rule beyond the small group. The responsibility of group to group is rarely expressed or implied. The social vision does not extend to large groups. (6) A comparative study of primitive social sayings indicates countless similarities, and testifies to the uniformity of human experiences and social needs, irrespective of racial distinctions. These resemblances do not imply collaboration, collusion, or imitation. They mean that the needs of primitive individuals in various and unrelated parts of the world have everywhere led the human mind out in search of socially satisfactory explanations. Primitive thinking produced fundamental social concepts, such as kinship, authority, dependence, and tribal loyalty.

Chapter III

The Social Thought of Ancient Civilizations

In this chapter the discussion of earliest social thought will be presented from the standpoint of the ancient civilizations of Egypt, Babylonia and Assyria, India, China, and Persia. The evidences of social thought are meagre and inchoate. Nevertheless, there are data which cannot be ignored. Inferential evidence and proverbial references constitute the main portion of these data.

(1) The ancient Egyptian social order was bureaucratic and autocratic. The king was supreme. With the rise of the Theban hierarchy, the priestly class came to power and established a theocratic régime. Then military leaders came into prominence and overthrew the theocracy of the priests.

With the historical rise of Egypt, about 4000 B. C., the emphasis upon law as the basis of the social order stands out prominently. The books of laws early acquired sacred significance. They were reputed to be of divine and monarchical origins; they provided courts of justice; and they prescribed punishments for offenses.

The social ideas are to be gleaned almost entirely

from proverbial sayings. Egyptian scholars refer to collections of these moral precepts as being of a practical rather than a systematic philosophical nature. The most frequently mentioned of the Egyptian books of proverbs are the Proverbs of Ptah-hotep, and the Prescriptions of Ani.

The social order was dominated as a rule by the king, who was supposed to be divine. The king and a relatively small number of nobles owned the land. The large percentage of the people were serfs and slaves. Throughout ancient Egyptian history, the middle class must have been weak, and small in numbers. When the lands passed under the control of the temple authorities no change occurred in the social conditions of the masses. The priests shared the authority with their auxiliaries, the soldiers. The unprivileged classes included the farmers, boatmen, mechanics, trades-people, besides the slaves.[1]

Egyptian life was rural. Commerce was undeveloped. Higher education was reserved for the very few, although it appears that elementary education was widespread. The priests often used their educational advantages to prey upon and excite the superstitions of the people, thereby strengthening the social control which they enjoyed.

An anomalous phase of the Egyptian mind was that it shifted back and forth from a hedonistic enjoyment of the moment to a serious contemplation of the future life. Amusements were fostered;

the drinking of intoxicating liquors was extensive, and music was promoted. The game of draughts was perhaps the national pastime. The people were not warriors. They employed mercenaries, who ultimately became socially powerful.

Polygamy was countenanced and practised, but only of course among the wealthy. A relatively high degree of freedom was granted the women among the privileged classes. They appeared in public with their husbands; they publicly engaged in religious ceremonies; and they were given unusual property rights. At one time it is reported that Egyptian women could not only own property, but could dispose of it as they wished, or could loan money at interest to their husbands. At another time the following injunction seems to have been issued: "Thou shalt never forget thy mother, and what she has done for thee, that she bore thee, and nurtured thee in all ways." Children were enjoined to obey their parents, to be respectful to their superiors, and to be reserved. Greatness was identified with kindness. Justice and kindliness were urged upon the leaders.[2]

The belief in the future world claimed a lion's share of the attention of the Egyptian. As a result, sculpture flourished. It was believed that if the human figure was copied and the copy preserved, the spirit and the body of the departed person could be more easily re-united. Architecture developed, but with the tombs or pyramids and other monuments as the chief forms. Urban mural divisions and fortified walls are still to be found as evidences of Egyptian social institutions.

It was taught that in the next world the individual would be held accountable for his deeds in this life. This belief acted as a powerful social control; it involved specific social obligations. The individual must deal openly with his fellowmen. He must observe the rights of the weaker members of society. For example, he must not make false charges against a slave to the master of the slave. He must show that he has respected the social rights that were invested in property. From the moral and social writings of the Egyptian scribes, it is apparent that in religious matters, the individual was moved to give thought to his duties as a citizen and as a neighbor.

(2) The ancient Babylonian and Assyrian social order was similar in many ways to Egyptian civilization. The Babylonian description of a great deluge resembles the account of the Flood that is given in the Old Testament, and indicates thought about morals and social life. Both Babylon and Assyria developed a religion which was expressed in terms of the nation-group. The boundaries of one, with Merodach at the head, and of the other with Assur in supreme control, marked the national group divisions. Merodach, it was believed, accompanied the king in the wars and fought for the nation. He was concerned entirely, according to

traditions, with the welfare of Babylonia as a population group.

The attitude in Babylonian society toward the institution of slavery was distinctly different from that in Rome, but similar to the Egyptian practices. The slave was considered in a more social way than by the Romans. He was frequently regarded as one of the family; he could even become a free member of society. "Slavery was no bar to his promotion." Moreover, slavery did not necessarily imprint a social stigma upon the slave.

The social rights of women were similar to the Egyptian customs. The married woman of the ruling classes possessed definite property rights. She could use the property that she owned as she saw fit; she could even bequeath it as she chose. Her dowry gave her economic independence; it was her absolute property, which she could bequeath by will in any way that she desired.

The earliest well-known Babylonian ruler was Hammurapi (2124-2081). He is known best through his famous book of laws, the Code of Hammurapi. The Code bespeaks for the author the desire to rule Babylonian society justly. There are minute regulations of private business and of labor conditions which give the Code some of the characteristics of modern mercantilistic thought.

The Code contains perhaps the earliest forms of labor legislation that were enacted. Hammurapi sought through legislation to determine wages for different classes of labor. The Code prescribed severe punishment for anyone who sheltered a runaway slave. In this and similar ways, property rights were protected and human elements subordinated. It was not until the Deuteronomic Code was written that the rights of labor received legislative recognition.

Hammurapi stood for a paternalistic control of society. His idea of justice was literally that of an eye for an eye. "If a man has caused the loss of a patrician's eye, his eye shall one cause to be lost."[3] Justice, moreover, was subject to the law of social gradation. An offense against a man of lower rank might be atoned by paying money. "If a man has caused a poor man to lose his eye, he shall pay one mina of silver."[4] Additional light is thrown on the concept of justice by other passages from the Code, especially by this one: "If a builder has built a house for a man and has not made strong his work, and the house he has built has fallen, and he has caused the death of the owner of the house, that builder shall be put to death."[5]

The intellectual progress and the inventions of the Babylonians are indicative of social status. The development along artistic lines, particularly in architecture and sculpture, must have exerted an indirect but important social influence. Significant advances in surgery had been made preceding the reign of Hammurapi. In medicine, however, the demonic theory of the causes of disease enslaved the people.

The Assyrians, who lived to the north of the Babylonians, were less social in type. They were little concerned about the future life; their religion was relatively undeveloped. The Assyrian artists gave their attention chiefly to the king, the court, and to war. They reproduced in artistic form the king and the soldier, but ignored the life and customs of the people.

(3) When we turn to early East Indian records, we find a higher development of social ideals than among any peoples which have thus far been considered. In the Vedic documents there is considerable evidence of communal life and of a remarkable degree of social spirit and brotherliness. In the East Indian account of a Deluge—similar to the Deluge that is described in Genesis—there is a conception of punishment that falls upon the group because of the sins of individuals. Sacrifice, among the Vedic believers, had acquired a positive social function. It was considered as a social act, in which the worshipper and the god took part. The food strengthened the god and the spiritual contact strengthened the worshiper. Hence mutual sympathy was generated.

With the rise of Brahmanism, the caste system developed. It divided society. It gave structure to the concept that some people are naturally—and artificially—superior to other people. In the laws of Manu, several social concepts are broached. The nature of marriage and the duties of a householder are explained. The duties of a woman are prescribed. The nature of private and public law is noteworthy, and the recognition of the obligation of one caste to another in times of distress marks the beginning of a reaction against the caste system. It was considered possible for an individual to fall from a caste to the one below, but not for an individual to rise in caste. The moral standards for individuals reached a level comparable to those represented in certain of the teachings of Jesus. For example, notice this instruction:

Let him patiently bear hard words, let him not insult anybody, nor become anybody's enemy for the sake of this perishable body. Against an angry man let him not in return show anger; let him bless when he is cursed.

Buddhism inaugurated a set of social ideas which involved the abolition of the caste system. In the fourth of the "Four Noble Truths" the principles which are formulated, are partly of social import. Commendation is extended to right speech—speech that is friendly, and sincere toward others. The requirements include right conduct—conduct which is peaceable and honorable toward other persons. Stress is placed upon right means of securing livelihood—methods which do not involve the injury or the taking of life. There are types of modern business enterprise that are extolled in our Christian America which would fall under the ban of the

"Noble Truths" in pagan India.

Among the "ten commandments" of Buddha, eight represent social ideas and obligations:

(1) Not to kill any living being.

(2) Not to take that which is not given (not to steal).

(3) To refrain from adultery.

(4) To speak no untruth (not to lie to other people).

(5) To abstain from intoxicating liquors.

(6) Not to slander.

(7) Not to covet.

(8) Not to be angry.

Buddha taught that hatred is to be repaid by love, that life is to be filled with kindness and compassion, that the widest toleration is to be practised. The teachings of Buddha engendered a delicate social consciousness regarding the relation of the individual to his fellows. The precepts were strong enough to break down rigid class barriers. The underlying conception was broadly human.

Additional light is thrown on the social thought of Buddha by the following sayings which are credited to him:

Pity and sympathy is the Buddha's mind.

Pity to his parents is the Supreme Law.

Honesty is the Paradise of the Bodhisattva.

O my Disciples, flee from fornication, know how to be content with your own wife, and do not even for a single moment lust after another woman.

A state without a ruler is like a body without a head; it cannot exist very long.

The king looks upon his subjects with a heart of mercy, as if they were his children; and the people regard the king as their father.

If there is no Buddha in the world, be good to your parents; for to be good to one's parents is to minister unto Buddha.

Nursing a sick man is the great field where the righteous tree of mind grows.

Even a strong man cannot lift himself.

Ten people have ten colors (opinions).

The paint which is painted by ten fingers (men) is accurate. (In the multitude of counsellors there is safety.)

The sayings of Buddha may be summed up in the statement that, like many of the teachings of Jesus, they accent the gentle virtues and the passive traits of a people bearing a yoke against which they are powerless to revolt, the virtues of obedience, respect to those in authority, long-suffering, patience, even resignation.

(4) The social thought of early China can best be gleaned from the writings of Confucius. This scholar was not a reformer or a religious leader, but primarily a conserver. He was interested in civil and political affairs. His books reflect not his own ideas, for his originality was not great, but the concepts which had been worked out before his time. In the *Li Ki,* or Record of Rites, there are

many social and domestic precepts. In a way the *Li Ki,* "the Chinamen's manual of conduct," is a treatise on social as well as individual ethics. Around the family group, Chinese social ideas revolved. On the death of his mother, Confucius, for example, went into seclusion for twenty-seven months. On sacrificial occasions the living members and the departed spirits of the household were accustomed to gather in one filial communal group. The welfare of the individual was completely subordinated to the interests of the family group of spirits.

The Chinese worship, or honor, their ancestors. The worship of the past has paralyzed new thought. Custom imitation has ruled and tradition has been reverenced.

Marriage receives special attention, but the arrangements are made by parents or "go-betweens." Socially, the sexes do not intermingle. The parents exercise complete control over the children; the mother bears a considerable portion of the burdens of parental discipline. Filial piety is the cardinal virtue. Although polygamy is discountenanced, concubinage is permitted. The sexes dress very much alike, except in headdress and footgear. The style of wearing apparel is not only simple and aesthetic, but it "minimizes the visible distinctions of sex."

Confucius, or Kung-fu-tsze, believed in the efficacy of setting good examples. Imitation would then accomplish the desired results. By these methods, Confucius expected that society would be improved. Fundamental principles of a stable social order, more than of social progress, were in the mind of Confucius. He conceived of the universe as a perfect order. Likewise, he thought of the state as a perfect social order. Confucius urged that the individual strive for perfection. According to the Confucian doctrine of the Superior Man, the individual should master his own passions and desires, substituting an enjoyment of music, ceremony, and of friendship, for the enjoyment that comes from the exercise of the bodily passions. He should seek salvation through the study of nature and of things. Moral character and intelligence if accompanied by bravery will produce the highest type of personality.

In Chinese social thought the family and state were early recognized as the two leading institutions in society. In the civil organization it is worth while to note the *hien,* or city district. The *hien* has been pronounced "the real unit of Chinese corporate life"; and the *hien* magistrate, "the heart and soul of all official life." Since this magistrate keeps closely in touch with the masses, he is called by the people "the father and mother officer." The *hien* contains some of the germ ideas of democracy; it emphasizes local self-government.

The ancient laws were elaborate, giving an unusual degree of power to the judges. Although customs ruled, the judges often possessed a liberal margin of freedom in determining the nature of punishments. Contrary to Western procedure, the Chinese consider an accused man as guilty until proved otherwise. Excessive corporate punishment is deplored.[6] Confucius objected to the maintenance of a government by the use of fear and of coercive measures. He predicted that capital punishment (even in a land ruled by custom) would be abolished in a hundred years.

The ideas of peace and harmonious social relationships have long held sway in China. Militarism has been scorned, and war held in contempt. It is ironical that as China begins to function as a world power in contact with Western and Christian nations, she is compelled to find her chief defense in an uncivilized and unChristian militarism.

Sympathy is a fundamental concept among the Chinese. Unfortunately, it has been instrumental in producing a highly specialized and professionalized class of beggars. Industry and patience are characteristic social virtues. Lao-tse, the founder of Taoism and a contemporary of Confucius, taught the social precept: Recompense injury with kindness. Confucius, who disagreed, taught that kindness should be paid with kindness, and injury with injury. This conception led Confucius to formulate his golden rule of human conduct: Do not do to others what you would not have others do to you.

Obedience to authority has been for centuries a cardinal social principle of the Chinese. It was enunciated by Confucius, who spoke as a representative of the ruling classes. In stressing obedience to temporal authorities and in shunning the gods, Confucius has been accused of fostering a materialistic philosophy. This charge is partly offset by his ethical teachings. Confucius was a humanitarian rather than a materialist; he was a utilitarian rather than an idealist. In these attitudes he reflects not his own opinions so much as the thought of the generations which preceded him.

Mencius, who lived shortly after Confucius, was an environmentalist in the sense that he believed that external evil influences have corrupted man's original good nature. On the other hand, Mencius urged progress through regeneration of the heart. Mencius was a more thoroughgoing humanist than Confucius, for he made the happiness of the people the supreme goal for the individual. He condemned war and warriors alike and declared that generals are criminals. He asserted that it is wrong to conquer a territory against the will of the people of that territory.

Additional sidelights upon early Chinese social thought are afforded by the following social proverbs of ancient Chinese origin:

If a cat cries after eating the mouse, this is false sympathy.

Follow good, learn good; follow beggar, learn to

beg.

Gentlemen use heart; lesser men use strength.

New clothes but old friends are good.

Within the four seas all are brothers.

If two people were 1000 miles apart and be like-minded, they will come together; if they sit opposite one another and are not like-minded there will be no mutual acquaintance.

Speak language fitting to station of man you meet.

All under heaven is one home.

Although a man is away from home, his heart is there.

The big fish eat the little ones, the little ones eat the shrimps, and the shrimps are forced to eat mud (applied to the classes of society who pay taxes).

He who praises me on all occasions is a fool who despises me or a knave who wishes to cheat me.

Govern thyself, and you will be able to govern the world.

The hearts of the people are the only legitimate foundations of an empire.

By nature all men are alike; but by education, widely different.

For the sake of one good action, a hundred evil ones should be forgotten.

To forget one's ancestors is to be a brook without a source, a tree without a root.

Rogues differ little; each began first as a disobedient son.

Of all man's actions, there is none greater than filial piety.

When they saw an old man, people walking or driving gave him the road. Men who had white hairs mingling with the black did not carry burdens along the highways (care for the aged).

When the man of high station is well instructed, he loves men; when the man of low station is well instructed, he is easily ruled.

Three friendships are advantageous: friendship with the upright, friendship with the sincere, and friendship with the man of observation. Three are injurious: friendship with a man of spurious airs, friendship with the insinuatingly soft, and friendship with the glib-tongued.

Who taught you politeness? The impolite.

To be a successful monarch, one must be a just monarch.

Of the different peoples which have thus far been considered, the Chinese have furnished the most elaborate degree of social thought. While the social ideals of the Chinese are largely unsystematic, they accent the family and the state as essential social institutions. They also reveal even a significant conception of world brotherliness. The Chinese have probably created more social proverbs than any other people, past or present. For the stage of civilization that is represented by proverbs and sayings, the social thought of the Chinese is unsurpassed. In this regard the Chinese have but one close competitor, the ancient Hebrews.

(5) The Persians, who after their defeat by Alexander the Great in 331 B. C. have been credited with having turned over the torch of civilization to the Greeks, made a contribution to social thought similar to that of the other ancient peoples. Under Cyrus the Great, Darius, and Xerxes a system of state education was fostered which was designed chiefly to train soldiers. It did not stress social and intellectual development, although it existed in a land that produced the Magi. The individuals who were not in the army received slight educational benefits.

It is in the teachings of Zoroaster of the sixteenth century B. C. that we first find the main trend of Persian social thought. The Zend Avesta, the document from which Zoroasterism and the modern Parsee religion have evolved, emphasizes the principle of kindliness in all important human relationships. Sanitation, business honesty, and chastity in family relationships are taught.

The ancient Hebrews and the Greeks each made such large contributions to social thought that separate chapters will be devoted to these peoples. In a summary of the social thought of the Egyptians, Babylonians and Assyrians, East Indians, Chinese, and Persians, it may be said that there is a rather uniform emphasis upon the elemental virtues, particularly upon kindliness. While the individual's salvation is given prominence, the individual is urged to be socially considerate and to cultivate sympathetic relationships with the gods and with his fellow human beings.

Chapter IV

The Social Thought of the Hebrews

Ancient Egyptian, Babylonian and Assyrian, East Indian, Chinese, and Persian records disclose a set of elemental and yet more or less passive social backgrounds against which the social ideals of the Hebrew prophets shine forth like stars of the first magnitude. The Pentateuch and the writings of the Hebrew wise men are rich in gleams of a social spirit, while the Hebrew prophets, notably, Amos, Hosea, Isaiah, and Jeremiah, uttered flaming indictments of social evils.

The Hebrews stood head and shoulders above their contemporaries in social thinking. They left a series of historical documents, covering several centuries and revealing a specific evolution in social concepts. They expressed the fundamentals from which Christian social thought developed, and from which much of the ethical and social thinking of Western civilization on its practical side has evolved.

The social thought of the Hebrews was born of group suffering. Through the mists of the earliest Hebrew traditions we discern that conflicts occurred in the Euphrates Valley which sent Abraham out on his perilous journey toward unknown and hostile Canaan. The gaunt spectre, famine, brought distress to the household of the domestic-loving Abraham and drove him to Egypt where he sojourned for a time. Abram, exalted father, or Abraham, father of a multude, became the founder in a sense of three world religions, for to him Judaism, Christianity, and Mohammedanism trace their origins.

Throughout the years of migration, exile, and suffering, Abraham maintained his religious faith and belief. By means of his simple religion he was able to interpret sanely the troubles and conflicts of life. Out of suffering interpreted religiously, Abraham developed a remarkably well-balanced and social personality. From this beginning, Hebrew social thought evolved. Ultimately, Israel created social concepts which has won for her the distinction of being " the leading social teacher of the human race."[1]

As a social entity the Hebrews were the result of "a titanic social struggle;" they arose out of an industrial crisis. The scene was laid in Egypt. The descendants of Jacob were working long hours with little pay, as slaves, and under harsh social conditions. One of their number, more favored than the rest by heredity and environment, saw a Hebrew workman being beaten by an Egyptian "boss." The favored one, Moses, felt the surging passions of social injustice rising within his breast—and he slew the boss. Moses thereby became the founder of the world's labor movement. By an act of violence in the impassioned days of youth, Moses became "a social agitator"; by years of patient service of his people in the name of Jehovoh, he became one of the world's greatest social seers.

Rameses II was "an unprincipled captain of industry." He was haughty, hard-hearted, and without social conscience. Moses was sympathetic, socially sensitive, and keenly religious. Rameses II was a leading representative of an ancient aristocracy; Moses was the first great exponent of an incipient democracy, and "the first man in history with a well-developed social consciousness."

According to the Exodus record Moses, as the murderer of an Egyptian boss, felt no qualms of conscience, but he did fear the mighty Pharaoh. At that time in history it was a minor matter to kill a slave; but to have killed a boss was vastly different. The slave represented weakness; the boss was the official representative of political and financial power. Consequently, Moses fled the country. In Egypt he was helpless, and in danger of losing his life. He fled to Midian.

In Midian, Moses pondered over the economic and social injustices to which his people were being subjected. He communed with God, from whom he received the motive power to correct a gigantic social wrong. His vision of Jehovah gave him the conviction that Jehovah is a God of justice and mercy who understands social and industrial evils and sympathizes with the socially defeated classes. Moses reports this remarkable social message from Jehovah:

"I have surely seen the affliction of my people that are in Egypt, and have heard their cry of anguish because of their taskmasters, for I know their sorrows, and I am come down to deliver them out of the power of the Egyptians."[2]

In other words, against the union of great wealth and political power in the hands of an unjust man, God revolted, and God said to Moses: "Rescue this Israelitish people from the heels of autocracy." Moses conceived of Jehovah as a God who is "full of sympathy for the afflicted and dependent and ever eager to champion their cause against cruel oppression." Moses' conception of Jehovah as a socially spirited God is unique for that day in human history. God is described as a lover of justice and even a lover of mankind. When God speaks, it is usually in terms of democracy. The first social teachings of the Old Testament, considered chronologically, are those against social and industrial oppression.

A momentous conflict ensued. Fired by the promises and presence and power of Jehovah, Moses journeyed back to Egypt. He proceeded to organize the first labor strike known to mankind. Thereupon, the angry Pharaoh commanded the workers to make brick without straw. And when the workers cried out against the impositions and burdens, the agents of "the first great captains of industry" taunted the workers and cried at them: "Ye are idle, ye are idle." But God and Moses won against the hosts of autocracy and plutocracy. The workers were freed.

Out of these struggles the Hebrew nation took form. Group loyalty, or patriotism, became a conscious Hebrew concept. The idea of kinship was supplemented by an appreciation of the meaning of national life. Furthermore, a sense of social and economic justice received a clear-cut and positive human expression and divine approval. For the first time the social problem was defined.

The major social chord which the Hebrew prophets kept vibrating was justice. Some of the recurring interpretations of the needs of the hour were: Let justice roll down like waters; Rulers shall govern in justice; Hear, I pray you, ye heads of Israel, is it not for you to know justice?

The Hebrew word for the English "justice" is *mishpat.* It is used in various senses, such as, justice, order, law, right, legal right. Amos wanted *mishpat* established in the land. Micah asserted that Jehovah requires the individual to do *mishpat,* and to love kindness, and to walk humbly with his God. Isaiah urged the people to do well and to seek *mishpat;* he pronounced woe upon those who turned aside the needy from *mishpat;* he declared Jehovah to be a God of *mishpat.* Jeremiah made plain that

Jehovah exercises mercy and *mishpat* among the people.

Amos protested vigorously against special class privileges. He denounced the wealthy classes because of their social arrogance and economic injustice. In describing them, he points out a fundamental principle of social procedure. By their repression of those who are protesting, they "are heaping up violence"; that is, autocratic repression will never right injustice, but will foster ultimate revolution. Amos charged the rulers and all persons in positions of social power with the primary obligation of seeing that the poor and the outcast are protected from exploitation. What satire in a day when rulers were noted for their exploitation of the weak social classes!

A special responsibility rests upon judges. Amos severely arraigned all who turn judgment to wormwood and cast righteousness to the ground. Anathemas were heaped upon the takers of bribes, especially if they sit in places of public authority and wear the robes of law and patriotism. Hot denunciation fell also upon the private doer of injustice; upon the merchant who makes smaller the measure and perverts the false balances; upon all who trample in any way upon the needy, who trample on the head of the poor, who sell the righteous for silver, who turn aside the way of the humble.[8] The concept of justice was vividly defined by Amos. Moreover, the shepherd prophet of Tekoa had the courage and ability to make the concept clear to all who would listen to him. Amos spoke for justice on the throne, on the judge's bench, in the activities of the wealthy, in the transactions of merchants, and in the daily dealings of individuals with one another.

The campaign against injustice is carried forward by the first Isaiah, the statesman and orator. In the Kingdom of Judah, Isaiah found the same social evils that Amos had earlier preached against in the Northern kingdom. The boldness of his attack is startling:

Thy princes are rebellious, and companions of thieves: everyone loveth gifts, and followeth after rewards: they judge not the fatherless, neither does the cause of the widow come unto them.[4]

Then Isaiah enters upon perhaps the most open, daring, and indignant challenge to doers of social iniquity that is to be found anywhere:

Ye have eaten of the vineyard; the spoil of the poor is in your houses. What mean ye that ye beat my people to pieces, and grind the faces of the poor?[5]

After the manner of Amos, Isaiah protested vigorously against the judges and officers of the law who for a bribe vindicate the wicked and deprive the innocent man of his innocence. He denounced in no doubtful language the scribes who devote themselves to writing oppression, who turn aside the dependent from securing justice, who prevent

Jehovah's followers from receiving honest treatment, who prey upon widows and despoil orphans. Special condemnation was heaped upon those who set up iniquitous decrees.

Isaiah was a forerunner in an indirect sense of Henry George, for he vehemently rebuked land monopolists. His new principle is contained in a pronouncement of woes upon the persons who join house to house and add field to field, until there is no land left except for the monopolist who dwells as a lord over all. Isaiah protested against social injustice not only because of the harmful effects upon the individual but also because of the destructive and enervating national results.

After the fashion of Amos and Isaiah, Micah conceived of Jehovah as a just God. Micah depicts the social injustice of his day in terms of the persons who hate the good and love the evil, who pluck off the skin of the weak, even the flesh from the bones of Jehovah's followers; "who also eat the flesh of my people, and flay their skin from off them; and they break their bones, and chop them in pieces, as for the pot, and as flesh within the caldron."[6]

Micah unhesitatingly condemns the priests who are giving oracles for a reward, and the prophets who are divining for silver and who are trusting in Jehovah to protect them. Micah was perhaps the first person to describe the activities of the criminaloid which have been so carefully analyzed by Professor E. A. Ross. He grasped the concept of the social sinner who keeps within the law. He attacked wealthy landowners who crush the small holders; he spared neither high officials, nor priests. He presented his social concepts with precision and effectiveness.

The invectives against social injustice are carried into the teachings of Jeremiah. They appear later in the Deuteronomic Code. The Psalmists deprecated injustice. The wisdom teachers uttered profound warnings on the subject. The writer of Job deplored injustice. Throughout the Old Testament the almost countless references justify the conclusion that justice is the leading social concept which is presented by ancient Hebrew thought.

The Old Testament parallels its denunciation of unjust social relationships with diatribes against luxury. The evil effects of great riches are again and again described. Amos boldly pointed the finger of scorn at the idle rich, at those who "lie upon beds of ivory and stretch themselves upon their couches."

The possession of vast wealth has usually been considered by those persons who are immediately concerned as an expression of divine favor. Amos exposed the fallacies in this belief, commanded the owners of wealth to assume social responsibility, and instantly to cease their unholy practices of securing gain.

Isaiah united with Amos in treating the possession of wealth not as a matter of favor or luck, but as a social trust. With one stroke Jeremiah tore off the gilded frame from about the life of the self-indulgent, luxury-loving King Jehoiakim. What powerful and autocratic monarch was ever charged with indulging in luxury in such relentless and uncompromising language as this?

Woe unto him that buildeth his house by unrighteousness, and his chambers by injustice. . . . .

Shalt thou reign, because thou closest thyself in cedar? . . . . .

But thine eyes and thine heart are not but for thy covetousness, and for to shed innocent blood, and for oppression, and for violence, to do it.

The ways of the dishonest rich are vividly described by Jeremiah. They set snares and catch people with lying. Their houses are full of evidences of their crooked dealings. They maintain themselves in luxury despite wanton expenditures by violating the needs of the fatherless and the needy.

Zephaniah was no less direct in pointing out the dangers in wealth. He declared that ill-gotten gains shall themselves become a prey and that the houses of the sinful rich shall become desolate. All their silver and their gold shall not be able to deliver them from their ultimate desolation.

In a beautiful and effective style the Wisdom writer in Proverbs unconsciously sums up the Old Testament philosophy concerning wealth:

Labor not to become rich; cease from thine own wisdom. Wilt thou set thine eyes upon that which is not? For riches certainly make themselves wings; they fly away as an eagle toward heaven.

The Old Testament with surprising uniformity supports the cause of labor. The welfare of the slave is frequently espoused. According to the Deuteronomic Code a runaway slave who was caught did not necessarily need to be returned to his owner. In fact, a person who harbored such a slave was expressly enjoined not to return him. By this injunction the rights of property and vested interests in slaves were ignored. Such an attitude was in opposition to the Code of Hammurapi and to the codes of vested interests throughout history. Slavery, however, was a well-established institution among the ancient Hebrews.[8]

Although the law book of Hammurapi fixed the wages of laborers, the Old Testament law book restricted the hours of labor. Not only is the master to limit his labor to six days a week, but he is commanded to see that his slaves, male and female, do not work more than six days. Modern industry, even twentieth century manufacturing enterprise in the United States, has been persistently violating the labor rules of the Hebrew law-givers. Employers are commanded not to take advantage of poor and needy hired servants. They shall not oppress labor simply because they are powerful and labor is weak. Even the poor immigrant laborer is not to be exploited!

The first legislation in behalf of immigrants is found in Deuteronomy. Employers must respect the needs of alien workers. The foreigner shall not be oppressed. In the ordinary dealings between citizens and foreigners, justice must not be perverted. The Hebrew law makers even went so far as to issue the command: Love ye therefore the strangers, for ye were strangers in the land of Egypt.

The institution of marriage is early accented in the Old Testament. In the second chapter of Genesis divine approval is placed upon marriage. In accordance with biological and social needs the institution of marriage is made sacred. Although the Hebrews are noted for their emphasis upon the responsibility of children to parents, the husband is ordered to forsake his father and his mother and cleave unto his wife. A man's obligation to his helpmate exceeds even his obligations to his father and mother.

The concept of a long-suffering, patient husband is extensively elaborated in the teachings of Hosea. This prophet of the eighth century, B. C., demonstrated the sanctity of the marriage relation by remaining true to it even after his wife bore children of whom he was not the father. It is remarkable that Hosea should not have divorced his wife at once when he learned of her unfaithfulness to the marriage vow. Hosea taught, by example, that divorce should be the last resort after all the means of love have been used in trying to win back the erring partner.

The description of Hosea's domestic difficulties, whether allegorical or not, is an early protest against the double standard of morals for man and woman. The attitude of people in modern society who blame and shun the fallen woman but permit the guilty man to continue to enjoy the company of respectable men and women is vigorously challenged by Hosea.

The last word against sex immorality was pronounced by Hosea. His description of the effects of widespread sex immorality is brief but incisive.

Whoredom and wine and new wine take away the heart.

Their glory shall fly away like a bird, from the birth, and from the womb, and from the conception.

Their root is dried up, they shall bear no fruit.

In the Deuteronomic laws we find the duties of parents to children and of children to parents carefully outlined. Parents, primarily, are made responsible for moral and religious education in the home; and children are under obligations to obey their parents. This teaching is summed up in the injunction:[10] Honor thy father and thy mother, that thy days may be long upon the land which the Lord thy God giveth thee; and in the imprecation: Whoso curseth his father or his mother, his lamp shall be put out in obscure darkness.[11]

The Wisdom writers dwell at considerable length upon the proper relationships of husbands and wives and of parents and children. They point the finger of shame at the quarrelsome woman. They warn against the woman whose chief asset is her beauty. A virtuous wife is a crown to her husband, but an immoral wife is as rottenness in his bones.[12]

The Wisdom teachers do not minimize the importance of parental discipline. On occasion parents must act with force. Correction of children is commanded. The situation is pictured in the following language:[13]

The word and reproof give wisdom; but a child left to himself bringeth his mother to shame.

In other words, it is necessary that parents assume a positive, definite attitude in regard to child nurture. They must see that their children are actually trained in the ways in which they should go. Even the loving parent must sometimes show his affection for his child by chastising the child. Only by such a procedure do children grow up to be a comfort to parents in their old age.

On the other hand the child must assume his share of responsibility. It is the part of wisdom for children to receive willingly the instruction that parents can give. The wise son loves parental advice. He listens gladly to his father; he does not despise his mother's counsels.

It has already been intimated that the Old Testament writers frequently stress the importance of high standards of conduct for women. Amos rebuked the wives of nobles and the wealthy who fritter away their best impulses in idleness and sinful living and who dissipate their deepest instincts in debauchery. Amos and Isaiah agreed, apparently, that a nation's welfare depends on the attitudes of its women. The wrath of God will fall upon women who are haughty, who walk with heads held high and with wanton glances, who go tripping along, "making a tinkling with their feet."

The anti-social character of sin was pointed out in Genesis. Cain was the first to raise naïvely and blandly the question: Am I my brother's keeper? Sinful living narrows the soul, increases selfishness, and vitiates a genuine social attitude. Sinning is repudiating social responsibility. Amos advanced the idea that selfish living was nothing less than disloyalty to one's country. To dissipate one's energy is to undermine one's usefulness to his country.

Intemperance was deplored. Isaiah has been called the first temperance reformer of the world. His impassioned and classic utterances are well represented by the following lines:[14]

Woe unto them that rise up early in the morning that they may follow strong drink; that continue until night, till wine inflame them.

Isaiah warned especially the priests and prophets of the evils of intemperance. Wine will swallow them up, it will put them out of the way, it will cause them to err in wisdom and to stumble in judgment.

In both Leviticus and Numbers the danger that lurks in the wine cup is recognized. The special servants of Jehovah are commanded to separate themselves from wine and strong drink. In Proverbs the Wisdom writer declares:[15] Wine is a mocker, strong drink is raging and whoever is deceived thereby is not wise. The same authority admonishes rulers and judges not to drink wine lest they forget the law and pervert the judgment of the afflicted. On the other hand, a reversion to a lower standard is made in Proverbs when the legitimacy of giving strong drink to the poor and miserable is recognized, so that they may forget their poverty and misery.[16] The general teaching, however, is that strong drink leads to social inefficiency and the disintegration of human personalities.

The cities of refuge represent a new social idea. A person who has taken life without intention may flee to and find protection in the cities of refuge. The altar and the sanctuary are designated as places to which persons may flee who are not wilful murderers.[17]

The social concept of democracy occupies an interesting place in the Old Testament literature. In the days of Abraham the kinship group prevailed. Within this group there were many households, ruled by patriarchs. Within the kinship groups high standards of honor were maintained, but antisocial attitudes toward outside and foreign groups were encouraged. It was justifiable, for example, to lie to foreign groups and even to kill the representatives of such peoples.

The concept of democracy developed *pari passu* with the evolution of the idea of Jehovah. In the minds of the Hebrews, Jehovah, or Jahweh, was first a tribal god, then a national god; and finally, a universal God, that is, a being who is interested in the welfare of all peoples, and not simply in the welfare of "the chosen people."

The Hebrew conception of the state contained several democratic elements. The fundamental purpose of the state was declared to be the welfare not of an irresponsible monarch, but of the people themselves. This idea stands out in marked contradiction to the practices of the Canaanites, who submitted themselves helplessly to capricious and autocratic rulers.

The Hebrews treated the state as a part of a theocracy. But when Jehovah spoke, he usually arraigned false wealth, arbitrary political power, selfish ambition of kings, luxurious living, and special privileges. Jehovah spoke for the oppressed, the poor, the defeated, the laborer,[8] in short, for humanity.

Consequently, loyalty to the nation was positive and persistent. Consider this statement from Psalm

137 of Hebrew patriotism on the part of exiled Hebrews who longed for their native land:

By the rivers of Babylon, there we sat down, yea, we wept, when we remembered Zion.

We hanged our harps upon the willows in the midst thereof. . . . . .

If I forget thee, O Jerusalem, let my right hand forget her cunning.

If I do not remember thee, let my tongue cleave to the roof of my mouth; if I prefer not Jerusalem above my chief joy.

According to Hosea, Jehovah charged the citizens of the land to deal with one another on the basis of fidelity and true love, and to stamp out all social evils, such as perjury, stealing, committing adultery, and mob violence. The writer of the Book of Job portrayed a good citizen as one who delivers the poor, who helps those about to perish, who causes the widow's heart to sing for joy.[18] He is eyes to the blind, feet to the lame, and a father to the needy. He searches out the cause of social evils. Moreover, he breaks the jaws of the unrighteous, and plucks the prey from their mouths. He defends the blameless. He does not put his confidence in gold or rejoice at his enemies when evils beset them or they are destroyed. It may be truly said that fundamental ideas of democracy were originated by the Hebrews.

Amos raised the question of internationalism. For the first time in history, the idea of a universal

God was postulated. Amos pronounced Jehovah the God of other peoples besides the Israelites. "Have not I brought up Israel out of the land of Egypt?" said Jehovah, "and the Philistines from Caphtor, and the Syrians from Kir?"[19] The day would come, according to Isaiah and Micah, when Jehovah would judge over many peoples and rebuke strong nations. The conception of Jehovah as a Being who transcends both time and space gave to the Hebrew mind at its best a broader cast and a more universal comprehension than the peoples of contemporary tribes and nations possessed.

The concept of universal peace was invented by the Hebrews. Isaiah and Micah share the honor of being the first persons to advocate world peace, and to predict the day when all nations shall worship a just God and thereby be enabled to beat their swords into plowshares and their spears into pruning-hooks, when nation shall not stand against nation, and when the methods of warfare shall no longer be taught. The spirit of hatred and of blind, selfish antagonism shall pass away. No modern writer has ever spoken the doom of militarism so trenchantly as the Old Testament prophet, Isaiah, who said, according to the translation by Charles Foster Kent:[20]

> "For every boot of the warrior with noisy tread,
> And every war-cloak drenched in the blood of the slain
> Will be completely burned up as fuel for the flame."

The Hebrews strongly emphasized laws as a social dynamic. Love will make socialized individuals. It will demonstrate to a person his responsibilities as a member of society and his duties to his fellow human beings. It will stifle hatred. It will even return good for evil. It is the cardinal virtue and an eternal principle of right living.

The Old Testament teaches social salvation. Jehovah is fundamentally interested in the improvement of social and living conditions. He commanded the socialization of all human relationships. His teachings, as given by the prophets and Wisdom writers, take cognizance of the influence of environment upon character.

Hebrew social thought deals largely with social injustice. Social evils are vividly described and evil-doers, chiefly kings and judges, are vigorously and fearlessly arraigned. The family is made the chief social institution, and love is crowned servant of all. Education is centered in the home, and moral discipline is made the keynote of education; hence the Hebrews survived the Greeks and Romans. A new and perfect social order, directed by a just Jehovah, and motivated throughout all its individual and social relationships by love, is prophesied.

CHAPTER V.

PLATO AND GRECIAN SOCIAL THOUGHT

In turning to a study of Grecian civilization we find a development of social thought which on the rational side excels in many particulars the social thinking of the Hebrews, but which in its affective elements falls far below the quality of Hebrew social thought. We may expect to find, therefore, in Grecian social thought important new contributions which are complementary to the legacies from the Hebrews, and which when taken in conjunction with the early Christian forms of Hebrew social thought constitute the main foundations of modern social thought.

The thought life of the Greeks reached the crescendo in the idealism of Plato (427-347 B. C.) and the opportunism of Aristotle (384-322 B. C.). In an idea-world Plato depicted an ideal society. After studying 158 constitutions, Aristotle formulated rules of practical social procedure. Plato's *Republic* and Aristotle's *Politics* are the two leading source books of Grecian social thought.

Plato and Aristotle were the first two thinkers in history who left definitely organized analyses of societary life. Although in point of time they stand close together, in content of social reasoning they are at many places antagonistic. However, their high rank as thinkers need not blind anyone to the fact that their social thought was in part an outgrowth of theories held by predecessors. Antecedent to Plato was Socrates and the Sophists; antecedent to these scholars was a large number of thinkers who, incidentally to their main intellectual efforts, gave expression to isolated but significant social ideas.

As early as the ninth century, B. C., Lycurgus declared that the state owned the child, and urged a system of education which would prepare the child for the state. Despite, however, of a similar emphasis by many later Greek leaders, "Hellas" never developed a genuine national unity. She experienced a temporary national patriotism only when attacked by the Persians and at the seasons when the national games were at their height.

It was Hesiod, the founder of Greek didactic poetry, who about 700 B. C. described the Golden Age and the subsequent ages of society. Hesiod protested mildly against the social injustice in his time.[1] In the following century, Anaximander, the philosopher, and Theognis, the elegiac poet,[2] discussed the value to society of providing that children should be well born and well trained—the fundamental concepts of current eugenics and euthenics.

Solon, the Athenian lawgiver, about 590 B. C.,

began to put into legislative practice certain ideas of social reform, thereby preventing revolution. At that time it was customary to sell persons into slavery who could not pay their debts—a procedure which Solon ended. The cost of living was very high, consequently Solon forbade the export of food products and thereby reduced prices for the consumer. He introduced a measure which today would be considered revolutionary, namely, the limiting of the amount of land which an individual might hold. For the classification of people on the basis of wealth, he substituted a classification on the basis of income. He lessened the severity of the laws of Draco, and in other ways increased the freedom of the individual. Although Solon's régime was followed by a tyranny, Solon is credited with initiating certain essential ideas of democracy.

After the Tyrants, Athens under the leadership of men like Cleisthenes became "a pure democracy." Cleisthenes democratized the Athenian Constitution. For the four phylae he substituted ten phylae, or units of government, thus securing a new and better distribution of authority. He is credited with introducing ostracism as a mode of punishment; he, it is alleged, was the first individual to be ostracised by his government.

The fifth century precursors of Plato and Aristotle were numerous. Aeschylus (525-456 B. C.), the first of the famous Athenian tragic poets, described in general terms the evolution of civilized society.[3] The artistic historian, Herodotus, developed through his imagination a world point of view. From an almost unlimited store of legendary and ethnological materials, he elaborated a planetary theme which had its beginning in the Trojan War and its culmination in the conflict between Eastern and Western civilizations. The basic social principle in the writings of Herodotus is that downfall awaits the insolent autocrats of earth. Herodotus describes the customs and habits of the peoples[4] whom he visited on his numerous foreign travels in such a detailed and elaborate fashion that he has been styled the world's first descriptive sociologist.

Pericles (495?-429 B. C.), perhaps the greatest statesman of Greece, furthered the cause of democracy. His conception of democracy led him to make the entire body of citizens eligible to office-holding. Pericles initiated a social program which in certain aspects was paternalistic. He instituted the plan of granting allowances for performing public duties. As a result, unselfish public service was minimized and political morale was weakened. Pericles was led into this error[5] by the desire to compete for public esteem with Cimon, who made extensive gifts to the poor in the form of dinners and clothes.

In his tragedies, Euripides (480-406 B. C.), aroused interest in the experiences, not of legendary characters as many of his predecessors had done, but of the ordinary members of Athenian society.

He was a spokesman for the emancipation of woman;[6] his writings reveal the social changes that were occurring in the fifth century in Athens. Likewise, the comedies of Aristophanes reflected social changes, and, in addition, caricatured social conditions.

Hippocrates, the so-called father of medical science, wrote several works which attracted the studious attention of Plato. He gave as the first of two chief causes of disease, the influence of climate, seasons, weather on the individual.[7] He might be called the first anthropo-geographer. At any rate he opened the field which has recently been so well covered by Ellen C. Semple in her *Influences of Geographic Environment.*

By their disconcerting and sceptical teachings the Sophists, who also lived in the fifty centucy, B. C., stimulated the intellectual activities of Socrates. The influence of the Sophist leaders, such as Protagoras, Gorgas, Callicles, Thrasymachus, brought forward the problem of training pupils to solve civic questions rather than scientific or philosophical questions. According to Plato, Callicles believed that government was an instrument for exploiting the masses. Thrasymachus argued that so-called justice is that type of activity which favors the interest of the strongest members of society, and that might determines what is called right.[8] Epaminondas, the Theban statesman, personified in his own career an unusually high interpretation of the concept of patriotism, perhaps a more unselfish expression of patriotism than is represented by any other political spokesman of the Hellenic states.

The argument of the Sophists that what is best for the individual is best for society aroused the antagonism of Socrates (469-399 B. C.), whose ideas are reported by Plato and Xenophon. Socrates, the son of an Athenian sculptor, asserted that the qualities of justice, wisdom, temperance, and courage, which make a person a good member of society and which increase social welfare, are the same qualities which make a person a good individual and secure his individual advancement. Socrates spent many years at the market places, on the streets where people congregate and at the public resorts in studying the actions of individuals and in engaging them in conversation concerning their moral life. As a result Socrates evolved a significant social philosophy. The heart of this philosophy is found in the statements that virtue is knowledge, not in the sense of mere memorized facts but of a thorough understanding. If a person understands completely the good and evil phases of a proposed act, he will choose the right. For example, when one is completely convinced of the harmful effects of poor teeth, he will employ the regular services of a dentist to keep his teeth in good condition. When he perceives the evil effects of dishonesty, he will establish honest habits. The conclusion might be drawn that social virtue rests upon societary knowledge.

Socrates was convinced that something was fundamentally wrong with Athenian society. Everywhere he saw that ignorance led to vice. Only in the mechanical and professional activities did he discover correct action, but this was preceded by correct knowledge.[9]

A good carpenter is an individual who thoroughly understands carpentry; a good man is an individual who truly knows the value of good actions. Similarly, it might be said that a good urban resident is an individual who deeply appreciates what it means to have a city of mutually developing people.

Socrates wished to make all men intelligent. His teachings raised the deep-seated social question: How can social organization be made highly advantageous to the individual, and the individual made so aware of these advantages that he will always act socially?[10] Inasmuch as Socrates left no writings, it is impossible to explain with certainty his teachings. Fortunately, he left a permanent impress of his personality on the lives of his associates, and particularly, upon his able and brilliant pupil, Plato.

In the fundamental dictum that virtue is knowledge, Socrates is theoretically correct, but practically he ignores the overpowering influence that oftentimes is exerted by the instincts and established habits. He underestimates the power that is represented by a deeply ingrained instinct or a habit which has existed for several years. Instincts and nearly all habits are firmly established neurologically, whereas knowledge is often new to the individual and merely a veneer on the surface of the individual's life. The acquisition of knowledge is no guarantee that instincts centuries old will be promptly overcome or re-directed.

Furthermore, with a young child the instinctive tendencies begin to assert themselves and to give direction to the growth of the character of the child, long before his mentality has unfolded and developed to the point where he is capable of genuinely understanding the real meaning of many forms of activity, and where many phases of knowledge are entirely beyond his ability to comprehend.

Little is known concerning Plato's early life and training. The most influential factors were the life and teachings of Socrates. The strong Socratic personality left its indelible impress upon the thought-life of Plato. As a young man, Plato became greatly interested in Athenian social and civic life. When he was perhaps twenty-three years of age, the self-styled "Fair and Good" rulers came into control of Athens. The failure of these men, whom history calls the Thirty Tyrants, to govern wisely, produced an attitude of thorough disgust in the mind of Plato. Further, the legalized murder of Socrates by the restored democracy in 399 B. C. aroused the bitter antagonism of Plato to the existing forms of government. In the years which followed the death of Socrates, popular rule produced loose and licentious social conditions. As a consequence, Plato turned to the realms of the thought world in order to find a perfect society. As a result of his contact with every-day life and government, Plato evolved in his mind an ideal republic.

The Socratic principle that virtue is knowledge was accepted by Plato. In Plato's thinking this proposition led to the generalization that education is the most important thing in the world. Upon this doctrine more than any other, Plato's twentieth century influence thrives.

What shall be the nature of a world-molding education? Theoretically, Plato gives his answer in his epistemology. Ideas are the ruling forces in life. Over against the uncertain fluctuating sense world, Plato set up a realm of eternal, changeless ideas. An individual man is simply an ephemeral expression of Man. Plato created a concept of unchangeable reality which he found in Ideas. These, alone, are the permanent, worth-while elements which man must seek to know and understand.

Because of his aristocratic attitudes and of his early disgust with the experiments in democracy in his day, Plato turned away in his social philosophy from the direct study of the people, such as had engaged the attention of Socrates, to a search for a just society in the world of ideas. This line of thinking found expression chiefly in the *Republic*, written during Plato's mature manhood. A discussion of these idealistic concepts is found in the *Laws* and the *Politicus,* the latter being written in Plato's old age and representing a partial reaction from the idealism of the *Republic.* Because of its consideration of nearly every aspect of social life from a specific viewpoint, the *Republic* may be called the first treatise in social philosophy. While it falls below the social writings of the Hebrews in its dynamic and practical phases, it excels them in its unity, its profundity, and its philosophic quality.

Inasmuch as Plato had turned away from an inviting though strenuous public career to a private life of scholarly thought, his perfect society assumed characteristics that were far from mundane. Because Plato lived in a day of small political groups and in a country of limited size, he limited his ideal society—to a group represented by 5040 heads of families. Consequently it is impossible to apply Plato's social ideas with accuracy to a modern metropolitan center of 5,000,000 people, or to a nation-state of 100,000,000 people. Several phases of Plato's thought, however, were given a practical turn in the *Laws.* In revealing Plato's social philosophy, the *Politicus,* or *Statesman* ranks third.[12]

In Plato's ideal society there is a hierarchy of rank, which includes three classes of people: the rulers, or true guardians; the soldiers, or auxiliaries; and the artisans, or the industrial and agricultural workers. In introducing the ideal state

Plato uses mature individuals.[13] Out of the needs and through the activities of fully-developed persons, Plato builds an ideal commonwealth.

No individual is self-sufficing. Each has his peculiar bias, or ability. By uniting, all will profit. There are not only specialized classes, but there is specialization within the occupational groups. An essential rule for the building of a just society is that each individual shall find his place in the social order and shall fulfil his special function. Plato recognized the need for correlating the diversities of nature and the different types of occupation.[14]

The common people are engaged in the foundational occupations as skilled artisans. The advantages of a special education are not open to them. They receive the common education, including gymnastic and music training. But, in accordance with the aristocratic strain in Plato's social philosophy, it is useless to try to give a higher education to that large proportion of the population who are mentally incapable of profiting by higher education. The logic is good but the major premise is faulty in this pedagogical rule.

The second class, the soldiers, will maintain order at home, repel invaders, and conduct territorial wars. The growth of population will create a demand for more territory. Other states likewise will need more territory, and war will become inevitable.[15] Plato frankly admits the territorial basis of wars. From this factor he sees no escape, although he declares peace to be better than war.[16] In his *Tamias* and *Critias* he pictured a peace-state, "Atlantis."

The soldier's occupation is an art which requires years of training. The chief physical trait of a true soldier is courage. The social psychological significance of a military régime is that soldiers are continually inciting their country to go to war. Such a régime raises up enemies against itself, many and mighty, and results either in ruining the specific people or in enslaving the foes of these people.[17] On the other hand, the non-soldier classes, since they prefer to lead a peaceful life and seek to conduct their affairs quietly, unduly endeavor to avoid war. By degrees they become unwarlike; their children develop a like attitude. Eventually, they find themselves at the mercy of their enemies and are enslaved.[18]

Among the members of the state there will be a few especially able individuals, destined by birth and reinforced by training to be rulers and true guardians of the welfare of all.[19] They are lovers of wisdom and philosophy. Flabbiness of character, drunkenness, selfishness are unbecoming to them.[20] Selfish living is condemned.[21] The guardians are characterized, according to Plato, by the greatest eagerness to do what is for the good of their country. They show utter repugnance to anything that is contrary to the best interests of the state.[22]

The guardians, however, rule aristocratically.[23] They do not inquire of the citizens the kind of laws which they want passed, for the same reason that a physician does not ask the patient the kind of medicine which he wants. In the *Republic,* the *Laws,* and the other dialogues where the nature of rulers and philosophers is discussed, Plato's "best men" show an indifference to earthly or material things and uniformly seek righteousness, even social righteousness.

The candidates for guardianship receive first the elements of education. At twenty years of age they must pass a general education in order that they may go on with a special course, including arithmetic, geometry, and astronomy.[24] At thirty they are subjected to a further examination, after which the successful individuals devote five years to the study of philosophy. At thirty-five they enter practical life, hold minor offices, balance their theoretical training by practical studies, and submit to diverse temptations.[25] They undergo a civil service examination which extends over a period of years. At the close they are subjected to a final series of threefold tests. The first test is that of logic; they must argue successfully that it pays an individual, especially a guardian, to serve society. The second test is that of fear; they are faced with dangers, for example, the dangers to life, which beset those who undertake to rule without favoritism and without compromising their principles when confronted with the ambitions and desires of powerful selfish interests. The third test is that of pleasure; they are submitted to all the pleasures which thrill the heart of man. In other words, they must show proof that the highest interest of the state is to be the ruling interest of their lives.[26] Neither pain nor threats must affect their loyalty. The temptations which come from pleasures and enchantments must not disturb their self-control or weaken their qualities of guardianship. From these requirements it will be seen that Plato provided for a long period of intensive and extensive training for the rulers. His idea varied widely from the ancient theory of the divine right of kings and from the current practice of distributing political spoils to friends.

Plato saw that the rulers when once selected and installed in office would be tempted to become avaricious at the expense of the state. Instead of becoming and remaining allied to all the citizens, they will be prone to become tyrannical.[27] Plato perceived that it would be difficult, after good rulers had been selected, to keep them on the plane of good rulership. In order to preserve their virtue as guardians and to remove the powerful temptation to wink at exploitation that is carried on by the economically powerful, Plato indicated certain protective devices. The guardians shall be permitted no private property beyond a few incidentals. They shall not live in private houses, but shall dwell and eat together. They shall receive a fixed salary, sufficient to meet necessary expenses but no more. They shall not be allowed to touch gold and silver or to wear gold and silver ornaments. They shall be taught that they are made of divine gold and silver, and therefore shall have no need of the earthly dross. They shall not be subject to pollution from any earthly contacts. If the guardians should acquire lands or moneys or homes of their own, they would be unable to give their undivided attention to the state, and they would become not guardians of the welfare of the citizens, but tyrants, plotting and being plotted against.[28] In his zealous care that the rulers might not be distracted from guarding with undivided attention the interests of the state, Plato advocated community of wives and children for the rulers.[29]

The question arose: Will the people be content to accept the division of the population into hierarchal classes? In reply, Plato suggested that the power of public opinion be utilized, and that all the inhabitants of the state be taught that they are brothers, that is, children of their common Mother Earth. This instruction will serve to keep the masses in a humble attitude. Further, they are to be told that different metals have been used by Mother Earth in making different individuals. Those persons in whose make-up gold has been mingled have the power of command and may become rulers. Others who are made of silver may become auxiliaries, or soldiers; while the masses, being made of brass and iron, are destined to become artisans.[80]

The objection is raised that people will not believe this "audacious fiction." The truth of the objection is admitted, and a solution of the problem is offered. Teach the children the gold, silver, brass and iron fiction; and they will believe it. When they grow to maturity, they will tell their children, who in turn will teach it. Posterity, thus, will accept it.[81] In this way Plato founded his social philosophy upon education. Plato made clear that any kind of social or economic theory can be foisted upon a whole people through the utilization of the educational processes. A few selfish exploiters, by controlling the educational system, can ruin a nation in a generation.

The guardians are instructed to examine the children in order to discover of what metals they are made. Plato admitted a democracy of talent in the sense that talent is likely to appear in the children of brass and iron parents, while gold parents may beget brass and iron children. If a gold child is found among the children of the artisans, he is to be encouraged and trained to become a guardian. If a brass and iron child is found among the children of the gold parents, he must descend the social scale and be trained for husbandry or artisanship.[82] Plato foresaw the fact, now scientifically established, that geniuses are born indiscriminately among all classes of society from the highest to the lowest. They are just as likely to be born in the hovel or overcrowded tenement as in the spacious and luxuriant palace. Consequently, society should seek out potential genius and give it opportunities commensurate with its possibilities and not allow its dynamic and divine spark to be snuffed out in a heavy-laden tenement atmosphere.

Furthermore, according to Plato, the guardians are to seek out the imperfect children and put them out of the way as easily as possible and without attracting public attention.[33] If the capable must devote their energies to the care of imperfect children, they would presumably be wasting their ability and would be prevented from devoting themselves to upbuilding the state. This doctrine neglects the consideration of the harsh, unsympathetic attitude which it would engender. Although rigorously eugenic, the doctrine is undemocratic, unchivalric, and unChristian. It is thoroughly aristocratic.

The guardians are to supervise marriage. Plato especially deplores the fact that almost all persons choose their life-partners in marriage without proper regard to the kind of children that will be procreated.[34] The marriage relationship should not be primarily an individual affair, but should be governed by the thought of the children that are not yet born and by due regard to the welfare of the state and society.[35] The true purpose of marriage is not found in wealth or power or rank, but in the procreation of healthy minded children. Marriage is sacred in the highest degree because it is socially necessary. Plato deplores class marriages, that is, marriage within temperamentally similar groups. Persons of gentle nature seek persons of gentle nature; the courageous seek the courageous. It would be better if the gentle would seek the courageous in marriage, and vice versa.[36] Marriage is sacred, and hence should be subjected to strict eugenic safeguards.

The guardians shall prevent the extremes of poverty and riches. With far-sighted social wisdom Plato points out that poverty is the parent of meanness and viciousness, and that wealth leads to luxury and indolence.[37] Both result in discontent and both cause the deterioration of the arts. The poor man cannot properly equip or train himself, or enter into his work painstakingly; the rich man will grow careless and no longer act diligently when he comes into the possession of unlimited wealth.[38]

In the acquisition of wealth the laws of imitation function powerfully. One person accumulates property; others are immediately stimulated to do likewise. In consequence, all the citizens may become lovers of money.[39] But a money-loving public would be disastrous to the state.

The larger the amount of wealth that an individual accumulates, the more he will want to accumulate. The momentum of the desire for money-getting is socially destructive. The more the individual is hypnotised by the wealth-getting delusion, the less attention does he give to the maintenance of virtue. When the desire for virtue is in competition with the desire for riches, the former decreases as the latter increases.[40]

When the state becomes established on a property basis, the rich exercise power and the poor are deprived of it.[41] In ordinary times the rich are as indifferent to the welfare of the poor as to the development of virtue, but in times of group crises they will not despise the poor. In the days of prosperity and peace the poor man is given the hindmost position, but when war comes, "the wiry, sunburnt poor man" is placed in battle at the side of the wealthy man[42]—and social democracy obtains. But in battle the poor man fights longer and better than the rich man "who has never spoilt his complexion and has plenty of superfluous flesh." In the words of the poor man Plato draws the astounding conclusion that many persons are rich because no one has had the courage to despoil them.[43] At this point Plato has given a striking explanation of the rise of socialism, syndicalism, and economic radicalism.

When you see paupers, according to Plato, you may safely conclude that somewhere there are also present thieves, robbers of temples, and malefactors.[44] The causes of pauperism are given as (1) a lack of proper education, (2) ill-training, and (3) unjust social laws and an unjust constitution of the state.[45]

Plato suggested two instruments for preventing extreme wealth and poverty—legislation and education. Each individual is to be guaranteed a minimum amount of property. He may acquire as much as four times this amount, but above the maximum a one hundred per cent excess tax operates.[46] Plato planned a form of communism, not primarily to secure the material well-being of the state, but to safeguard the rulers against falling before selfish temptations. Plato also wanted to protect the state from splitting asunder because of the distractions that arise from labor-capital controversies. By educational means the children are to be trained to be satisfied with the necessaries of life[47]—at least some children are to be so trained. Parents should bequeath to their children not riches but the spirit of reverence.[48]

The guardians shall be censors. They shall establish a censorship over the arts in order to protect the children from seeing indecent sights and hearing vulgar sounds. The works of fiction shall be censored in order to prevent the children from reading and adopting bad ideas. The creative artists shall be prevented from exhibiting forms of vice and intemperance, in order that the future guardians may not grow up in an atmosphere contaminated by images of moral deformity, and in order that all children may develop in an environment of fair sights and should and may receive unhindered and unhampered the good in everything.[49]

The guardians shall protect the *mores*. When Plato described a perfect state, any change in the established customs would mean retrogression.[50] Hence, the rulers should jealously guard the customs, allowing no insidious innovations. Further, if any change is permitted to take place in small things, there may be no stopping the spirit of change.

Plato rested his argument for an ideal society upon the education of wise leaders. Their judgment is better even than government by law. Law is too rigid and inflexible. In view of the changeable character of human conditions, which Plato recognized, no final or absolute laws can be laid down.[51] The chief advantage of laws, however, is not that they make men honest but that they make men act uniformly, and hence in a socially reliable way. Laws are to be respected because they represent the ripe fruits of long experience.[52]

Considerable attention is given to penology in the *Laws*.[2] In view of the sanctity of custom and of the necessity of law, obedience is a highly important social virtue. In theory Plato is modern and scientific, for he advocated punishment, not as a vindictive but as a preventive and reformatory measure.[54] Reformation is the true aim of punishment.[55] In practice Plato is rigid and harsh. For example, beggars are simply to be sent out of the city and out of the country.[56] The death penalty is utilized freely.[57]

Plato opened all occupations to women as well as men, even the highest, that of ruling.[58] The only difference between the sexes that needs to be recognized occupationally is that men are stronger physically than women.[59] Women, like men, vary in occupational temperament. One individual is fitted for one kind of vocation; another, for some other type of work.

Although the fundamental importance of bearing children is appreciated, Plato observed that it is unnecessary that a woman devote her whole life to the rearing of children. All women should have opportunities for the development of their personalities. Those women who have special talent for public service should enter thereupon. Although a social conservative Plato admits an innovation in the ideal republic—universal woman suffrage.

Since women have the same duties as men, they receive the same opportunities for training. Women must share in the toils of war and the defense of their country.[60] Women are priestesses;[61] they serve on committees for the regulation of marriage, and for deciding divorce cases.[62]

Although Plato was averse to change, he advocated a dynamic type of education. This educational system, however, is to be definitely controlled by the guardians. It is also paternalistic. Common education shall be of two kinds: gymnastic, for the body; music, for the soul.[63] Gymnastic training will produce a temper of hardness, and music will lead to gentleness. The extreme of the one is ferocity and brutality; the extreme of the other is softness and effeminacy.[64] When taken together, they produce a well-ordered personality. The one sustains and makes bold the reason, the second moderates and civilizes the mildness of passion.[65] Gymnastic exercises provide for the care and training of the body through childhood and youth so that in maturity the body may best serve the soul.[66] Music, including literature, trains through the influence of its qualities of harmony and rhythm. For example, through exercises in harmony the child develops a harmonious temperament.

Education is not a process of acquisition, but of the development of the powers within the individual.[67] It is a life-long process; it begins with birth and continues until death. It, however, slows up as the individual grows old. An aged person cannot learn much, no more than he can run much.[68] Education in the early years of life is the most important. As a child is educated, so will his future be determined.[69] A child should be taught early to respect his parents. Great care should be given to the first years of life. From three to six years of age the children in Plato's republic come under the supervision of chosen matrons and nurses.

Education shall be universal, but not compulsory, that is, all shall be taught, but not compelled to learn. Education shall be made attractive, almost a form of government.[70] The laws of imitation shall be utilized. The tutor shall carry out his teachings in practice.[71]

A well-trained individual is a replica of a just society. Plato draws a parallelism, which is inaccurate, between the three classes in society and three traits of the individual. The rulers, soldiers, and artisans are compared respectively to the reason, the spirit, and the passions of the individual. The passions must be subordinated to the spirit, and both must be controlled by reason. The result will be a just individual.[72] In society a similar hierarchal relation shall hold between the rulers, soldiers, and artisans. The fundamental aim in education shall be to secure a change in the attitudes of people. Such changes are more important than modification in external matters. Thus, according to Plato, the divine foundations of a state are laid in education.

Religion plays a basic rôle in the ideal Republic. Plato held that belief in God superseded in importance the doctrine that might is right. Impiety undermines the strength of the social kingdom. God created the individual for the whole, but not the whole for the individual. The worship of God is necessary for the individual in order to prevent him from reverting to selfishness and from making his humanitarian beliefs purely egoistic phenomena.

Inasmuch as Plato outlined at the start a perfect

republic, any change would likely constitute a deterioration. But even an ideal state is not immune to the entry of destructive ideas. The wise men, the rulers, are not proof against the temptations of absolute power. To remove the stirrings of self-interest in the minds of the guardians, Plato planned a communistic order. He overlooked, however, the weaknesses of communism, but these were pointed out at a later time by Aristotle.

In spite of excellent safeguards the wisdom of the best rulers will occasionally fail them. Sooner or later they will err. In examining the youth they will allow warrior youth to be trained for the guardian class. With their spirit of contention and of ambition for honor these adventitious guardians will start the perfect state upon the downward road.[74] When the rulers seek personal power and honor, the ideal republic will be superseded by a timocracy.

In a timocracy the ruler with the most private wealth will possess the greatest personal power and receive the highest honor. Moreover, other persons will be stimulated, thereby, to acquire wealth and power. In the meantime the masses will lose nearly everything. The result is an oligarchy in which the wealthy are honored and made rulers.[75] The poor are treated with dishonor and deprived of position.

In such an oligarchic state there is a fundamental division; there are two states instead of one. In spirit, the rich and the poor comprise separate states. They live in the same territory but are conspiring against one another.[76] Social stability is destroyed by the conflicts between the extremes of countless riches and utter poverty. The propertyless hate and conspire against the propertied.[77] Civil war ensues. Because the wealthy have fallen into carelessness and extravagance, and because the poor possess superior numbers, the poor are the victors. A democracy—the rule of the Demos—comes into being. Everyone rules.

But the populace is not fitted to rule. They are without experience. Since the drones are numerous among the common people, the drones manage almost everything in a democracy.[78] Excess of liberty among people untrained for liberty leads to anarchy. Individuals will set themselves up as the special friends of the common people. These self-appointed friends of the people will prove to be self-seeking tyrants; the democracy will be transformed into a tyranny—the lowest state of all in Plato's five-fold devolution.

With distrust of the masses and with a paternalistic government, Plato coupled a belief that the individual must participate in the life of society. Social justice does not consist in doing good to one's friends and ill to one's enemies, or in catering to the interests of the most powerful. The theory that might is right is repudiated.[79] A just society is one in which every person has found his place of greatest usefulness to the state and fulfils his entire obligations in that place. On the whole Plato exhibited an impassioned faith in the moral and social order.

Plato believed that Ideas are real and that they are the tools with which the world is made over. He perceived perfect Forms, even a perfect social Form. Through intellectual control, Plato planned a new social order.

CHAPTER VI.

ARISTOTLE AND GRECIAN SOCIAL THOUGHT

Aristotle (384-322 B. C.), the distinguished pupil of Plato, did not make, like his master, a unified contribution to social thought. He sacrificed unity for the examination of parts. Aristotle was an opportunist, a pragmatist, and a practical student of conditions and constitutions. Unlike Plato, Aristotle did not look for Ideas separate from but in things.

Aristotle studied 158 constitutions inductively and comparatively. His primary attention was given to what is, rather than to what ought to be. His eyes were directed first of all to the parts, and then to the whole. In this examination he found that the parts are related, and further, that they hold a developmental relation. Instead of Plato's perfection, we shall now consider Aristotle's process of becoming. Although unsystematic, the social ideas of Aristotle reveal the concepts of process and progress.

In Aristotle's *Ethics* the discussion of virtue is socially valuable. Virtue is a mean. Virtue is an impulse which is expressed neither in excess or in deficiency. It is an impulse expressed temperately until it becomes a habit. Excess and deficiency are equally fatal. The coward is he who avoids and fears anything; the foolhardy is he who rushes into danger anywhere.[1] Liberality is the mean between prodigality and avarice; civility is the mean between obsequiousness and insolence. Virtue itself is the mean between self-indulgence and asceticism. In virtue, lies happiness, man's *summum bonum.*

Aristotle's *Politics* affords a searching analysis of many phases of societary life. The family and the state are by nature prior to the individual, since the whole must exist before any individual part.[2] When isolated, the individual is not self-sufficient. Thus, the state is founded on the social needs of the individual. By virtue of these social needs, man possesses the gregarious, or social, instinct. By nature, man is a political animal,[3] that is, he is a being who by nature or necessity lives in association with his kind. Man can attain his highest good only as a member of society.

Property is accorded by Aristotle a fundamental social position. Physical necessities can best be provided through the efforts of individuals. Communal ownership of property on a large scale will fail. In referring to Plato's communism, Aristotle declared: "For that which is common to the greatest number has the least care bestowed upon it."[4] Further, when one feels a thing to be his own, how much greater is his pleasure in it.[5] Then, if one has private property, he may have the great pleasure which comes from making gifts to others. Moreover, communism will lead to an unusual amount of quarrelling; those who work faithfully will feel aggrieved when they see that those who work dilettantishly receive and consume a full portion.[6]

Aristotle deprecated land equalization. Equalization of the desire for land is urged. Instead of dividing land equally or of establishing communism in land, Aristotle advocated that the higher classes be trained not to desire more land. He also stated that speculators and land schemers should be prevented from getting more land.[7]

The communism in wives and children that Plato suggested, Aristotle denounced as impracticable and foolish. Such a procedure will weaken friendship and destroy love. Moreover, it will break up the unity of the state.[8]

Aristotle held the prevalent disdainful attitude toward manual labor, and theoretically justified slavery. A slave is a person who by nature is a slave, a person who by nature expresses himself through bodily action. He is unable to guide himself by means of reason.[9]

The subject of social control and government received extended treatment from Aristotle. After considering a great variety of forms of government, he avoided a dogmatic choice of any particular form. He arrived at what is the modern, scientific conclusion, namely, that no one form of government is to be worshipped to the exclusion of all other types. A successful, or virtuous, government depends on the attitude of the people. Human nature must be changed. All people must become socially virtuous before a perfected government can be established.

Theoretically, Aristotle believed that the best government would come through the absolute rulership of one man, provided that there is available a man pre-eminently wise and virtuous. But practically, Aristotle held that in choosing a form of government which will succeed, it is necessary to consider the actual social conditions, the state of development of the people, and the attitude of the ruler or rulers. It does not matter whether one person, or a few persons, or a large number of persons perform the function of ruler so long as the best interests of the state are kept uppermost. If the interests of the entire group are the guiding principles, then royalty, aristocracy, or constitutionalism is commendable. The one, the few, or the many are good rulers, providing they are dominated by the common interests. In these declarations Aristotle overlooked the fact that participation in government by the governed is essential. He also neglected the fact that a "best" ruler would be subject to very many temptations as a result of personifying in himself all the forms of political, economic, and social power that exist within the state. After a period of time he would probably yield to some interests which are inimical to the welfare of the whole.[10]

When private interests control the government, the resultant forms of government are either tyranny, oligarchy, or democracy. According to Aristotle the chief difference between oligarchy and democracy is that an oligarchy is the rule of the rich and a democracy is the rule of the poor. Evidently, he believed that the poor are as selfish as the rich and that the poor are incapable of being trained to the levels of virtuous citizenship.

Although Aristotle is aristocratic in his political science and advocated frequently the rule of the best few, he endorsed a constitutional republic. Such a form of government will succeed where there are many wise and virtuous individuals. He admitted that in large numbers there is a stability of judgment and that common sense bulks large. Under constitutional government, the extremes will cancel one another, and the virtuous mean will rule. Large numbers of persons are less likely to be corrupted than a few persons or even the one best person.[11]

There are two fundamentals in a good government: first, actual obedience of the laws by the citizens; second, the social goodness of the laws. Aristotle's formula for an ideal society is this: virtuous people and good laws, both judged by the common welfare. And practically, the form of political organization—a monarchy, an aristocracy, or a constitutional republic—depends upon the place of the members of the social order on the incline of socialization.

If a constitutional republic is established, then rotation in office should be practiced. The tenure of office should be restricted to six months.[12] An office should rarely be held more than once by the same person.

On the other hand, the laws should be changed slowly.[13] Law has no power to make people obey in spirit, except through force of habit. The state must guard itself against small changes in laws. Any apparently slight neglect or disregard of law is insidious; transgression creeps in unperceived.[14] At first, small transgressions may not be observed; then, they may gain such momentum that they will ruin the state. Hence, there should be at all times strict observance of laws.

The major chord in Aristotle's ideal society is the social mean. The existence of two classes only, the very rich and the very poor, will bring disaster to the state. The very wealthy consider themselves above legalistic or social authority; the very poor are too degraded to understand the necessity for and the reason for authority.[15] In fact, all who possess, not simply an unusual degree of wealth, but great beauty, great strength or a "noble" birth feel that they should be accorded special privileges. Further, not only those who are very poor, but also the persons who are very weak, or very disgraced find it difficult to follow the dictates of law or of social reason. With the privileged characters who possess a superabundance of advantages, the arrogant attitude developed when they were yet children. At home, they received special considerations; they did not learn obedience within the small family group. In consequence, how could they be expected to be obedient citizens within the larger nation-group? The rich are likely to become insolent and avaricious; they will rule despotically.[16] Not everyone can bear either prosperity or adversity. An increase in prosperity in any part of society should be carefully noted, and that part of society should be placed under surveillance. No one should receive extraordinary power, either from friends or through money. Even the pre-eminent are not above egotism.

A society is safest when the middle class is in control.[17] The states will likely be well administered in which the middle class is numerous. Persons of about equal condition do not plot against others; neither are they plotted against. A middle class prevents both the arrogant wealthy and the impetuous proletariat from dominating the state. "Inequality is the source of all revolutions."

Poverty is a cause of revolution and crime.[18] In time of war, it is important that the poor be well fed else they will cause disturbances. Aristotle might have added that in time of peace the poor should be able to feed themselves well else they will in due season cause revolution.

But poverty is not the only cause of crime. Riches often lead to crime. Wealth causes the commitment of greater crimes than does poverty. The greatest offenses are not occasioned by necessity but by excess.[19] In order to gratify some passion or desire, crime is often committed. Of the passions ambition and avarice are the chief causes of crime.[20] Intoxication produces crime.[21]

The causes of social revolution are manifold. The desire for equality and the desire for inequality are common factors.[22] Inferiors revolt in order that they may attain a state of equality with other persons. Equals revolt in order that they may gain superior levels of honor and status. Aristotle cited a long list of additional factors in social revolution: insolence, fear, political graft, a disproportionate increase of wealth in some part of the state, neglect of trifles in the observance of laws, dissimilarity in elements such as racial. The fundamental cause, however, of social revolution is love of gain and honor.

Aristotle was not a militarist, for he believed that war in itself is not a social good. No people should be trained to conquer and obtain dominion over neighboring states.[23] Military states are safe only when they are at war. After they declare peace the weight of their military burdens brings about their downfall.[24]

The principle of social telesis, which has been recently developed by Lester F. Ward, was foreseen by Aristotle. A society of individuals, like the individual himself, has a work to do.[25] It should adapt itself to its task.

Aristotle was a public health advocate. The location for an ideal city should be carefully chosen. It should be selected, first of all, with reference to the health of the citizens. This point is of greater importance than that of locating a city wisely for the purpose of public administration or war.[26] The importance of a pure water supply is given almost a modern emphasis.

The question of eugenics received the attention of Aristotle. In order that children may be as physically sound as possible, legislators should give special attention to the institution of marriage. Youthful marriages are condemned because the children that are born to such unions will be wanting in respect for their parents.[27] Late marriages will be unsatisfactory because there will be too great difference between the ages of the parents and their children. The marriage of a man and a woman whose ages are widely disproportionate will lead to misunderstandings and quarrels. According to the rigorous, unsympathetic dictum of Aristotle, no deformed child shall be permitted to live.[28] Even the advocates of modern birth control may turn for encouragement to Aristotle.

In the marriage relation there is inequality. The man is by nature better fitted to command than the woman.[29] The chief characteristic of a good wife is obedience to her husband—a doctrine which is patriarchal. Unfaithfulness of either sex in marriage is disgraceful.[30]

Aristotle, like Plato, considers education the leading social force. There is a fundamental educational problem: Shall youth be trained primarily (1) to do useful work, (2) to be virtuous, or (3) to gain higher knowledge?[31] No final answer is given. Aristotle's conception of education, however, is paternalistic.

Utilitarian education possesses a danger line. To be seeking always after the useful prevents one from developing a free and exalted soul.[32] Utilitarian education should cease when it cramps the body or spirit and makes either less fit for the practice of virtue.

Gymnastic education should never be professionalized or allowed to hinder the individual's higher education.[33] The excessive training which leads to Olympic victories is anti-social, because the constitution of the given individual is exhausted. Music is valuable inasmuch as it has the power of forming character.[34] The persons who are engaged in seriously-minded occupations need amusements which will give relaxation.

In summary of Aristotle's social thought it may be said that the Stagirite introduced the comparative method of studying human institutions. He demonstrated the relative value of institutions, showing that those which are best for one age of society will be worthless for a later period. In order to meet changing social needs and conditions, institutions must change. There is a fundamental evolution in social changes.

A communistic social organization, according to Aristotle, is psycho-sociologically untenable. The importance of the middle classes is socially inestimable. Laws should be respected in small particulars. The attitude of the members of society toward their social organizations is more important than the type of organization itself. Human conduct in the mass is to a degree predictable.

After the time of Aristotle, Hellenic life degenerated. Political corruption, military intrigue, and intellectual scepticism vitiated the Hellenic morality that was founded on custom. The ideal, held by Plato and Aristotle, of man as an integral part of a constructive social order was supplanted by a philosophy of pure individualism.

In Athens, Epicurus (341-270 B. C.) became the leader of the popular hedonistic philosophy with its emphasis upon pleasure. Self-sacrifice and noble conduct in the social sense are foreign to Epicureanism. Friends should be sought, not for the sake of cultivating their friendship, but for the pleasure to the seeker. If you treat other persons unjustly, they will retaliate; therefore, treat others justly.

Stoicism which was founded in Athens by Zeno reached its culmination among the Romans and hence will be discussed in the following chapter. Polybius (203-121 B. C.), known as the last Hellenic social philosopher, developed a theory of social evolution, based on the belief that people associate because of the selfish benefits that accrue, and on the fact that group approval and disapproval play a leading part in the development of human attitudes.

Grecian social thought is noteworthy because of its intellectual foundations. It ignored many affective elements, and for that reason it became one-sided and unbalanced. It was rational rather than affective or supernatural. It was designed to meet the needs of this life. It moved away from authority and towards opportunism.

Economically, Hellenic social thought assumed or justified human slavery. It postulated a democracy, but a democracy builded on the backs of thousands of slaves. In practice at the height of the Athenian democracy there were only about 25,000 free Athenians as against 300,000 slaves. Women were not enfranchised. The governments put slaves into the armies, and ultimately attempted to throw out a commercial net over the other Mediterranean states. As a result they lost the spirit of democracy. The whole system and concept of democracy was undermined by the debilitating influences of an industrial autocracy. The social thought of the Greek was limited in its actual application largely to the privileged few, who aristocratically ignored the needs of the helpless many.

Grecian social thought at the height of the Athenian democracy did achieve, however, for its day and epoch, a unique degree of expression among the free citizens. For example, in the matter of athletics and recreation, the Athenians worked together in furnishing themselves organized group activities. Their athletic contests were of a free community nature, untrammelled by commercialized motives. In furnishing recreation for themselves, they co-operated, they acted as community units. Moreover, in these community activities they generated in themselves the spirit of a genuine democratic consciousness.

The fundamentals of Grecian social thought were preserved by the Romans, without being augmented by them. Together with the Hebrew and early Christian social thought, Grecian social thought laid the foundations for the rise of modern social science, and even of sociology.

Chapter VII

Roman Social Thought

Roman social thought is an outgrowth of Hellenic philosophic movements. It is represented in part by the codification of important phases of societary control—the product of the legalistic genius of the Romans. Stoicism, moreover, greatly affected and conditioned the meager social thinking of the Roman scholars.

Lucretius (99-55 B. C.) was the chief Roman exponent of Epicureanism. In his story of social evolution he began with the various phases of the biological struggle for existence, and proceeded to depict in a remarkably significant fashion the origins of social practices and customs.[1] Although his data are of questionable value, his descriptions of social origins often run strangely parallel to modern findings.

The ideal commonwealth of Cicero (106-43 B. C.) is founded on the belief that Rome has the possibility of becoming an ideal state.[2] The best ideas in this connection were selected by Cicero from the Aristotelian, Epicurean, and Stoic philosophies. Cicero was apparently an exponent of honest statesmanship and finally gave his life for civic efficiency. He argued that a child should not be punished by either a parent or a teacher in a fit of anger. Corporal punishment should be considered only when other methods fail to discipline.

The descriptive studies of Julius Caesar (100-44 B. C.) are noteworthy. The *Commentaries* present social studies of contemporary conditions; they possess modern value. In a large number of instances the accuracy of Caesar's social notes has been verified.

The teachings of the Roman Stoics may be traced back to the Socratic formula: Virtue is knowledge. Virtue is knowledge which grows out of practical human conduct. Unlike Aristotle, the Stoics believed that sympathy is a disease. It is pathological and hence must be overcome. In helping other people the wise individual does not allow the emotion of pity to appear.

Contrary to the theory of the Epicureans, the Stoics taught that pleasure is a tiresome and sickly goal. Seneca (4 B. C.-65 A. D.), a leading Roman Stoic, declared: "I am seeking to find what is good for a man, not for his belly."[3] Virtue, according to Stoic philosophy, consists in living a free and undisturbed life. A line was drawn between the virtuous and non-virtuous, between a few virtuous and a multitude of fools. This doctrine tends to engender in the few virtuous a contemptuous regard for the pig-trough philosophy of the many.

This tendency, however, was offset by the Stoic

belief that all persons originally possess the same nature and that all are children of the same universal Spirit. Social differences, hence, are external and superficial. Beneath the surface of human nature there is a cosmopolitanism which constitutes a passive brotherhood of man. Brotherly love should rule, according to the Stoics, but it should rule temperately, and not in such a way as to disturb the individual's self control. Brotherly love should be not a passionate but an intellectual element.

In his treatise on Benefits, Seneca makes benevolence the most social of all virtues; and ingratitude the most venal of all crimes. Marcus Aurelius (121-180 A. D.) gave the social injunction: Love mankind.[4] Living should consist in passing from one social act to another.[5] This is a social world; men exist for the sake of one another.[6]

The Stoic Emperor declared that God is social and that individuals are part of God's universe. Each individual is a component part of the social system, and hence every act of the individual is an integral phase of social life.[7] Inasmuch as the Intelligence of the universe is social, human society functions as a phase of the cosmic co-ordination. We are all co-laborers and co-operators. Even the persons who find fault and who hinder what happens, are performing useful co-operative functions.[8] That which is harmful to the swarm is likewise harmful to the individual. Man is a citizen of the world.[9] The services of a good citizen are never lost. The good citizen does good chiefly by the example he sets.[10]

But the cosmopolitanism of the Stoics never extended beyond a passive interest in the world of affairs. It meant that the individual should be agreeable with other persons, that he should be tolerant of the weaknesses of others, and that he should be aware constantly that others are watching him and likely to copy the example he sets.[11] Stoicism requires the suppression of anger and the exercising of clemency toward all human beings. While Stoicism does not extend so far in its profession as Christianity's doctrine of brotherhood of man, it represents a broader viewpoint of life than any code of conduct which previously had developed in the non-Christian world.

The purpose of punishment, according to Seneca, is two-fold: either to reform the evil-doer; or to prevent the operation of his evil influence and to stop him from setting harmful examples.[12] The social medicine must be determined, quantitatively and qualitatively, by the nature of the offender and the offense. Above all things else, he who administers punishment must not act in anger. Justice cannot be angry.[13] Lynch procedure is entirely contrary to the teachings of Stoicism.

First of all, thieves and robbers should be instructed in the error of their ways. Obtain their point of view and administer punishment accordingly. Pity them. The individual who understands why criminals commit offenses is prevented from becoming angry with them.[14] Aurelius, like Jesus,[15] gave the injunction: Love even those who do wrong. Aurelius, like Paul,[16] urged an attitude of charity toward wrong-doers.[17]

The Stoics condemned luxurious living and fashion racing. True riches consists not in augmenting one's fortune, but in abating the desires for securing material wealth.[18] The words of Emperor Aurelius regarding ostentatious living do not seem out of place when applied to the modern display of wealth. Seneca asserted that he would despise wealth as much when he has it as when he does not possess it.

Stoicism urged the Aristotelian social mean regarding property. Much property is a burden and a cause of worry and fear. It excites envy in others. The best society is that which is characterized by neither poverty nor plenty. The poor should not condemn riches, and the wealthy err in extolling the benefits of poverty—each is speaking of a situation which is objective to him and outside his sphere. Since it is objective to him, he is not qualified to speak concerning it. The individual is a great man who is not corrupted by his wealth; but he is a greater man who is honestly poor in the midst of plenty.[19] Riches constitute a power to do evil, hence mediocrity of fortune with a gentleness of mind represents the best status.[20]

Stoicism enunciated excellent social ideals, which

were, however, passively intellectual. They were not affectively dynamic. Despite their implications, they begat social inertia. The teachings of the Stoics removed rather than instilled a sense of public responsibility. The doctrines are available to the few rather than to the masses, although a Roman slave, Epictetus, as an exception, rose to a full interpretation of Stoic principles. The social ideals and concepts of the Stoics did not possess enough power to regenerate a degenerate society. They had sufficient strength, however, to maintain themselves in a voluptuous and pleasure-seeking world. They performed the exceedingly useful function of preparing the way for the invasion of the Roman Empire by the new and active Christian propaganda. The teachings of the Stoics made easier the conquest of Rome by Christianity. They softened a little an otherwise hard-hearted world.

As a class the Romans were men of action. They were soldiers and administrators. The name of Rome is still synonymous with power. On the whole it must be said that the Romans made little contribution to societary thought.

The constructive work of the Romans was legal and administrative. They built up a special social science—legal science. The legal genius of the Romans emphasized the rights of contract, of private property, of interest. Although this attention to the development of individualistic institutions was fatal to the rise of new social attitudes and to an increase in the sense of social responsibility, it nevertheless was instrumental in constructing a stable framework for the evolution of the social process.

The Romans preserved a portion of Hellenic culture. The teachings of Plato and Aristotle were saved to modern civilization. Credit is due the Romans for receiving, keeping, working over, and handing on a part of the best Hellenic civilization.

Roman thought accentuated military principles of authority, even to the point of autocracy. It tended to crush the unprivileged populace. It tried to keep the masses contented by generous state aid. It denied to personality its complete individual and social expressions. In building an individualistic framework which would provide an orderly *milieu* for the rise of the institution of private property, it ignored the needs of the uneducated and poverty-enslaved masses for a full measure of liberty.

Rome.developed the concept of organized power. The organizing ability of the Romans was marvelous, an organizing power that lives today in and through the Catholic Church.

The greatest gift of Rome was its Stoic concepts. Although these originated in Hellas, they attained their maturity in Rome. They opened the way for the reception of the Christian social concepts of love, service, brotherhood of man.

CHAPTER VIII

EARLY CHRISTIAN SOCIAL THOUGHT

Christian social thought is the direct outgrowth of Hebrew social concepts. Amos and Hosea and Isaiah paved the way for the social teachings of Jesus. The social commandments of the Old Testament were the progenitors of the modified social injunctions of the New Testament. Job, the social citizen, was not an unworthy precursor of Jesus, the lover of humanity. Out of the love and tender care for children which thrived in Hebrew homes there arose the concept of the brotherhood of man and the Fatherhood of God—the two cardinal principles of Christianity.

Jesus gave expression to no system of social thought, but uttered social principles and concepts which, when put together, constituted the basis of a new social order. He dealt with personalities rather than with institutions. He looked to the individual rather than to the mass. He emphasized functions rather than structures. He proclaimed the need for socio-religious personalities. If he could get these, he was sure of the ultimate societal results. He foresaw a perfect society—the Kingdom of God.

Unlike Plato and Aristotle, Jesus was a continual student of everyday life. Like Socrates, Jesus was fond of people. He was a student of individual and social affairs. He mixed with all types of human beings. Like Socrates, he wrote practically nothing. Unlike Socrates, Jesus had a dynamic element in his nature which forbade him to remain content to argue with people (after the Socratic manner), but which drove him to help and to heal. He went about doing good. The Gospel records are replete with instance after instance of his work in healing the sick of their infirmities. He was not, however, a physician but a teacher and a savior from sin and evil.

Behind all the teachings of Jesus, there is the concept of a perfect human order. This Kingdom begins in the hearts of individuals.[1] It is a spirit or an attitude of mind which leads the individual toward co-operative living. The Kingdom may come on earth as well as in heaven. Consider the picture of a harmonious community life which Jesus gave when lamenting over Jerusalem: "How often would I have gathered thy children together, as a hen doth gather her brood together under her wings, and ye would not!"[2]

Jesus extended the concept of brotherhood. Whoever shall do the will of God is a brother to me.[3] The world, under God, is one family. The Kingdom, therefore, is to include all human beings, who worship God in spirit and in truth and who at the same time love their fellowmen in justice and co-operative living.

The ideal society is organic. It grows from good examples. Live so that other persons, seeing the helpfulness of your life, may live likewise. The Kingdom grows like a grain of mustard seed, which finally becomes a tree in whose branches the birds find homes.[4] Love grows, and like leaven, permeates and transforms the whole mass,—the result is the perfect Kingdom.

God is the spiritual leader of the new society, to whom Jesus prayed in the social term, Our Father. God is the personification of love. God loved the sinful world so much that he gave his only son to the task of saving not simply the Jews or modern Europeans, but the whole world from all sins. The Star which guided the Magi was God's service Star, announcing that he had given his only son in the war against sin.

Love is the new note that is to re-form the world. Love is the scientific principle from which all other true sociological concepts are derived. Love received the most perfect human expression in the personality and life of Jesus, who came not for self glory but to save people from hate and sin; who sought not the sheep to oppress and slay them for his own gratification, but to direct them, when lost, back to safe living; who sought not to weigh down the burdened with unjust taxes and harsh living conditions, but to relieve and give rest to the heavy-laden; who cared less for the upper Four Hundred than for the lower Four Hundred Million.

The principle of love compels the members of the Kingdom to show mercy. God is full of mercy, therefore, let his followers show mercy. Love forgives. The Christian citizen is instructed to become reconciled with his brother citizen before worshipping at the altar of God.[6] If the individual would be forgiven of his sins, he must acquire the habit of forgiving other persons. He must be careful not to judge harshly, lest other persons judge him harshly. He should forgive others seventy times seven times, that is, without stint or measure.

St. Luke, the physician, recites the story of a loving father. The prodigal son impetuously demanded his share of the inheritance, and going into a far country, wasted his substance in riotous living. But upon showing true remorse for these exceedingly grave offenses, his father received him back with a loving, forgiving heart, a feast, the best robes, and music and dancing. One of the malefactors who was crucified with Christ, showed a penitent heart at the last moment and received forgiveness from the loving, dying Christ. Since no one is without sin, no one has a right to be unforgiving. Even the woman taken in adultery came within the law of forgiving love.

The societary principle of love is the major chord of Christianity. It is Christianity's unscientific but greatest gift to sociology. It has become the fundamental concept of sociology. To the Old Testament type of love which urged the individual to love his neighbor and to love the alien and stranger, Jesus repeatedly insisted upon a love that is still greater, namely, a love which will include enemies. Love your enemies.[7] Jesus himself exemplified this form of love. He made no idle interpretation of an impossible love, but demonstrated and lived a love which forgave his enemies, even those who mockingly, shamelessly nailed him to a cross. So great is the drawing power of this almost superhuman love which Jesus expressed in deeds that he himself predicted that if he were lifted up he would draw all people unto him.

Love fills people with compassion. The Gospels are replete with references to the fact that wherever Jesus saw sickness, poverty, sin, he was moved with compassion. The illustrations range from the blind men by the wayside to the bread-hungry multitudes, from the unclean leper in Galilee to murderous Jerusalem.

Love is cosmopolitan. All peoples are entitled to know the meaning of Christian love.[8] Both Jew and Gentile shall feel its warming glow. The Samaritan lives it. Loving neighborliness includes more than priestly and Levitical acts; it involves Samaritan kindness. The love in the heart of Jesus reached first to a few close friends, then to sinners and outcasts, then to the Samaritans and the Gentiles, and finally to the whole world. It led ultimately to that most unselfish of all human enterprises—the missionary movement.

Love leads to humility and self-sacrifice. Almsgiving is done in private, not for social plaudits. The individual prays, not to be seen of men and thereby to be accounted good.[9] He who seeks to save his life shall lose it; whoever loses his life for the sake of the Kingdom shall save it. He who stores up for himself the wealth of the world shall lose himself. Salutations in the market places and chief seats in the synagogues in themselves are unworthy. The poor in spirit are blessed.

Love shuns positions of worldly power, lest they be secured at the loss of one's soul.[10] The best positions in life are not to be seized; they are obtained through the exercise of love; they are bestowed in recognition of merit and worth. He who exalts himself will be abased; the humble will be exalted.

Love creates true greatness. The members of the society of perfect love are characterized by the sincerity, purity, humility of little children.[11] He who serves most is greatest. The Kingdom of God is an aristocracy, not of Might but of Service. The Son of God came to serve, not to be served. For the sake of those outside the Kingdom, Jesus sanctified himself, sacrificing even his life in that cause.

Love makes the Golden Rule the best sociological proposition in Hebrew and Jewish literature. "Whatsoever ye would that men should do to you, do ye even so to them." In reply to a lawyer of the Pharisees, Jesus enunciated a twofold commandment, the first part of which invoked complete love to God; and the second part, to man. The love of the individual for his fellow man as shown in both attitude and deeds is the test of the love of the individual for God. Love means service. Love does not connote lip-service; neither does it mean divided service. No one can serve two masters, God and mammon.

Christian love implies definite and continued public service. Social service is the test of entrance to the Kingdom, and of the sincerity of the individual's religious profession.[12] On the judgment day those on the right hand will be blessed and given life eternal, and to them the king of the judgment will say:

I was an hungered, and ye gave me meat;
I was thirsty, and ye gave me drink;
I was a stranger, and ye took me in;
Naked and ye clothed me;
I was in prison, and ye came unto me.

Then the righteous, with surprise, will inquire of the Lord of the judgment: When did we see you hungry and feed you; or thirsty, and give you drink? When did we see you a stranger and take you in? Then the Lord of the judgment will answer them that when they had served the weak and poor and the heavy-laden on earth, they had been serving him and thereby had proved their loyalty to

God and earned the rewards of everlasting life. And those who fail to measure up to the social service test, whether professing Christians or not, will be turned away.

The importance and nature of religio-social service is indicated by Jesus when he symbolizes the giving of a cup of cold water in his name as a test for receiving eternal life.[13] He who has two coats should give one to him who has none. The share-ing of food with those who have no food is commanded. Give liberally; give all thou hast.[14] It is blessed to give under all circumstances. Material riches are insignificant in value when compared with spiritual wealth. To give the things of this world is to receive the greater things of the spirit. He is richest who gives most, both of material and spiritual goods. As an expression of his love for God, Jesus lived a life of social and human service.

Whenever Jesus mentioned the ten commandments—all three synoptic writers agree on this point—he omitted the four commandments of individual import and repeated only the social rules, or principles:

(1) Thou shalt do no murder,
(2) Thou shalt not commit adultery,
(3) Thou shalt not steal,
(4) Thou shalt not bear false witness,
(5) Honor thy father and mother,
(6) Thou shalt love thy neighbor as thyself.

After the fashion of the major social prophets, Jesus cried out vehemently against social injustice. He denounced the persons who devour widows' houses, or who lay unnecessary economic burdens upon their fellowmen.

Anti-social religion, above all things else, angered Jesus. He wanted no followers who were practicing social or political injustice. Cursed are those persons who appear righteous, who make long prayers, or who go about in long robes, but who inwardly are hypocrites, are full of dead men's bones, of uncleanness, of extortion and excess.[15] The shedding of innocent blood is condemned. The paying of money in order to expiate sin will avail nothing. Such money is tainted; it is blood money.[16]

Anti-social and commercialized religion so angered Jesus that, contrary to his customary attitudes toward sinners, he committed violence on one occasion against offenders. He overthrew the tables of the money changers in the temple, and, making a scourge of small cords, he drove out the money changers. In so doing, he declared that the worship of God should not be commercialized.[17] He would not have the house of worship turned into a cultured den of thieves.

So furious were the scribes and the chief priests because of the attack of Jesus upon anti-social religious practices that they planned how they might kill him.[18] It appears that as a direct result of the antagonism of Jesus to the anti-social practices of the religious, or temple, authorities and of the other religious leaders the conspiracy against Jesus finally brought about his death. Jesus went about stirring up the common people in a democratic movement against the autocratic, hypocritical, anti-social religious leaders among the Jews. He met his death while championing the needs of the masses who were being exploited in the name of religion.

Jesus was the highest type of social democrat. The perfected social order which he foresaw is a democracy, ruled by the principles of love and service in the name of God. Furthermore, no one shall be compelled to come into the Kingdom. The good tidings shall be presented to all individuals, but the liberty of the individual shall not be violated. The principle of voluntary assent, not compulsion or conscription, rules in recruiting for the Kingdom. Moreover, within the Kingdom, compulsion is unknown. Love sufficeth.

Jesus hated sin. To him, sin was anything which overcomes love and which causes the individual or society to disintegrate. Sin is that which defeats or hinders the coming of the Kingdom of Love. Sin breaks up or holds back the social process. Sin, like love, is organic. Sin grows. An evil tree brings forth evil fruit; grapes and figs are not gathered from thorns or thistle-bearing plants.

Jesus forgave sinners; even social sinners. By means of his imagination, he put himself in the place of the sinner and sought to understand the causes of the sinning. As his mind filled with an understanding of sin, his heart overflowed with pity and forgiveness for the sinner. He sought primarily to reclaim; he thought secondarily of punishment. Even in the case of the adulterous woman, he sought to save what was left of the broken spirit rather than to punish. His cardinal penological principle was reformation.

It is significant that the social institution which Jesus supported above all others, even above the church and the state, was the family. Jesus spoke frequently for the family. He commanded that children should unwaveringly act loyally toward parents; he used not only the clear-cut terms of the writer of Exodus but added a curse of death upon those who abuse their parents.[19]

An even stronger command was given by Jesus concerning loyalty to the marriage relation. A man's genuine loyalty to his parents, undiminished in intensity, must be subordinated to faithfulness to his wife.[20] This social theory is opposite in character to that of Confucius concerning attitudes toward parents and wives. The conception which Jesus urged leads to social progress, while the teaching of Confucius leads to social stagnation.

A man and woman who have been spiritually joined together in wedlock are one flesh, above and beyond separation by civil authorities. Jesus uttered the stern and awe-inspiring sanction: What therefore God hath joined together, let not man put asunder. The family as an institution is accorded a sacredly fundamental place in the social order.

Jesus recognized woman as equal with man spiritually. His attitude toward his mother and the other women of his day was one of respect, chivalry, and gentleness. He laid the foundations of a social process in which women function on terms of equality with men.

Honor to parents and honor to wife must be supplanted by honor to children. Jesus worshiped little children. In them he saw the innocence and purity of God. When he wished to describe the attributes of the Kingdom, he selected a little child and held him up as typifying the simple, natural spirit of perfect living. Although without children himself, Jesus loved little children, choosing them for special honors, and declaring that of such is the Kingdom of God. It is not God's will that one of these little ones should perish; it is the stupidity of man and the lack of social conscience that causes a high mortality rate of little children. He who harms the trustful child shall be cursed. It were better for such a miscreant that a millstone were tied about his neck and that he were thrown into the sea.[21]

In regard to the influence of private property Jesus was fearful. His zeal for and whole-hearted loyalty to spiritual values made him suspicious of vested interests. He repeatedly warned in vigorous language against the lure of gold and the baneful influences of material wealth upon the attitudes and acts of the individual. He himself showed no interest in owning property. He lived without a home of his own and without private means. If he had possessed these, his life-work probably would have failed. He urged his disciples to remain free from the desire for money; he even commanded them to rely for the means of material subsistence upon the people with whom they labored. Jesus believed that private property hindered the realization of the principle of brotherhood of man. He made a sharp distinction between the interests of God and mammon. He believed that these two sets of interests are diametrically opposed to each other. To the extent that the individual relies upon property, he separates himself from God and the things of the Spirit. The disciples were instructed to scorn, not only the earning of wealth, but if they possessed earthly goods, they were to sell these and give the proceeds to the poor.[22] The disciple of the spiritual life must divorce himself from the love of monetary gain.

Toward the poor, Jesus was sympathetic. The Gospel shall be preached chiefly to the poor, not because the poor, *per se,* need it more than the rich and not because the poor should be specially favored, but because they recognize their needs. They are in a receptive attitude whereas the attitude of the rich has been calloused by their wealth.

The response to the Gospel is not likely to be whole-hearted by persons who possess an extensive interest in riches.

Jesus taught a spiritual socialism. He thought in terms of spiritual love for all persons, not of material well-being for the proletariat. But he seemed to prefer the company of the poor. Blessed are the poor, was his attitude; for they are in a frame of mind which makes them fit subjects for the perfect Kingdom. The possession of property gives the individual a feeling of self-exaltation; poverty gives rise to humility—a cardinal virtue of the Kingdom.

Jesus did not attack poverty with preventive measures. Poverty will continue to exist.[23] Perhaps it is well that it should continue, for a nation of economically satisfied people might not be religiously minded. It is harder for a camel to go through a needle's eye than for a rich man to get into the swing of an untrammeled social process. Woe unto the rich, because they are self-centered, materially inclined, and pleasure-loving. The man who pulled down his barns in order to build larger barns, saying to himself, "Take thine ease, eat, drink, and be merry," is scathingly condemned by Jesus.[24] He is ostracized from the ideal society. In the story of Lazarus and the rich man, the former is carried to Abraham's bosom, but the latter, in torments, begs for a cup of water and the company of Lazarus. He wanted Lazarus sent to him; he longed for the company of him whom he once ignored. The attention of Jesus was continually centered on the dangers of wealth, but rarely on the need of preventing poverty.

Zaccheus, a rich man, was called as a disciple of Jesus. But before the discipleship began, the superintendent not only had to come down from the mulberry tree and declare his allegiance to God, but he had to become socially converted as well. He promised to give one-half of his wealth to the poor and to restore falsely acquired possessions fourfold.

Then there was the rich young man who came to Jesus, asking how he might obtain admittance to the Kingdom, declaring that he observed the commandments. One more thing, however, was required of him, namely, that he sell all his possessions and give the returns to the poor. Only by so giving might he have treasure in the social Kingdom.

The teaching of Jesus concerning the Sabbath throws light on the exceedingly human element in his thought. The Sabbath is a special day for doing good deeds.[25] The Sabbath is to be treated not primarily from the standpoint of religious rites but from the viewpoint of human welfare. Works of necessity, and deeds of mercy and kindness to man and beast are proper to the Sabbath.[26] Man was not made for the Sabbath, but the day of rest and good deeds was designed for the benefit of man.

The attitude of Jesus toward the problem of peace versus war has aroused considerable controversy. There are certain of his sayings which seem to contradict each other. But an analysis of all his teachings demonstrates that his emphasis was on peace. The exceptions to the rule will be stated first.[27] On one occasion he said: I came not to send peace, but a sword. The context shows that Jesus was speaking in an individual and not a national way. He had in mind the conflicts which arise between the individuals who are converted to the ideals of the Kingdom and those who are not. Jesus explained that those who love him must do so even at the expense of forsaking father and mother.[28] Loyalty to the Kingdom may mean that the son will oppose the practices of his father in business, the daughter will object to the time wasted in the un-Christian practices of her mother, the parents will protest the sowing of "wild oats" by son or daughter.

In the temple, on one occasion, Jesus displayed anger and used violence. He was dealing, however, with a group of criminals, cultured criminals, who apparently would respond to no treatment except violence. They would not cease their nefarious practices except through compulsion.

On the other hand, the illustrations are many where Jesus used love in order to change the ways of people. He never used force in his own behalf, even to save his life. He rebuked Simon Peter for drawing his sword and cutting off the right ear of the servant of the high priest who in company with others were seeking Jesus in order to bind him and kill him.[29] At another time Jesus specifically enjoined: Resist not evil; and instructed his followers when smitten upon the right cheek to turn the left also. Those who take the sword shall perish by the sword; the nation that builds itself up by the sword shall be destroyed by it.

The birth of Jesus was accompanied by glad tidings and song, proclaiming peace on earth and good will toward men.[31] Blessed are the peacemakers. In the perfect society, good will by all to all will be shown, perfect love will reign, and permanent peace will prevail.

Jesus may or may not have expressed himself on several important issues of his day. The incomplete records do not indicate his attitude upon many vital social problems. It appears that Jesus usually spoke in remedial rather than preventive social terms. However, beneath this remedial terminology there are fundamental social principles, which, if put into common practice, would solve all social problems. Jesus proposed to build an ideal society by re-making and regenerating individuals. He dared to promulgate the radical program of re-making human nature itself. He commanded that all selfish impulses and instincts be completely subordinated to the altruistic and socializing desires.

Jesus insisted throughout his life-work upon the

principle that material factors must be subjected to spiritual values. In order to make this principle clear he often took particular pains to treat material goods with the utmost insignificance. He perceived that individuals are made slaves by the worship of wealth, either on the part of themselves, of the privileged classes, or of society itself. He inaugurated a program of spiritualization which would free the world from the slavery which may come from economic forces.

Although a religious teacher above all things else, Jesus insisted upon the necessity of the existence of something more than saving faith alone. He required a social attitude of mind, a heart of social love, and a spirit of service. Give freely to others. Serve others. By giving himself for others, the individual will function in the Kingdom of perfect love, and win other individuals to that Kingdom.

Jesus required that love be substituted for hate. Unkind deeds must be supplanted by kind deeds. According to this principle, employers and employees must learn to love one another; and business must be put upon the basis of love and service. Government must be a series of mutual services. Religion must harbor no selfishness. In all human relationships, Jesus reiterated the principle: Love, love, love. This is the spiritualizing and socializing principle by which Jesus proposed to make over the social process.

Paul, the apostle to the Gentiles, by virtue of

unique experiences and many travels, possessed a cosmopolitan attitude of mind. He gave a practical application of the teaching of Jesus concerning the brotherhood of man. He urged the equal treatment of Jews and Gentiles, bond and free.[32] He preached the essential unity of mankind. God is no respecter of persons; his Kingdom is a spiritual democracy. We are all—Jew and Gentile—children of the same Father, who gave his son in service for all.[33] To the call to come over into Macedonia for the purpose of rendering aid, Paul responded immediately and favorably. By so doing he believed that he was carrying out the true implications of the love of God.

The greatest tribute that has ever been paid to love as a social force was given by Paul.[34] Although possessing the highest educational qualifications and being able to speak with the greatest eloquence, any individual leads a practically useless life unless that life is motivated by love. Giving one's possessions to the poor and sacrificing one's body counts little if one does these things in any other spirit than that of love. Love protects the individual from envying his neighbors, from becoming proud and haughty and boastful. Love is the greatest principle of life.

The members of the Kingdom of God should love one another under all circumstances.[35] They should bear one another's burdens.[36] They should do good to all men, even to those who persecute.

Above all, they should not recompense any man with evil for evil, or fail to feed their enemies if the latter hunger. Love is the law of God. Perfect love is more powerful than principalities and powers and even death.[87] Love conquers all evil. Love is more powerful than might. A practical, cosmopolitan brotherhood of man is one of the fundamental concepts of Paul's teachings.

Paul taught the organic unity of mankind. In the perfect Christian order each individual has a specific function to perform which is a part of the whole process. Paul compares this situation to the human body in which there are many organs, each performing its individual but correlated function.[88] No one liveth to himself, no one dieth to himself.[89] Every individual, even in dying, influences the social equilibrium and affects group progress. All individuals in the perfect Kingdom are co-laborers and co-operators. Whatever weakens one individual weakens society; whatever strengthens the individual strengthens society, providing that strength is used societarily.

Another fundamental element in the social thought of Paul was his concept of sin. Sin is socially and individually destructive. The wages of sin—a generic term—is death. Paul made a long list of social sins, namely: covetousness, maliciousness, drunkenness, wantonness, dishonesty, fraud, stealing, fornication, murder. In nearly all his letters, Paul warned his followers against the evils which beset mankind. He urged people to beware of the appearance of doing evil. Paul's rule of conduct was the Aristotelian mean: Be temperate in all things.

On the other hand, Paul cited long lists of virtues. Love is continually urged. Temperance, meekness, gentleness, honesty, purity, and justice are repeatedly stressed. Paul's description of a good man and bishop is the delineation of the character of a social citizen, who is temperate, a good husband, who is not mercenary nor covetous, and who ruleth well his household, with good reputation and character.

In all Paul's thought, righteous living was uppermost. Cheerful giving was commended. The strong should bear the infirmities of the weak, not only for the sake of the weak, but in order that the strong may not become self-centered.

Paul taught a gospel of peace. He deprecated strife between individuals. He trusted in the operation of the law of love. Love will bring order out of confusion, and peace out of discord. The social Kingdom of God, motivated by love, moves orderly, harmoniously, and constructively.

Paul firmly supported the family as an essential institution of society. He admonished children to obey their parents, to honor their fathers and mothers. He commanded wives to obey their husbands, and husbands to love their wives even as Christ loved the church and as men love themselves.[40] He commanded men to remain true in the marriage relation, and to keep the single standard of morals inviolate.

The dangers of wealth were frequently pointed out by Paul. We brought no riches into this life; we can not take any riches out. Riches continually subject us to temptations, snares, and lusts. The love of money is the root of all evil.[41] The greatest wealth which any person can acquire is the wealth of good deeds done to other persons.

The thought of Paul concerning law is exceedingly modern. Law is not for the righteous; law is for the lawless and disobedient. The honest and righteous and just are above the law in the sense that a well-mated husband and wife are above the law of divorce. If there were none other than happily-mated husbands and wives, there would be no need of divorce laws. In a similar way, if perfect love prevailed among all people, law could be entirely discarded. The teachings of Paul run the gamut of brotherly love. Paul thought in terms of concepts such as these: being well-grounded in love; abounding in love; let brotherly love continue; the love of Christ constraineth. Paul carried a message of love to all men, and established the church as a home for all who would accept Chirst's message of love.

The apostle James spoke in no uncertain terms of the democracy of God, the need of helping the weak, the dangers of riches, the evils of strife, and the social commandments. James made social service a fundamental test of religion.[42]

Peter attacked the same social sins that Jesus and Paul had flayed, argued in behalf of the justice of God, and proclaimed with new vigor the law of love.

John is the chief exponent of the principle of love. God is love. The reign of God is a reign of love; the Kingdom of God is a Kingdom of perfect love. In the Book of Revelation, John describes two cities; one wicked; and the other, perfect. The first is elegantly clothed in purple and gold, bedecked with precious stones. But her heart is rotten. Lust and vice have ruined her. Her dominating sins are sex immorality and luxury. The perfect city is the new Jerusalem, a community of happy people, motivated in all things by love. Nothing that defileth is permitted in the New Jerusalem, nor anything that worketh abomination, or maketh a lie.[43]

The fundamentals of early Christian social thought may now be summarized. The New Testament authorities offered no system of sociology; they did not submit a scientific program for the social reorganization of the world, but made, however, substantial contributions.

(1) Early Christian social thought represented a system of changing the attitudes of individuals. By making over individuals the world can be improved. The individual is exalted. The individual

must be re-educated. The right sort of men will produce the right sort of social structure and the proper type of social process and society. Christianity indicated socialized principles of conduct which the disciples of Christianity must accept.

(2) The Fatherhood of God is made a cardinal principle of the Kingdom. When all persons recognize the Fatherhood of God, they will have a strong tie binding them together and impelling them to regenerated living.

(3) The universal brotherhood of man is a natural corollary of the principle of the Fatherhood of God. When everyone recognizes the underlying brotherhood of all individuals, the prejudices of race which now so bitterly divide mankind will begin to dissolve.

(4) Marriage is a divine right, and husbands and wives shall work together in behalf of their children. The family is the chief social institution which the New Testament writers supported.

(5) Little children set examples of simple faith and trust. They call for sacrifice and transform parents into altruistic beings.

(6) Early Christian thought was missionary. It was not self-centered. It said: Go. It drove out its adherents unto all forms of unselfish living. It required that its followers help the sick, preach the gospel, travel into foreign lands. It was an activity religion. It defined in living terms the dynamic and driving principle of love.

CHAPTER IX

SOCIAL THOUGHT IN THE MIDDLE AGES

The social thought of the Middle Ages was in part a reflection of the unsettled social conditions, and in part an outgrowth of the thought and life of the five centuries which intervened between the beginning of the Christian Era and the Fall of Rome. During these centuries the Church Fathers moved away from the pristine Christian teachings. While they accepted the underlying social nature of mankind and believed that government and social organization were necessary in order to curb evil tendencies, their teachings treated government as a divine institution and transformed rulers into super-powerful beings with divine rights. The autocratic rather than the democratic element in government received support.

The strong Roman bias for organization and administration was builded into the church—the result was the powerful Church of Rome with its hierarchal structure. After the Fall of Rome, the Roman proclivity for centralization of government lived on and produced within the Church a center of power that has been the marvel of church history.

The Church Fathers directed the attention of the people to the next world and to preparation therefor. Sacramental and sacrificial methods of salvation were elaborated. The importance of improving social conditions was ignored. In fact, the injustices in the current social order were considered as disciplinary measures for the soul in its preparation for the next world. The improvement of living conditions was considered to be wasted effort, if not indicative of heretical tendencies of mind.

By the third century, loyalty to creed had become a dominant note in Christianity. The poor constituted a decreasing influence in church life; wealth was exerting unChristian influences. The aristocratic elements in church organization began to transform the poor into a special class within the church. Poverty was not viewed preventively. By the time of the Fall of Rome the poor had become objects upon which to bestow alms as a means of expiating sin.

The greatest of the Latin Fathers was Saint Augustine (354-450). Among other works, he wrote a large set of twenty-two volumes under the title of *The City of God*. In this gigantic undertaking social thought was submerged beneath theological discussions. A part of the argument is devoted to an explanation of the Fall of Rome. The leading causal elements are described as economic factors, such as the rise of luxury; and religious unbelief, such as the worship of pagan gods. Augustine describes two cities, one of this world, materialistic and debasing; and one of the next world —the City of God, which through the will of God will finally triumph.

During the first half of the Middle Ages the dominant tendencies are Roman and Christian. The Roman power of organization gains increasing strength in its new form—the Church. The Christian influences were expressed in high ideals, new duties, and asceticism. The church acted as a soothing and quieting force in the centuries of unrest. It built elaborate monasteries and gathered together under its protecting wing large numbers of people, chiefly the poor. Under the supervision of the church, these religious believers lived in communal and sympathetic fashion. Along with these developments the church also manifested grave abuses. At the expense sometimes of the ignorant and the poor the church grew powerful.

Out of the period of social disorder which characterized the early Middle Ages there developed educational movements, such as that which Charlemagne sponsored, and the system of Feudalism, which gave to the Middle Ages its most distinctive set of characteristics. Feudalism made land the central institution of society. The ownership of land gave power; land constituted social and political power. Land was parcelled out upon the receipt of oaths of homage and fealty. Under this land system there were three classes of people: the nobles, the clergy, and the peasants. The nobles were the rulers and exercised military prerogatives. The clergy were either the privileged subjects of the nobles, or else through the institution which they represented they acquired land power. The peasants often despised the nobles, although they worked for and supported them.

As an outgrowth of feudal industry various forms of guilds or industrial organizations flourished from the tenth to the fifteenth centuries. Sometimes the masters and workmen jointly belonged to guilds, as in the case of the merchant guilds. Sometimes the guilds became local monopolies. Always they possessed the aim of improving the conditions of the membership.

The religious wars, or Crusades, of the eleventh to the thirteenth centuries inaugurated many changes. They gave the restless nobility major themes of attention and even removed many nobles through death in battle from the European arena. They created intellectual unrest. They enlarged the horizons of many individuals and gave rise to skepticism. They led to the Reformation.

Social thought in the Middle Ages received a considerable stimulus from Teutonic sources. The barbarous Teutons contributed ideas of freedom. They increased the emphasis upon the individual. They were rough, bold exponents of "personal liberty," and disregarded mere churchly procedure, social traditions, and some of the finer ideals of life and character. On the other hand, chivalry and knighthood were perhaps of Teutonic origin.

The church utilized chivalry. It became the duty of the knight to defend the church and that which belonged to the church. Chivalry became a form of social discipline which ruled in the latter part of the Middle Ages. It softened manners and became the sponsor for virtue. It remained, however, a modified military structure with military traditions.

The rise of scholasticism took place in opposition to monasticism. In the ninth century the leading thinkers had not advanced beyond the conception of a natural social state, characterized by chaotic conditions, and organized by political machinery. By the twelfth century only the faintest glimmerings of a doctrine of popular sovereignty had begun to appear. The thought of the day was largely theological.

The church through its systems of monasteries had maintained centers where religious and intellectual traditions had been preserved. These centers were undoubtedly important factors in conserving much that was valuable in an age when ruthless disregard for civilized values prevailed.

Because of the abuses which sprang up in connection with the monasteries, certain positive reactions against the monasteries arose. St. Francis of Assisi (1181-1226) turned from the monastery to actual life. He inaugurated a method for the regeneration of society. He and his followers lived and spent themselves among the actual poor, subjecting themselves to the economic conditions of the poor. They helped the poor, not by giving alms as an expiation for sin and to secure self-salvation, but by the first-hand giving of their lives. St. Francis ignored the regular ecclesiastical conception of charity and gave it all the reality of a new and genuine social force. By renouncing the possession of property and living as the poor live, he obtained what he could secure in no other way—the poor man's point of view. In this way, also, he secured an entrance into the poor man's mind and heart that could not be had so well by any other method. By renouncing wealth and accepting literal poverty he reached the core of the problem of poverty. St. Francis was motivated by a desire to live a life of love. He spent not wealth but his life for the poor.

Scholasticism developed as a reaction against churchly asceticism. According to scholasticism the individual should look to reason rather than to church dogma for religious and spiritual guidance. Scholasticism repudiated church traditions as a guide for individual action; it turned to Aristotelian logic for its technique. Thomas Aquinas (1226-1274), the best known of the scholastic philosophers, pushed forward the Aristotelian premises as follows: Man is a social being; he unites with other individuals in a social organization in order to gain his own purposes. The individual looks to able rulers for wise political guidance; he accords the requisite power to these rulers. Aquinas thus recognized a tacit social compact, or contract, foreshadowing Rousseau.

In religion, scholasticism reduced religious mysticism to rational forms. It based religion on learning rather than on authority; it pursued the methods of reasoning rather than of contemplation.

Scholasticism furthered the advancement of learning; it aided and developed the life of the universities. It encouraged the growth of independent thinking, although its decline set in about the fourteenth century, before it had had a fair opportunity to inaugurate a movement which would lead to an inductive or a positivistic philosophy, or sociology.

Various other thought elements appeared in the closing centuries of the Middle Ages. As early as the ninth century a maritime code, a military code, and a rural code were formulated in the Byzantine Empire in order to meet new social needs. Until the fall of Constantinople the Byzantine influence was a deterrent against the forces from the East. Byzantium preserved and gave a new impetus to Grecian literature, art, architecture, and law.

In Arabia the celebrated historian and philosopher Ibn Khaldun (1332-1406), made a detailed and surprisingly accurate description of the social life of the Arab tribes. With the evolution of the life of the individual, he compared the development of the successive stages in social life. This distinguished historian urged that history should consider not simply rulers, dynasties, and wars, but also racial factors, climatic forces, the laws of association, and the stages of associative life. He wished to make history scientific, even a social science. He formulated an evolutionary doctrine of social progress. He evolved a spiral theory of social evolution, beginning with the crudest primitive life and ending with the most civilized urban life.

In the latter part of the fourteenth century, England's great popular poet, William Langland, wrote an allegorical poem entitled, *Piers Ploughman.* In this work the oppressed laboring and peasant classes cry aloud their longings for improved conditions. They are personified in Piers the Ploughman, who as a dignified laborer, plays for the first time the leading rôle in serious thought. He is the leader of a field of all types of people who are laboring together and longing for a better social order. Along with the agricultural laborers we see weavers and tailors, friars and minstrels, merchants and knights. Labor of every sort is dignified. All living laborers who work with their hands and minds, truly earning, living in love and according to the laws of social order and progress, will become the pure and perfected leaders of truth.

Langland depicted well the living and working conditions of the English laboring classes. Productive toil, he argued, will receive its crown of glory. But he did not indicate practical solutions. Langland was sure, however, that the service of labor to society is sacred. He pronounced patient poverty to be the prince of all virtues. He personified Jesus in the form of a working man. Langland's fourteenth century social message was that the individual should renounce wealth, join the honest laboring poor, and follow Christ's example of living a life of labor and love.[1]

Social thought in the Middle Ages is fragmentary. While several centuries are included in the period, new social ideas are very few. The centuries of unrest and transition, the paucity of great leaders, the intellectual stagnation, and the prevalent illiteracy of the masses produced situations in which little social thinking of importance was stimulated. New thought of any type was almost negligible except as an isolated individual stood forth, such as Augustine, Charlemagne, Ibn Khaldun, Aquinas. A portion of the social thinking of the preceding age, however, was preserved, constituting a foundation for the renaissance of social thought that was coming.

Chapter X

More and Utopian Social Thought

Shortly after the close of Middle Ages with its modicum of social thinking, the idealism of Plato appeared in a new form, namely, in descriptive utopias. Of these, the chief and subtlest was the work of England's sane, shrewd, tolerant student of society, Sir Thomas More (1478-1535). More's *Utopia* deserves a degree of attention which is not customarily accorded it.

More mediated Plato to modern social philosophy; he moved in the field of Platonic ideas and ideals. He was also indebted to Plutarch's account of Spartan life. At the dawn of the Renaissance he presented the concept of a perfect commonwealth.

If one would understand the social thought of More, a contemporary of Columbus, he must put himself under the spell of fifteenth and sixteenth century conditions in England. He must remind himself of Henry VII and Henry VIII, two autocratic rulers whom it was difficult for any individually-minded person to please. The living conditions of the peasants were almost intolerable. Unemployment was common. Punishments were severe and brutalizing. Even thieves were subject to capital punishment. If an individual stole a loaf of bread, he might as well kill the person who saw him steal the bread. In fact, by so doing, he might be better off—the only witness to his theft would thus be unable to testify against him.

Sir Thomas More could not have openly criticised the unjust social conditions of his day, and long escaped death. It was necessary for him to put his radical ideas into the mouth of a fictitious traveler, Raphael Hythloday, and thereby disown them. At is was, More became a martyr to his religious faith and to the cause of social freedom.

More wrote the *Utopia* in two parts. Part one was written as an explanation, or introduction, to part two. In part one a conversation involving three persons is reported. A conservative Dutch citizen of Antwerp converses with Raphael Hythloday, an experienced traveler, and with More. Hythloday, however, is the chief speaker. He is well versed in Latin and especially in Greek culture. Moreover, he has traveled extensively, even with Amerigo Vespucci, the Florentine navigator. In this way he is given prestige in the mind of the reader. It is not impossible in part one of *Utopia* to recognize a distinct resemblance to the dialogue form of Plato.

Part one describes certain factors in the political situation in England. The untoward phases of poverty and the vicious forms of punishment that prevailed are painted in gloomy colors. The reader is glad to turn from this unpleasant social picture to the description in part two of *Utopia,* where the people are living under well-ordered conditions.

The ideal commonwealth is located on the mystical island of Amaurote, where Raphael Hythloday lived for five years. On this island the economic and social life is communistic, somewhat after the manner of Plato's *Republic.* It is a fundamental communism which More postulates. Complete communism of goods exists on Amaurote.[1] All possess equal portions of wealth. The Utopian communistic state implies a radical change in human nature. More justifies communism on the grounds that it roots out that serious social evil, covetousness.[2] Likewise, the incentive for stealing and plundering is removed. If there is a scarcity of economic commodities in any part of Utopia, the surplus in any other part is immediately drawn upon to meet the need. Thus the whole land conducts itself as if it were one family or household.[3] The guiding principle in regard to economic goods is that of human needs.

In Utopia everyone finds his greatest pleasure in giving to others. The strongest league of peoples or of nations is not that which is united chiefly by covenants or treaties, but one which is knit together by love and a benevolent attitude.[4] The strongest league in the world is that which is based on the fellowship of kindred natures—a genuine

Christian brotherhood of nations.

In Utopia, agriculture is the most highly respected occupation. Agriculture is a science in which all Utopian men and women are expert. In the harvest days the urban people, both men and women (farmerettes) go out into the country and help gather in the crops.[5] Urban and rural co-operation at harvest time solves the farmer's employment problems to the pleasure, good feeling, and advantage of all concerned. The food question is considered of paramount national importance. The agriculturist is equipped with the best tools and follows intensive methods.[6]

In addition to agricultural science, every citizen of Utopia learns at least one trade or craft.[7] Even every woman learns a skilled trade. The advantages of learning a trade by every citizen are obvious—they include a great increase in the potential industrial resources of a people. The question may be raised here, if it would not be a worth-while asset for every citizen in our modern days to learn a trade. Such an accomplishment would give a sense of economic independence to every individual; it would afford to everyone the point of view of the skilled workman; it would add a gigantic potential force to production.

In Utopia, there is one leader, or syphogrant, to every thirty families. Although there are other officers, including a prince for each city and a king for the island, the syphogrants are in reality the leading officials. It is noteworthy that no public matters are to be decided until they have been considered and debated for at least three days. By this scientific procedure the necessity of rescinding hasty legislative action is reduced to a minimum.

An important duty of the syphogrants is to regulate employment. Not only is everyone in Utopia to have a trade, but all are to work. There are no idle poor or idle rich. All rich men, commonly called "gentlemen," all women, priests, monks, and friars (except a few) engage in productive labor. Even the syphogrants, or officials, work spontaneously. All useless occupations are prohibited. In countries where the dollar rules, there are many vain occupations which serve only to augment riotous superfluities.[8] Thus, since all persons work and since only needed occupations are permitted in Utopia, the working day is shortened to six hours.

In the case of a season of unemployment, the simple device is adopted of shortening temporarily the labor day. By cutting down the hours of labor to four a day during an unemployment period, work is provided for all. When an individual, it may be added, visits his friends, he works the same as if he were at home. He sets himself to the task in which his friends are engaged. No one in Utopia is encumbered with visitors who sit about doing nothing and at the same time hinder their hosts from productive activities.

The syphogrants prevent idleness; they also prevent overwork. They permit no one to work at a task like a laboring and toiling beast; they allow no one to become a slave to his labor.

Laws in Utopia are few in number. Inasmuch as all the people are well instructed and socially minded, many laws are needless.[9] Each citizen is above the law in the same way that an honest person is above the law against stealing. In the case of those disputes which must necessarily arise, the plaintiff and defendant go before the judge and plead for themselves. Utopia is noted for its scarcity of laws and the absence of attorneys. No crafty and subtle interpretation of laws by attorneys is permitted. Every man is his own attorney and simply states the facts in the given dispute; the judge knows the law and decides the case.

The organization of the cities is interesting. In the middle of each quarter of each city there is a market place for the exchange of all manner of goods. Public *abattoirs* are in operation. Splendidly appointed hospitals are located outside the cities in a quiet environment. Contagious wards are provided. So excellent is the care which is afforded the patients in the public hospitals that any person who falls sick prefers to go to a hospital than to be cared for by the kindly ministrations of relatives at home. It may be noted that every city is provided with a hall of fame.

Every urban community is a garden city; every

house has a garden plot. Furthermore, the people take much pride in their gardens; they compete with one another, endeavoring to excel in the fruitage and in the beauty of the gardens.[10]

City planning rules in Utopia.[11] Overcrowding is not permitted; whenever a city exceeds the norm, a new city is established. New urban communities are established by public action.

Social centers are common on the island of Amaurote. In the winter when the people cannot work in their gardens after the supper hour, they gather in their community halls, where they engage in music, wholesome conversation, and games. Dice-play and similar foolish and pernicious games are unknown.[12] Wine taverns, alehouses, "stewes," lurking corners, and places of wicked counsels are prohibited.[13]

Good health is a virtue in Amaurote; great pleasure is derived from possessing a well-ordered state of public health. Health is considered a sovereign pleasure in itself.[14] Preventive measures are substituted for remedial medicines.

Fashions are regulated rigidly. Fashion imitation is prevented. The garments for men are all of one mode; and for women, of another mode.[15] The married are distinguished from the unmarried by the style of wearing apparel. Thus, there are simply four sets of styles in Amaurote. Coats of uniform colors—the natural color of wool—are worn. It is argued that coats of many colors are no warmer and hence no more practical than coats of the one natural color; they are more expensive and hence more wasteful.

In Utopia, gold and silver are held in reproach. They are not considered to be as useful as iron. Consequently, the Utopians load down their slaves with gold and silver ornaments and pearls.[16] In this connection the description of the visit of a group of ambassadors to Amaurote is amusing. The ambassadors from an adjoining country were dressed in gorgeous apparel like the very gods. They came to Amaurote wearing chains of gold and displaying peacock feathers. The citizens of Amaurote, coming out to meet the guests, rushed past the ambassadors and saluted the plainly dressed slaves of the ambassadors. They mistook the ambassadors for fools and knaves. Even the little children of Amaurote, when they saw the jewelry of the ambassadors, looked at their mothers and said: "See, how great a lubber doth wear pearls and precious stones, as if he were still a little child."[17] After being in Amaurote a short time, the ambassadors perceived how foolish it was to set emphasis on the doubtful glistenings of trifling stones. They recognized that it is foolish to consider oneself nobler than other selves because one can wear clothes that are spun from finer wool than the clothes of other persons. After all, whether the wool is coarse or fine, it may have come from the self-same sheep.

An individual does not become a god by wearing precious stones. The more the individual burdens himself with heavy stones and gorgeous apparel, the more insignificant he is.

Although in Utopia no man is wealthy, yet in a sense, all men are wealthy. All live joyfully, without worrying, and without fearing that they or their children will fall into poverty. Amaurote is a gigantic household, wherein the more able take a personal interest in the less able and in the unfortunate. No one lives in idleness and no one lives by virtue of any form of unnecessary economic enterprise. Rich men are not permitted by either private fraud or common law to snatch away from the poor man some portion, great or small, of his daily earnings. There are no idle rich, conniving how they may keep their unearned wealth or how they may grind down the poor in order to get more wealth. Since the love of money is unknown in Amaurote, other passions are also absent. Since the people do not love money, they have lost the desire to perpetrate the money crimes, such as fraud, theft, murder, treason. Likewise, pride which measures its satisfaction, not in terms of its own merits, *per se,* but by comparison with the poverty of human beings, is destroyed. The Utopians have conquered materialism. They are not subject to the death grapples which are caused by the love of money. Luxuries have been suppressed and the leisure class has been eliminated. Social extremes are unknown.

People are honored, not for their wealth but for their serviceableness to the community.[18] In the halls of fame, to which allusion has already been made, benefactors of the commonwealth are rewarded by having images of themselves set up in perpetual memory of their good deeds to their fellows.

The family is the fundamental social unit, but it is of the patriarchal type. Pure monogamic love is idealized. Especial care is taken that neither of the parties of a marriage vow possesses any hidden vices. Adultery is the chief justification for breaking the marriage bond. A single standard of morals for both husband and wife is set. Love may be won by beauty, but it can be kept and preserved only by virtue and obedience.

Because of freedom from long hours of monotonous labor, nearly every one in Utopia is able to maintain his intellectual interests and to experience intellectual growth throughout life. It is the solemn custom to have daily lectures early every morning and it is the habit of multitudes of people of all types to attend.[19] All of the time that it is possible to spare from the necessary occupations is devoted to the development and garnishing of the mind.[20] Nearly all the citizens devote their extra-occupational hours throughout their lives to the arts and sciences. The chief felicity of life is said to be found in learning. In training the mind, the Utopians never weary. As a matter of course, a common school education is provided for every individual. Classes for adults and adult education are made the outstanding features of the public school system in Amaurote. One must learn to live and must go on learning throughout life. Hence, the provisions of public education should be adequate for the adult as well as for the adolescent.

Religious education and practice are considered essential. More's tolerant attitude in an age of brutal intolerance is shown by the fact that the Utopians are permitted whatever religion they prefer. Superstitious beliefs are taboo. More makes a subtle thrust when he observes that the priests of Amaurote are possesed of great holiness and hence are few in number.[21] It is no esoteric or monastic religion which More endorses. Future happiness may be secured best by busy labors and social efforts in this life.[22] Public service, including the care of the sick, is religiously emphasized.

War is beastly. Contrary to the attitudes of the people in all other countries, the people of Amaurote count nothing so inglorious as the glory that is obtained in fighting and killing.[23] No imagination is necessary in order to understand the courage which More displayed in making a vigorous attack in the sixteenth century upon war.

Under limited conditions, however, war is justifiable. More gives three worthy reasons for declaring war: (1) the defense of one's own country;

(2) the defense of the country of one's friendly neighbors; and (3) delivering oppressed peoples anywhere from the yoke and bondage of tyranny.[24] From the twentieth century point of view, these justifications of war are sound.

These reasons are all "defense" factors,—which is remarkable in view of the fact that they were enunciated in an age when "offensive" wars were common. The only reason for assuming the offensive in matters of war is the social one of taking land away from people who deliberately withhold land from cultivation and fail to produce food for the nourishment of mankind.[25] By this plan, More severely indicts the holders of large landed estates which are held chiefly for the selfish gratification of the owners.

Hired or mercenary soldiers are employed in war. The people of Amaurote employ hideous, savage fighters from the wild woods and the high mountains to do their fighting for them. The larger the number of these impetuous barbarians who are killed in battle, the better off is the world.

More opposed conscription. Ordinarily, no one is forced to fight, because under such circumstances he will not fight well. In the case, however, of defending Amaurote, the cowards are distributed among the bold-hearted. In warfare, the people of Amaurote do not allow their warriors to lay waste or destroy the land of their enemies. Neither foraging nor the burning of food supplies is permitted. No one who is unarmed is to be hurt.

More's penological ideas are modern. He points out the folly of making theft a capital offense the same as murder. The temptation will be to steal, or rob, and to kill also, whereas under a more reasonable law the temptation in many cases would be to steal only. A law which makes theft a capital offense is harsher than even the harsh Mosaic law of an eye for an eye, a life for a life, because the former justifies the government in taking the life of an individual who is guilty of stealing money. In Utopia the thief is compelled to restore the stolen goods to the person from whom he stole, and not to the king, as in many lands in More's time. The thief is put at common labor, not thrown into a city or county jail and left in idleness. Compulsory labor is the common method of punishment.[25]

The fundamental penological principle which More developed was that crime should be prevented by taking away the occasion of offense.[27] He condemned the prevailing method in England of allowing wickedness to increase, and then of punishing the sinners after they had been permitted to grow up in an environment of sin. He objected to taking men from the trades for war service and then later irresponsibly discharging them, leaving many of them industrially stranded, unemployed, and subject to the temptation of stealing. More's dictum was: Show people how to live; do not let them steal and then take their lives away. Life in Utopia is more or less equally divided between five factors: industry, study, music, travel, and domesticity.

In the *Utopia,* Sir Thomas More made a direct criticism of conditions in England; he showed himself an able student of social problems; and his ideas are noted for their "modernness." Altogether, the *Utopia* has made a remarkable impression, not simply upon social idealists but also upon practical thinkers. As a literary invention for shrewdly suggesting criticisms of vicious but entrenched social wrongs it has been followed by imitations, but remains unparalleled in quality.

In the *New Atlantis,* Sir Francis Bacon (1561-1628), wrote an unfinished description of a utopian island where there is a high degree of social welfare and where "social salvation by scientific education" obtains. An Order or Society of "Solomon's House" is established which sends out every twelve years merchants of light (intellectual) who travel for the following period of twelve years, gathering facts in all branches of science and art.[28] Upon being relieved by the next group of traveler scholars, they return home and contribute their knowledge to the acquired store, which in the meantime has been added unto by many trained experimenters and research scholars. Airplanes, horseless wagons, and submarines are not unknown in the *New Atlantis.* Superstition is banished. Social knowledge will lead to a nation of socialized persons,—this is the Baconian implication.

Tommaso Campanella (1568-1639), a monk, a philosopher, and an Italian contemporary of Francis Bacon, urged that human nature should be studied rather than books. Because of so-called heretical ideas, he was imprisoned for twenty-seven years. Shortly after his release he fled to Paris, where he died. In prison he wrote *The City of the Sun,* a crude but significant psychological analysis of society. It is a social order based on the balanced relations of the three principles of Power, Intelligence, and Love. These forces are equally ex-expressed in the social process and produce a perfect society.

Oceana, "a Midsummer Night's Dream of politics," is the title of a romance which was written by James Harrington (1611-1677). His social order rests on economic factors, chiefly landed estates. However, the author advocates the election of rulers by ballot every three years and the choosing of the rulers from the intellectually élite.

In this chapter it is impossible to note all the "utopias" that have been written. The utopian and communistic systems of socialists, such as Fourier, Saint Simon, and Owen will be referred to in Chapter XIV. There are other important utopian contributions, such as those by William Morris and Edward Bellamy. In *News from Nowhere,* William Morris (1834-1896), an English artist and socialist, describes his native England as a perfected society under a régime of socialism. Because of its American setting, Bellamy's *Looking Backward* will be presented in some detail in the following paragraphs.

In recent decades the utopian postulates of Edward Bellamy (1850-1898), in *Looking Backward* and *Equality* have had a wide reading. The author was the first American to command attention in the field of utopian thought. Bellamy presents a plan of industrial organization on a national scale with individuals sharing equally in the products of labor, or in public income, in the same way that "men share equally in the free gifts of nature." Bellamy protests against an economic order whose chief evil is summed up in the following question: How can men be free who must ask the right to labor and to live from their fellows, and seek their bread from the hand of others?

Society is likened to a gigantic coach to which the masses of humanity are harnessed, toiling along a very hilly and sandy road. The best seats are on top of the coach. The occupants of the elegant seats are constantly in fear of falling from their cushions of ease, splendor, and power,—and hence their interest in the toilers.

In *Looking Backward* the entire social process is made an expression of service. Service is a matter of course, not of compulsion. No business is so fundamentally the public's business as the industry and trade on which the livelihood of the public depends.[29] Therefore, to intrust industry and commerce to private persons to be managed for private profit is a folly "similar to that of surrendering the functions of political government to kings and nobles for their personal glorification."

Buying and selling are pronounced anti-social. They are an education in self-seeking at the expense of others.[30] Citizens who are so trained are unable to rise above a very low grade of civilization.[31] They are sensible chiefly to such motives as fear of want and love of luxury. For buying and selling, credit books are substituted which are good at any public warehouse. In place of higher wages, the chief motives to activity are honor, men's gratitude, the inspiration of duty, patriotism, the satisfaction of doing one's work well—in other words, the same motives that now influence, for example, the members of the teaching profession.

The arduousness of the trades are equalized, so that all shall be equally attractive, by making the hours of labor in different trades to differ inversely according to arduousness.[32] Everyone works as a common laborer for three years and then chooses an occupation—agriculture, mechanics, the professions, art. The working life is twenty-four years long, from the ages of twenty-one to forty-five, after which all may devote themselves to self-improvement and enjoyment, but subject to emergency calls along industrial and other social service lines.

Bellamy challenges an individualism which incapacitates people for co-operation. He builds his society upon solidarity of race and brotherhood of man. He does not fear corruption in a society "where there is neither poverty to be bribed nor wealth to bribe."[83]

All cases of criminal atavism are treated in hospitals. There are no jails. Under capitalism nineteen-twentieths of misdemeanors are due to economic inequality. The remainder are the outcropping of ancestral traits. In Bellamy's ideal society there are no private property disputes and no lawyers.

The educational system in *Looking Backward* does not educate some individuals highly and leave others untrained.[84] It gives everyone "the completest education that the nation can give," in order that individuals may enjoy themselves, in order that they may enjoy one another, and in order that the unborn may be guaranteed an intelligent and refined parentage.

Bellamy holds that human nature in its essential quality is good, not bad, and that men are naturally generous, not selfish; pitiful, not cruel; godlike in aspirations, moved by divine impulses of goodness, images of God and not the travesties upon Him which they have seemed.[85] It is our economic order which has fostered shameless self-assertion, mutual depreciation, a stunning clamor of conflicting boasts, and a stupendous system of brazen beggary.

In three utopias, H. G. Wells portrays societary conditions that are kinetic rather than static and world-wide rather than local in scope.[36] While the author provides a changed economic system, socialistic in nature, he urges that changed social attitudes are also needed.

In the utopian social thought that has been presented in this chapter and in similar works which are not mentioned here there is generally displayed (1) a common weakness of impracticability under current circumstances, (2) an over-emphasis upon simply changing the economic order, and (3) static rather than dynamic principles. The strength of utopian social thought is found (1) in its drastic criticism of current social evils, (2) in its relative harmlessness at the given time, (3) in the force of its indirect suggestion, (4) in the widespread hearing which it secures, and (5) in its social idealism.

CHAPTER XI.

INDIVIDUALISTIC SOCIAL THOUGHT

At the dawn of the Renaissance, tradition and dogmatism were ruling mankind. Here and there, however, individuals were perceiving the nature of the bondage. Occasionally a cry for individual freedom was uttered. Petrarch dared to say that the world was made for man's enjoyment. The early Teutons crudely developed the idea of personal liberty. In France a movement arose which culminated in the doctrines of natural rights and "Back to Nature." The stress upon individualism in England became so deeply ingrained that it exists today as a powerful form of traditionalism. The United States was founded, in part, upon a doctrine of natural rights.

Absolutely unlike Sir Thomas More in many ways, Niccolo Machiavelli (1469-1527), an Italian contemporary, broke with tradition and received the sobriquet, the Galileo of social science. Unfortunately, many people think of the Italian writer in terms of the adjective which bears his name, Machiavellism, or political intrigue. While he deserves this reputation, he also should be considered in another light. He cut loose from the customary ways of thinking of his time and asserted that it is not necessary to take all things on fiat or alleged divine decree. Although this may be dangerous doctrine, it serves a useful and constructive purpose when people are ruled by political and ecclesiastical autocrats. Machiavelli was no idealist in the accepted sense of the term, but a man who mixed with people, traveled extensively, and studied actual conditions. He declared that people should be considered as they are, and not according to false teachings about them.

A century before the time of Sir Francis Bacon, the inaugurator of the so-called inductive or scientific method of study, Machiavelli was observing human conditions and upon the basis of these observations was drawing conclusions. He believed that it does not pay to be guided in one's conduct by abstract ethics or impracticable ideals—and said so, in an age when imprisonment, exile, or death awaited anyone who opposed the autocratic authorities. From abstract ethics, Machiavelli swung to the extreme of concrete expediency. He lived and thought in the exigencies of the moment. He is an example of one who reacts so strongly against the stress and strain of the hour that he cannot get the larger vision that is necessary for balanced thinking on fundamental issues.

Machiavelli wrote on the subject of leadership and government. He advocated either an autocratic or democratic form of government—according to the conditions of the time and place. In the *Prince* he described with noteworthy accuracy the traits and methods of a leader whose constituents must be treated with absolute authority. In the *Discourses* he dealt with a democratic-republican type of leadership and control.

The succesful prince, or leader, in the selfish sense, makes himself both beloved and feared by his people.[1] On occasion he uses force and even fraud. Sometimes he must either exterminate or be exterminated. He must repeal or suppress old laws and make new ones to fit the social situation. He seeks to be considered merciful rather than cruel. He exercises universal pity in order to prevent social disorders from occurring and producing rapine and murder.[2] He does not allow his mercy to be taken advantage of by ungrateful and hypocritical persons. He is strong-minded; he is either a sincere friend or a generous foe. He is paternalistic, urging that his subjects be well-fed and have a good livelihood,[3] thus gaining and maintaining the affection of the people. In international affairs he acts with a strong hand, fortifying well his city or nation, and providing good laws for internal growth.[4] He errs grossly, however, in his fundamental philosophy that any plan or action that is for the welfare of the state, or nation, considered as a supreme unit of authority in itself, is morally sound.

Sir Francis Bacon, whose contribution to utopian

social thought has been indicated in the foregoing chapter, placed all social and sociological thinkers under deep obligations by his emphasis upon inductive reasoning. He helped to free the individual from control by dogma and superstition. He provided the individual with a technique for securing a new sense of individual freedom. In freeing himself the individual discards his irrational pre-judgments, whether socially inherited or individually developed. He protects himself from anthropomorphic judgments, i. e., from judgments which he makes because he looks upon life and the universe through human eyes. These pre-judgments are common to all mankind—they are "the idols of the tribe." On the other hand, the individual avoids purely personal preferences, which he is likely to hold because of his own peculiar experiences, and which thus place him outside the pale of common experience—these are "the idols of the cave."

Then there are "the idols of the forum," which cause the individual to give undue dependence to words and language. "The idols of the theater" are traditional systems of thought. Bacon's dictum has been stated as follows: Get as little of yourself and of other selves as possible in the way of the thing which you wish to see.

Having eliminated human predispositions, the individual is ready to gather facts, arrange them in groups, draw conclusions from them, and act according to the resultant laws. Knowledge gives power.[4] Social knowledge gives power to improve human conditions and makes possible wise social control. Thus, Bacon opened the road to individual freedom.

Too much individual freedom, however, destroys government and the social order. If each individual is a law unto himself, anarchy reigns and progress is prevented. Consequently, the question arises: How can individually free persons unite in a society without giving up their freedom? The answer to this question took the form of a controversy on the subject of the social contract, i. e., the contract or agreement of individuals, as units, to form and maintain societies. This controversy arose in the seventeenth century and was waged vigorously in the eighteenth century.

Thomas Hobbes (1588-1678), the distinguished social philosopher of England, introduced his analysis of society with the idea that man was originally self-centered, egoistic, and pleasure-loving. He was an independent center. His interest in other people was based on their ability to cater to his own good. He and they desired the same things in life. His hand was thus raised, in competition, against every other man. This state of continual conflict became mutually destructive and unbearable.[5] In consequence, each individual agreed to give over some of his precious, inalienable rights to a central authority or sovereign, whose decrees should constitute law and serve as the guide for conduct. The war of each against all, with the concomitant state of fear, was thus supplanted by a mutual contract, conferring sovereignty by popular agreement upon the ruler. In this way Hobbes met the dilemma of supporting an absolute form of government in which he believed and of denying the divine right of kings which he abhorred. Hobbes performed a useful service in intellectually destroying the idea of the divine right of kings, but urged after all an undemocratic political absolutism. Hobbes conferred humanly derived but irrevocable authority upon the king. He, however, traced sovereignty back to the people rather than to a divine right.

In getting away from the conditions "of Warre of every one against every one" in the natural state where "every man has a Right to everything," Hobbes swung to an undemocratic extreme. His Puritanic training gave an undue severity to his social thought. The Puritans, however, believed in the complete eradication of the savage human tendencies and also in the ultimate elimination of kings. Hobbes did not analyze deeply the instinctive bases of human nature. He built his *Leviathan* out of natural human qualities and tied its units together by means of a strong, central will—this was his perfect society.

Baruch Spinoza (1632-1677), the Portuguese Jewish philosopher of Holland, improved the social contract idea. He believed that man was originally of an anti-social and a tooth-and-fang nature, possessing only incipient social impulses. Hence, man is not naturally bad, but naturally anti-social. Social organization was effected for purposes of individual gain and glory; it was promulgated and furthered by individuals in order that they might escape the miseries of unregulated conflict. Agreements were made whereby sovereignty was embodied in a ruler, but if the ruler abused the sovereignty entrusted to him, it reverted immediately to the people. This democratic conception was vastly superior to the idea of Hobbes, that sovereignty is delegated by the people to the king as an irresponsible monarch.

John Locke (1632-1704) strengthened the social contract theory, elaborating the idea that sovereignty reverts to the people whenever the king becomes a tyrant. He held that the natural state of individuals is a condition of perfect freedom to order their actions, not asking leave of any man.[6] This state of liberty is not a state of license to individuals to destroy themselves or their neighbors.[7] The state of liberty has the law of nature to govern it. Since all are equal, no one ought to harm another in his liberty or possessions.

Locke affirmed that men are in a state of nature until by their own consent they join in a political society.[8] In order to meet their needs effectively, they join in societies. One of these important needs is the preservation of property. Locke defended private property on the ground that it is a normal expression of individuality and necessary to individuality.

Right and wrong are not determined by the ruler or the state; they existed before society developed. Here the Puritanism of Locke enters. He stressed moral values. He made the natural rights of individuals supreme; individuals may even overturn the government and still keep within their rights.

Locke's justification of revolution is his most startling doctrine. Imagine the heart-throb of the common people who heard Locke's contention that the end of government is the good of mankind, that people should not submit to tyranny, that whoever uses his force without right and law puts himself in a state of war with those against whom he uses it, and that in such a state the people have a right to resist and defend themselves.[9] Further, the people have a right to act as the supreme social force and to put legislation into new forms and into the hands of new executives. By these bold declarations Locke created a new public opinion, and aroused new moral power in the minds and hearts of the common people.

By the middle of the eighteenth century the con cept of individual freedom became crystallized in the doctrines of the natural rights of the individual, the contractual societary relationships between independent individuals, and the *laissez faire* principle in governmental science. The physiocrats, who took up the ideas of natural liberty and economic freedom, exercised a tremendous influence in France during the three decades following 1750. Their leaders were Quesnay, de Gournay, Condorcet, and Turgot. They believed that there was a natural law ruling human lives, just as there is a natural law ruling the physical world. They chafed under social restraints. Under the natural law, every individual has natural rights, chief of which is the right to the free exercise of all his faculties so long as he does not infringe on the similar right of other individuals. Unlike John Locke and other English thinkers who accepted the idea of individual liberty, the physiocrats argued that this natural liberty could not be abridged by a social contract.

According to the physiocrats the chief function of governmental control is to preserve the natural liberty of individuals. Industry and commerce must not be governmentally regulated, for by such regulation the rights of some men, chiefly employers, will be infringed upon. Employees, on the other hand, who are being treated unjustly will freely quit a harsh employer and obtain employment with considerate masters. Thus, an unjust employer will be unable to secure workers and be forced to discontinue his unjust practices—without government regulation. Likewise, a dishonest merchant will lose his customers and be forced to become honest or to close his shop—and again without government regulation. The physiocrats became known by their famous phrase, *laissez faire, laissez passer*.

Jean Jacques Rousseau (1712-1778), an able but baffling character, is the best known champion of the social contract idea. Although he advocated the family as a social institution and praised fatherhood, he reports that he carried his own children to a foundling asylum. He deprecated the disintegrating elements in civilization and urged a return to nature's simple ways. In his chief works, the *Contrat social* and *Emile,* he attacked civilization vigorously. He asserted that civilization had almost destroyed the natural rights of man. His dictum was: Trust nature.

According to Rousseau the early life of mankind was nearly ideal in its simplicity and pleasantness. War and conflict were relatively unknown. In his later writings, Rousseau modified his belief and asserted that primitive confusion made necessary some kind of social organization. On the other hand, it became the belief of Rousseau that civilization generates social evils and results sooner or later in social deterioration. Corruption in society has become notorious. Social inequality is rampant and unbearable. "Man is born free, and is everywhere in chains." People have become so engrossed in the artificialities of social life and so bewildered by its complexities that happiness has been lost.

Leave the individual free to carry out his own plans, untrammelled by complex social rules, restrictions, and duties. There is no social sanction at all; there is no authority except nature, which is necessity. In *Emile,* Rousseau takes his two leading characters to an island, where they live alone—happily! Liberty not authority reigns. But Emile, who has declared for liberty as opposed to authority, insists in his discussions of domestic relationships that "woman is made to please man." The "unselfish, unsocial life" of Emile and Sophie turns out to be more than purely individualistic—it is anarchic and sensual. Emile fails to demonstrate the merit of Rousseau's own theories, such as "Man is good naturally but by institutions he is made bad," and "Everything is good as it comes from the hands of the Author of Nature; everything degenerates in the hands of man."

Slavery is wrong, according to Rousseau.[11] It is a contract or agreement, at the expense of the slave and for the profit of the slaveholder, in which the slaveholder asserts: I'll observe the agreement and you will observe it—as long as it pleases me.

Strength does not make right. Strength and moral force are not necessarily the same. Strength may often be ironically accepted in appearance and established in principle. By a social contract man loses his natural liberty and gains civil and moral liberty.[12] In this connection Rousseau was simply the spokesman of a point of view which found frequent expression in the seventeenth and eighteenth centuries. For example, in 1635, John Winthrop, the first governor of the Massachusetts colony, made a clear-cut distinction between natural liberties, and civil and moral liberties. Natural liberty is liberty to do what one lists, to do evil as well as good. Civil, or moral, liberty is liberty under the covenant between God and man, under the political covenants between men and men, and under the moral law. It is a liberty to do only that which is good, just, and honest.[18]

It was Rousseau who contended that life, liberty, and the pursuit of happiness are man's inalienable rights. It was this doctrine which profoundly influenced Thomas Jefferson, as evidenced in the Declaration of Independence. Sovereignty rests not in a ruler or monarch but in the community of people—this was perhaps Rousseau's main contribution to social thought.

Before Rousseau, however, wrote the *Contrat social,* the social contract theory had been overthrown. The writings of Montesquieu (1689-1755) offer an elaborate analysis of social and political processes. These analyses are similar, in some ways, to Aristotle's analyses of 158 constitutions. Montesquieu discussed the doctrine of natural rights, but did not believe that the natural state of mankind was one of conflict, in which social organization was forced as a means of meeting the needs of individual protection. He asserted that there was a natural, innate tendency in man toward association. In the support of this belief, Montesquieu drew facts from the lives of the individual members of the primitive tribes which were extant in his day. The influence of Montesquieu was clearly inimical to the social contract doctrine.

In the *Esprit des lois,* Montesquieu dissected the laws of many nations and tried to show the relations between these laws and social and political conditions. The general implication is that laws are a natural outgrowth of life conditions rather than of formal contractual agreements. Hence, society is a natural evolution rather than a contract.

Perhaps the chief antagonist in the eighteenth century of the social contract theory was David Hume (1711-1776), the father of social psychology. According to Hume, the origin of society was not in a contract arrived at by intellectual processes; it was instinctive. Man is a social animal. At the basis of this sociability lies the sex instinct, which resulted in the establishment of the family. The sex instinct is strongly supported by the sentiment of sympathy, which also is innate, and which may develop into intelligent co-operation. Man is not entirely self-centered; he takes pleasure in other people's pleasures and suffers when others are in pain, or the victims of disease, or are dying.

Sympathy, like the sex instinct, is a genuinely fundamental element in human nature and in society. However, the combination of sympathy and the sex instinct is not strong enough to support the family in either its simple or complex stages from the attacks upon it that are made by inherent human selfishness. Hence, social and political organizations are necessary to hold the selfish impulses and interests of mankind in check. Intellectual control of society thus becomes necessary and consciously recognized. Environment alone does not cause people in a given community to act alike. It is imitation, primarily, which operates to bring about group conformity.[14]

Man in a large measure is governed by interest. It is impossible for men to consult their interests "in so effective a manner as by a universal and inflexible observance of the rules of justice, by which alone they can preserve society, and keep themselves from falling into that wretched and savage condition, which is commonly represented as the state of nature."[15]

According to the contract theory, people expect protection and security. If they meet with tyranny and oppression, they are freed from their promises and return to that state of liberty which proceeded the institution of government. But Hume maintained that if people entered into no contract and made no promises, government would still be necessary in all civilized societies. The obligation of submission to government is not derived from any promise of the subjects.[16]

Adam Ferguson (1723-1816) wrote an *Essay on the History of Civil Society* and *The History of the Progress and Termination of the Roman Republic.*

He argued that social institutions and social convenience lead to inherent sociability, and pointed out that competition and conflict are vital to social development. Thomas Paine (1737-1809) asserted that man is inherently social and that social organization is a natural development.

The natural rights theory and the resultant individualism not only repudiated their false derivative, the social contract concept, but also wrestled with considerable success with the socio-economic concept of mercantilism. Mercantilism was a system of regulating industrial enterprise by governments in order to build up strong nation-states. Mercantilism reached its strictest form in France in the writings of Colbert (1619-1683). It prevailed in Europe during the sixteenth and seventeenth centuries, and the first four decades of the eighteenth century. It was a system which grew out of feudalism and the city-state type of society. It operated to bring together towns and cities into national unities. Under feudalism, the town had regulated industry for its own advancement and against the welfare, perchance, of neighboring towns. Mercantilism served to unite towns and to create in townspeople a national loyalty.

Under mercantilism, the nation entered upon the task of regulating industry and finance so as to build a strong state. A favorable balance of trade was sought in order to add to the bullion within the state. High tariffs were enacted, which sometimes defeated the intended purposes. A dense population was favored as a means of securing cheap labor, and hence of furthering manufacture, which in turn would develop foreign trade and bring in the coveted bullion—the heralded strength of a nation.

In the eighteenth century, mercantilism in France and England met defeat in the contest with the *laissez faire* theory, with which the names of the physiocrats and of Adam Smith are inseparably connected. It often fathered too stringent regulations. Instead of supporting national ends, mercantilistic measures frequently furthered private interests. Mercantilism, however, played a strong part in building up the concepts of national unity and loyalty.

In the German states and Austria, cameralism represented the ideas for which mercantilism stood in England, France, and elsewhere in Western and Southern Europe. Among the leading cameralists were Seckendorf, Horing, Justi, and Sonnenfels. Cameralism obtained a far deeper hold upon the German states than mercantilism did, for example, in England. The *laissez faire* philosophy was never able to make a deep inroad upon cameralism. In fact, the *laissez faire* philosophy did not receive serious consideration in the German states before 1800, and did not strike deep. National self-sufficiency, paternalistic control, minute regulation of internal affairs, rearing of large families, and subordination of the welfare of the state—these are the concepts which ruled in Germany.

Adam Smith (1723-1790), primarily an economist and often referred to as the father of political economy, exerted a profound influence upon social thought. He coupled a modified natural rights theory with a doctrine of sympathy; he spoke for the natural rights of the individual, of the poorer classes in society, and of the smaller nations. He vigorously attacked mercantilism with its system of minute regulation of individuals. He objected to promoting unduly the interests of one class of men in a country, for by so doing, the interests of all other classes in that country and of all persons in all other countries are harmed.[17] He pointed out the fallacy of building a nation of shopkeepers, for in so doing the government of such a nation will be unduly influenced and controlled by the interests of shopkeepers. The interests of other classes will be more or less ignored. Adam Smith protested against Great Britain's methods of regulating the American colonies. To prohibit the American colonies from making all they could of every part of their own produce or from employing their stock and industry in the way that they judged most advantageous to themselves, was "a manifest violation of the most sacred rights of mankind."[18]

Mercantilism made use of monopoly of one kind or another, and hence is objectionable, according to Smith. Mercantilism is regulation, and regulation is often carried on for the benefit of the rich and powerful, thus neglecting and oppressing the poor.[19] Smith failed to note, however, that the *laissez faire* policy likewise favored the rich and powerful and neglected the poor. Mercantilism, according to Smith, considers production and not consumption as the end of industry and commerce, and thus favors one class at the expense of other classes.

"Wherever there is great property," said Smith, "there is great inequality." For every very rich man there must be at least 500 poor men, and the affluence of the few supposes the indigence of the many.[20] But no society can be flourishing and happy wherein the greater part of the members are poor and miserable.[21] The laboring men should have "such a share of the produce of their own labor as to be themselves tolerably well fed, clothed, and lodged." Poverty does not prevent the procreation of children, but is on the other hand extremely unfavorable to the rearing of children.[22]

Smith pointed out four causes of social inequality:[23] (1) Superiority in personal qualifications, such as strength, beauty, agility of body; or wisdom, virtue, prudence, justice, fortitude, moderation of mind. (2) Superiority of age and experience. (3) Superiority of fortune. Riches give social authority; riches possess power to buy. (4) Superiority of birth, based on family prestige.

Smith extolled the merits of division of labor in industry with the resultant increase in the quantity of work. There are three sets of causal circumstances:[24] (1) the increase of dexterity; (2) the saving of time in passing from one kind of work to another; and (3) the invention of a large number of machines. Smith, however, deplored the deadening effect upon the individual of repeating over and over a simple process, hundreds or thousands of times daily. In summary, Adam Smith (1) applied the concept of natural rights to industrial conditions; (2) developed Hume's concept of sympathy into a theory of mutual aid between individuals, classes, and nations; and (3) supported the necessity of division of labor.

The natural rights and social contract theories affected in one way or another the thinking not only of the men who have already been considered in this chapter, but also of many other individuals. Blackstone (1723-1780) held that man's weakness in isolation led to association. The primary group was the patriarchal family. Blackstone was not an advocate of social regulation. His exposition of English law in the *Commentaries* stood for law itself, and became the bulwark at once of the doctrines of individual rights and property rights in both England and the American colonies. In the United States, its influence remained dominant for more than a century after the founding of the republic.

Although Edmund Burke (1729-1797) believed in a corporate unity of society, he became in his century the chief spokesman of humanity for humanity's sake. He pleaded for justice for and conciliation with the American colonies; he spoke for the benighted Hindus who were being plundered by English stockholders; and he championed the rights of slaves. He failed, on the other hand, to appreciate the struggles of the French people which culminated in the French Revolution.

Immanuel Kant (1724-1817) declared man in a natural state is both social and unsocial and referred to the "unsocial sociableness" of man. "Man cannot get on with fellows and he cannot do without them." Man has an inclination to associate with others and also a great propensity to isolate himself from others. He wishes to direct things according to his own ideas and thus courts resistance and conflict. It is this conflict, however, which leads to individual advancement.

Kant laid great stress upon a good will.[25] The individual may have intelligence and sagacity, power and wealth, but he may still be a pernicious and hurtful member of society. He is not even worthy to be happy unless he possesses a good will. A man's will is good not because of the end he seeks nor because of the results of his activities but because he inherently wills the good. It is this "good will" of Kant which is in conflict with the utilitarianism of Bentham and Mill, and also with modern behavioristic psychology and objective sociology. To Kant, morality is subjective. Social laws may regulate and control man's conduct but they cannot control his motives.

Johann Fichte (1762-1814) joined with Kant in the interpretation of a good will. He held that property is essential to the development of freedom. However, he pushed the social contract idea to an extreme and developed a doctrine of an idealistic state socialism, including the superiority of Germany among the nations of the world.

Hegel (1770-1831) supported cameralism by developing the State idea, with the implication that Germany would become the supreme State in the world. Hegel even asserted that man has his existence and his ethical status "only in being a member of the State."[26] Morality is not a matter of striving independently to realize one's inner self, but of living in accord with the traditions of one's State.

Perhaps the individual rights theory never manifested a greater aberration than in the mind of Friedrich Nietzsche (1844-1900). Power is supreme. The individual or the nation with the greatest power has the greatest right to live. Against this idea or the expressions of this idea, the weaker individuals tend to combine and to extol their weaknesses as virtues, even building a religion out of these glorified weaknesses, for example, Christianity. Nietzsche's doctrine of the superman and the superstate will be discussed in Chapter XXI.

Closely related to the discussions concerning

natural rights and the social contract is the doctrine of utilitarianism, a modified form of individualism with certain objective standards. Jeremy Bentham (1748-1832) made utilitarianism well-known, and particularly the standard: The greatest good of the greatest number. In accordance with a formal idea of social change, Bentham urged that social improvements be made by legislation. He demanded objective standards as opposed to Kant's emphasis on the inner motive. Where Kant accented the "how" of conduct, Bentham insisted on the "what" of conduct. He pointed out the need for improved forms of government, apparently ignoring or at least greatly underestimating the fact that real progress comes chiefly through modifying organic processes. However, Bentham may be rated a virile social reformer, for he strongly advocated such measures as the secret ballot, woman suffrage, trained statesmancraft. He made social welfare a main goal.

The doctrine of utilitarianism was carried forward by James Mill (1773-1836) and was brought to its highest fruition by the son, John Stuart Mill (1806-1873). The elder Mill contended that utility is morality. Like Bentham the elder Mill urged many social reforms.

John Stuart Mill adopted a modified form of the natural rights theory. He asserted that the individual should have all the rights that he can exercise without infringing upon the equal rights of other individuals. Mill recognized a gradation in the pleasures which satisfy individuals. He declared that it is better to be a man dissatisfied than a pig satisfied; he objected to the prevailing classification of people on the basis of poverty and wealth, and urged the substitution of standards of personal worth, honor, and true leadership as bases for social classification.

Sir Henry Maine (1832-1888) invented the phrase: From status to contract. He applied this phrase to a program of social welfare. There are many illustrations, he pointed out, in business and industrial life, and even in political and fraternal activities where people make social contracts. The marriage contract also has many of the characteristics of a genuine social contract. Maine pushed the social contract idea to its furthest practical point; but deprecated the possibility that the masses might come into power. His individualism deprived him of a faith in the possible social development of the uneducated.

Herbert Spencer, whose ideas will be discussed more extensively in a subsequent chapter, became one of the chief exponents of the doctrine of *laissez faire* in governmental matters. He brought a vast reading knowledge and able arguments to the support of individualistic doctrines. He added very little that was new to individualistic and *laissez faire* theories although he was at one time perhaps their leading exponent. One of his chief contributions to social thought was indirect and unintentional, namely, the way in which his writings challenged the attention of an American paleontologist, Lester F. Ward, and led him to point out the psychical nature and hence telic possibilities of civilization. In consequence of this challenge Spencer fell, and Ward rose to the rank of dean of American sociologists. An entire chapter will be devoted to the sociology of Lester F. Ward.

William G. Sumner (1840-1910) was the last noted champion of a governmental *laissez faire* doctrine. He held that the State owes nothing to anybody except peace, order, and the guarantee of rights. It is not true that the poor ought to care for each other, and that the churches ought to collect capital and spend it for the poor; it is not true that if you get wealth you should support others; and that if you do not get wealth others ought to support you. In a society based on contract there is no place for sentiment in public or common affairs.[28] Every individual will develop the self-reliance of a free person, if he is not taught that others will care for him in case he fails to care for himself. Sumner spoke vigorously as well as harshly in support of liberty, contract, and private property. Although he took an extreme and untenable position his ideas will bear careful, unbiased study, for they contain a large amount of common sense. His ethnological work will be indicated at some length in another chapter.

A noteworthy statement which has come from a current American school of legal thinkers concerning individualistic social thought, is found in the writings of Professor Roscoe Pound of Harvard Law School. In "A Theory of Social Interests" he has summed up the new point of view.[29] In the last century all interests were thought of in terms of individual interests, all were reduced to their purely individual elements and considered as rights.

In this century, Dean Pound indicates that law, for example, aims primarily to conserve some general social interest. It conserves the social interest in the general security, that is, in public health and in peace. It conserves the social interest in institutions,—domestic, religious, political. It conserves the social interest in natural resources, preventing the waste of oil and gas and protecting water rights. In conserves the social interest in general progress, in economic, political, cultural progress, although its main contribution in other fields, such as promoting the esthetic interests, are yet to be made. It conserves the social interests in individual life and in seeing that people live humanly and that the will of the individual is not trodden upon. Legal processes have thus become types of social engineering.

The doctrine of natural rights reached its largest degree of acceptance in England, France, and the United States. It was not only reflected in the thought of Thomas Jefferson but in the fundamental principles upon which the United States was established. It suffered an aberration in the form of the social contract theory which in its extreme forms was later repudiated. Its greatest weakness was the exaggerated form which it assumed, especially in England and the United States. In the latter country it became greatly magnified through contact with the spirit of discovery, invention, and pioneering which prevailed for over a century. Consequently, it dominated the thought life of the United States throughout the nineteenth century. It permitted captains of industry to exploit the helpless masses, and encouraged politicians to pursue selfish practices until governments became honeycombed with graft. It nearly capsized the good Ship of State—Democracy.

Theories of natural rights have been supplanted by considerations of natural needs, both individual and social. Human needs are now considered the only imperatives, but even they are relative and changing.

CHAPTER XII

MALTHUS AND POPULATION CONCEPTS

A unique and distinctive trend in social thought with important sociological implications developed in the closing years of the eighteenth century, namely, Malthusian thought regarding population. Malthusianism, however, was preceded by the ideas of William Godwin and Adam Smith. In 1775, Adam Smith had stated that "every species of animals naturally multiplies in proportion to the means of their subsistence, and no species can ever multiply beyond it."[1] Scanty subsistence, however, destroys a large percentage of offspring. Inasmuch as men, like all other animals, multiply naturally in proportion to the means of their subsistence, food is always, more or less, in demand; and food, or the cost of living, regulates population.[2] City people must depend upon the country for their subsistence, whereas seaport towns can command food resources from all parts of the earth.

The population ideas of William Godwin (1756-1836) were the immediate stimuli which set Malthus at work. In 1793, Godwin's *Enquiry Concerning Justice* was published. Godwin elaborated several radical social ideas of the French Physiocratic philosophers. He declared that human misery is caused by coercive institutions. Government, he asserted, is an evil and should be abolished. He urged also the abolition of strict marriage relations, although he personally acquiesced in the custom and in his last days he commended marriage. He thought that no social group should be larger than a parish, and that there should be an equal distribution of property. Godwin thus carried the doctrine of natural rights to the verge of anarchy and licentiousness. His ideas furnished a basis for the nineteenth century experiments in communism. But what is more important, Godwin's ideas regarding the reconstruction of society stimulated Thomas Malthus, who developed what is commonly known as the Malthusian doctrine of population.

In 1798, under an assumed name, Thomas Robert Malthus (1766-1834) offered to the world the first carefully collected and elaborated body of data, dealing with what he called *the* social problem, namely: What is the underlying cause of human unhappiness? This study may be counted, in a sense, the beginning of modern sociological study. Early in life Malthus showed an interest in social questions. Godwin's ideas had centered Malthus' attention on population. Malthus' well-known treatise entitled, *An Essay on the Principle of Population as it Affects the Future Improvement of Society,* undertook two important tasks: (1) To investigate the causes that have impeded the progress of mankind toward happiness, and (2) to examine probabilities of a total or partial removal of these causes.[3]

Among both plants and animals there is a constant tendency to reproduce numerically beyond the subsistence level. Wherever there is liberty, this power of increase blindly asserts itself. Afterwards, a lack of nourishment and of room represses the superabundant numbers.[4] It appears, therefore, that the ultimate check to population is lack of food, due to the fact that population increases faster than food supply. Nature, in other words, sets a harsher law over the increase of subsistence than she does over the birth rate. Man fails to take cognizance of this law and brings untold misery upon himself. The lower economic classes are the chief victims, and the giants of poverty and pauperism rule over whole sections of human population. Malthus considers the question of population the fundamental social problem.

Since population outruns food supply, dire human consequences naturally follow. Food supply, as a check upon population, operates harshly; it is but representative of an entire series of rigorous natural, or positive, checks upon population. In this list there are unwholesome occupations; forms of severe labor; extreme poverty; damp and wretched housing conditions; diseases, epidemics, plagues, poor nursing; intestine commotion, martial law, civil war; wars of all forms; excesses of all kinds.[5] These positive checks upon population are the results of two main causes, namely, vice and misery. As a result of the operation of these factors, population is being continually cut down and kept near the mere subsistence plane.

Malthus pointed out another check upon population, the preventive. The fear of falling into poverty causes many young people to postpone marriage until they can safely marry—economically. This check so far as voluntary is peculiar to man and, to the extent that it is not followed by irregular sex gratification, is prudential. The actual pressure of population upon food supply, or the fear of this impingement, prevents people from marrying earlier than they do and from reproducing their kind faster than they would do otherwise. This pressure, or the fear of it, cuts down the marriage rate in times of economic depression. But let prosperity come and the marriage rate leaps upward, especially among the poorer classes.

The positive and preventive checks upon population hold a definite relation to each other. "In every country where the whole of the procreative power cannot be called into action, the preventive and the positive checks must vary inversely as each other."[6] That is to say, when positive checks, such as famine and war, slay large numbers of people, moral restraint is diminished and the population numbers rapidly increase. When the preventive check expresses itself strongly, the population is kept down numerically, and positive checks, such as famine or even war, are defeated.

Malthus attempted to establish three propositions:

(1) The limitation of population by the restriction of the means of subsistence.

(2) The invariable increase of population whenever the means of subsistence increase, unless prevented by powerful checks.

(3) The factors which keep population on a level with the means of subsistence are all resolvable into three: moral restraint, vice, and misery.[7]

No one can gainsay the importance or the seriousness of the problem of population. Plato wrestled with it, and urged that procreation when it goes on too fast or too slow should be regulated by the state—through a proper distribution of marks of ignominy or of honor. The number of marriages should be determined by the magistrates.

Aristotle suggested that the ages of marriage for both sexes should be regulated; he even advocated the regulation of the number of children for each marriage. Additional children should be aborted.

Malthus, however, was wiser than either Plato or Aristotle, for he observed that the cause which has the most lasting effect in improving the condition of the poorer classes is the conduct and prudence of the individuals themselves.[8] Malthus asserted that it is in the power of each individual to avoid all the evil consequences to himself and society which result from the principle of population, "by the practice of a virtue clearly dictated to him by the light of nature and expressly enjoined in revealed religion."[9]

Malthus demonstrated clearly the weakness of liberal poor-laws. Give more food to the poor, and they will produce more children, and suffer more misery. Poor-laws increase the numbers of children of the poor, and hence increase the amount of misery. Both private benevolence and poor-laws increase the number of marriages and of children.[10]

Education is the solution which Malthus demanded.[11] Educate the poor to postpone marriage, to keep the birth rate down, and to practice economic thrift. To a great extent education will secure the operation of the prudential check upon population. The science of moral and political philosophy should not be confined within such narrow limits that it is unable to overcome in practical ways the obstacles to human happiness which arise from the law of population.[12]

There are factors in the population situation which did not exist at the time of Malthus, or which he did not see. Today there are additional preventive checks upon population, for example, the rise of democracy in the family whereby the wife and mother no longer is dominated by the husband and father, but has a voice of her own regarding domestic matters, such as the number of children. Closely related to this tendency is the feminist movement, or woman's rights movement, whereby women are demanding that they not be confined to the sphere of bearing and rearing children. Increasing intelligence and foresight has served as a powerful preventive check upon population. The current emphasis upon luxury is inimical to the birth rate. A higher economic status almost uniformly cuts down the birth rate. Within the last score of years the new science of eugenics has attracted widespread attention. Eugenics stresses quality of population. It would effect a decrease in the numbers of children born among the lower classes, among the poorer stocks, and prevent procreation among the mentally deficient. It would increase the birth rate among the cultured and the high grade stocks.

Malthus appreciated the dependence of urban population upon rural districts, but he could not foresee the degree to which cities would grow in the nineteenth and twentieth centuries. The relative decrease of agricultural labor and the proportional increase in non-agricultural labor has thrown a burden upon the food supply which even Malthus could not forecast.

On the other hand, Malthus did not realize the extent to which new countries such as the United States, Canada, Australia, Argentina would contribute to the world's means of subsistence. He could not predict the way in which invention would be applied in solving agricultural problems, and how today one man with improved machinery and intensive methods can produce a hundred ears of corn where one was produced a century ago. Nevertheless, the "new country" argument against Malthus' principle of population is ultimately fallacious, for new countries soon become old, the supply of new countries becomes exhausted, and there is even a limit to soil productiveness. The very pressure of population against means of subsistence is, however, a cause of inventiveness, so that unanticipated increases in food supply may occur at any time.

Socialism has criticized Malthus severely. Socialism holds that at a given time the food supply is sufficient to meet human needs but that it is poorly or unjustly distributed. With just distribution of the returns from industry, food supply would not impinge strongly on population. But socialism might greatly endanger the prudential check on population, and hence result in an increased birth rate; which in turn would more than balance any release from human misery that a just distribution of the returns from industry would effect.

Another point which Malthus did not observe is that the increase in technical skill which comes with vocational education is overcome by the tendency of the world's population to overtake the world's food productiveness. With increase in population, the price of land rises, the rent for land increases, the cost of living mounts upward, and the purchasing power of the dollar, or its equivalent, declines.

Some of the followers of Malthus have advocated birth control as an artificial means of regulating population. Birth control prevents by physical means the birth of children. It is a useful weapon against sexually brutal husbands. It does not provide for self control or moral control of the sexual impulses. It encourages rather than controls gratification of the sexual desires. By it a gain is made in protecting helpless women and in cutting down the birth rate among the lower moral classes, whether wealthy or poor, but the gain is more than lost by the opportunity which birth control gives to the irregular gratification of sexual impulses and by the resultant weakening of moral fibre.

Thomas N. Carver, whose work will be referred to again in subsequent chapters, has developed an interesting population theory which is partly Malthusian.[13] The increase in population from both immigration sources and the birth rate should be cut down, thereby decreasing the percentage of unskilled labor. Further, persons should be trained out of the unskilled group into the skilled group and then into the *entrepeneur* class. Thus, by greatly decreasing the number of unskilled laborers and by increasing the number of entrepreneurs, wages will advance and profits will be increasingly subdivided. The poor will become well-to-do, and poverty as it is now known will tend to disappear. This theory underestimates the importance of psychological motives and of social attitudes under a system where a marked degree of competition is encouraged.

In conclusion, it may be stated that the principle of population as given by Malthus is fundamental to an understanding of the problems of social progress.[14] There is a positive relation between population and means of subsistence. Positive and preventive checks upon population are continually at work. Moral restraint and self control, based on scientifically devised human laws, create a better moral fibre than birth control. The quality of personality is far more important than mere numbers of population. The struggle for quality in personality must be supplemented by justice in industrial and social processes before the population problem can be solved.

CHAPTER XIII

COMTE AND POSITIVE SOCIAL THOUGHT

An organized foundation for the field of social thought was not laid until near the close of the first half of the nineteenth century. At that time Auguste Comte (1798-1857) gave at least an organized groundwork, if not a synthetic introduction to sociology. He was the first to stake out the territory of social thought, to show the relation of social thought to other fields of knowledge, and to separate social statics from social dynamics. He was the first important social philosopher, and his *Positive Philosophy* the first treatise roughly to outline the field of sociology.

Auguste Comte invented the term, sociology, by which he meant the science of human association. While he did not contribute much to the science itself, he laid important foundation stones. He reacted against all forms of loose thinking about man, rejected metaphysical and theological speculations, and insisted upon the observation and classification of social phenomena. He repudiated attempts to discover causes of social uniformities, and coined the name, positivism, for the philosophical system upon which he founded sociology. The bases of positivism may be found in the ideas of Bacon, Galileo, and Descartes. As each of these three men broke with tradition and sought observed facts in their respective fields, so Comte was likewise prompted to do in the field of social thought.

Auguste Comte was born at Montpelier, France, the son of humble and law-abiding Catholic parents. At the age of nine he displayed unusual mental ability, a strong character, and a tendency to defy authority. He is described as brilliant and recalcitrant. He possessed a wonderful memory and a remarkable avidity for reading. In school he won many prizes, and took a position of leadership among his fellow students, who called him "the philosopher." At the age of sixteen he was devoting his energies and abilities to the study of mathematics.

As a youth Comte demanded the resignation of one of his instructors, criticized Napoleon, and disregarded both ecclesiastical and parental authority. He especially enjoyed to point out the stupidity of his superiors and to oppose tyranny.

At the age of nineteen Comte made the acquaintance of Saint Simon, the well-known socialist. The friendship lasted for only a few years, but long enough to exert a deep influence upon the youthful mathematician. Saint Simon (1760-1825) had indicated the need for a scientific classification of the sciences with political science at the head of the list, and had developed a new fraternalism under the name of *Le nouveau Christianisme.* This system was optimistic and humanitarian, but dreamy. Comte was dissatisfied with it, and undertook to work out a better scheme of social analysis and organization.

In 1822, Comte's first important work was published. It contained an introduction by Saint Simon, and was entitled *A Prospectus of the Scientific Works Required for the Reorganization of Society.* It represented an important beginning of the task on which Comte was to spend his life. Upon the problem Comte read and worked assiduously, save as he was interrupted by an unhappy married life and by mental aberrations, due to overwork. He gave courses of public lectures, but insisted upon working gratuitously. He would not accept royalties from the sale of his books, despite the fact that he lived continually on the verge of starvation. His friends, however, made him gifts and established a subsidy. He insisted upon the rule that all his literary productions should be given to the public gratuitously.[1]

His method of composition has been commented upon by his biographers. As a result of his unusual memory and the high degree of mental concentration to which he attained, he was able to plan chapters and volumes in their smallest details, and then from memory to put them into written form. This method enabled him to secure "an extraordinary unity of conception and organic symmetry of plan."

Comte manifested an unusual regard for the truth. This attitude required him to modify and qualify statements of fundamental principles at great length. As a result his works are often tedious reading. He preferred, however, to write meticulously and thus to safeguard truth, rather than speak in epigrams and sacrifice truth.

Comte's two leading works are: the *Positive Philosophy* and the *Positive Polity.* The first appeared in six volumes during the years from 1830 to 1842. The second work, in four volumes, was published in the years from 1851 to 1854. It is not the equal of the *Positive Philosophy,* which was translated into English in 1853 by Harriet Martineau.

John Stuart Mill has referred to Comte as among the first of European thinkers; and, by his institution of a new social science, in some respects the first.[2] George Henry Lewes called Comte the greatest of modern thinkers. John Morley, the English statesman and author, says of Comte: "Neither Franklin, nor any man that has ever lived, could surpass him in the heroic tenacity with which, in the face of a thousand obstacles, he pursued his own ideal of a vocation." Harriet Martineau summarizes his methods as follows: "There can be no question but that his whole career was one of the most intense concentration of mind, gigantic industry, rigid economy, and singular punctuality and exactness in all his habits."[3]

In laying the foundations for a new social science, Comte began with an analysis of types of thinking. (1) Primitive and untrained persons everywhere think in supernatural terms. They suppose that all physical phenomena are caused by the immediate action of capricious supernatural beings. The primitive man believes in all kinds of fetiches in which spirits or supernatural beings live. Fetishism admitted of no priesthood, because its gods are individual, each residing in fixed objects.[4]

As the mind of primitive man became better organized, fetishism became cumbersome. Too many fetishes produced mental confusion. A coalescence of gods resulted and polytheism arose. The polytheistic gods represented different phases of life. This state in human thought is well illustrated by the Homeric gods.

But a large number of capricious divinities are mentally unsatisfactory. They create mental contradictions. Consequently, the gods are arranged in a hierarchy. Finally, the idea of one God, or of monotheism, developed. The belief arose that every phenomenon is produced by the immediate action of the one God. As man's vision widened and his observations increased in scope and depth, the concept of a monotheistic universe became clarified. Monotheism is the climax of the theological stage of thinking.

But rationalism argues that God does not stand directly behind every phenomenon. Pure reason insists that God is a First Cause or an Abstract Being. Pure reason speaks in terms of inalienable rights; metaphysical explanations, however, are unsatisfactory to the mind.

Hence, Comte developed his concept of positivism, which is a purely intellectual way of looking at the world. Comte held that the mind should concentrate on the observation and classification of phenomena. He believed that both theological and metaphysical speculations, as he used the terms, were as likely to be fiction as truth, and that there is no way of determining which is the case. Thus it will be more profitable if the individual should direct his thoughts to the lines of thinking which are most truly prolific, namely, to observation and classification of data.

Comte even took the position that it is futile to try to determine causes. We can observe uniformities, or laws, but it is mere speculation to assign causes to these uniformities. Positivism deified observation and classification of data. Its weaknesses should not hinder the student, however, from seeing the importance of its emphasis upon the scientific procedure of observing and classifying data in an age when dogmatism and speculation were rife.

The three stages of thought which Comte described are not three levels of thought, as Comte contended, but, as Herbert Spencer indicated, they may represent the same plane of thinking. Each requires about the same degree of thinking ability. Moreover, as John Fiske argued, the three methods of approach to problems are often pursued simultaneously by a given person. Some phenomena are explained theologically; others, metaphysically; and others, positively.

A second main contribution which Comte made to social thought is that each of the three modes of thinking determines and corresponds to a type of social organization. Speaking from the standpoint of his own religious contacts, he declared that theological thinking leads to a military and monarchial social organization, with God at the head of the hierarchy as King of kings and a mighty warrior, and with human beings arranged in a military organization. Divine sanction rules. As expressed through the human leaders, this divine sanction must not be questioned. Dogmatism must be meekly endured, or else its threatened punishments will be turned loose upon helpless offenders. Divine rights rule.

Metaphysical thinking produces a government dominated by doctrines of abstract rights. Natural rights are substituted for divine rights. A priesthood is furthered. Social organization becomes legalistic, formal, structural, without adequate content.

Positive thinking produces practical results in the form of industrial enterprises, and ushers in an industrial age. It inquires into the nature and utilization of natural forces. It transforms the material resources of the earth, and produces material inventions.

Comte failed to postulate a fourth mode of thinking, namely, socialized thinking, or a system of thought which would emphasize not simply the use of natural forces, but the use of natural forces for social ends, for the purpose of building constructive, just, and harmonious societies, and of developing personalities who will evaluate life in terms of the welfare of other personalities. Comte, however, should be credited with opening the way for the rise of socialized thinking.

A third phase of Comte's system was his classification of the sciences, with sociology as the latest and greatest of the group. The Greek thinkers, it will be recalled, undertook to classify all knowledge under three headings: physics, ethics, and politics. Bacon made the divisions correlative to the so-called mental faculties of memory, imagination, and reason, namely: history, poetry, and science.

Comte chose as his principle of classifying knowledge, the order of increasing dependence. He arranged the sciences so that each category may be grounded on the principal laws of the preceding category, and serve as a basis for the next ensuing category.[5] The order, hence, is one of increasing complexity and decreasing generality. The most simple phenomena must be the most general—general in the sense of being everywhere present.[6]

Comte began with mathematics, the tool of the mind. Accurate thinking is always done in terms of mathematics. With mathematics as its chief tool, the mind of man can go anywhere in its thinking. Mathematics is the most powerful instrument which the mind may use in the investigation of natural laws.[7]

Mathematics is not a constituent member of the group of sciences. It is the basis of them all. It holds the first place in the hierarchy of the sciences, and is the best point of departure in all education, whether general or special.[8] It is the oldest and most perfect of all the sciences.[9]

Mathematics is the science which measures precisely the relations between objects and ideas. It is *the* science.[10] The Greeks had no other. Its definition is the definition of all science. Its function is that of ascertaining relationships, a process which is basic to scientific thinking in all fields. Education that is based on any other method is faulty, inexact, and unreliable. It is only through mathematics that we can understand science.

The highest form of mathematics is calculus. There is no scientific inquiry in which calculus is not used. Even the physician in prescribing for the cure of a disease, must provide for the mixing together of different quantities of different medicines, so that, when taken at determined intervals of time, they will possess the right qualities for bringing the human body back to its normal state. Calculus is the branch of science which has the highest intellectual dignity. In it the proportion of reasoning to observation is greater than elsewhere.

With mathematics as the tool, the classification of knowledge may proceed. All natural phenomena fall into two grand divisions: inorganic and organic. The inorganic are more general and should be considered first. Inorganic phenomena are of two classes: astronomical and terrestrial. Astronomical phenomena are the most general of all. The stars and planets appear under the least varied aspects.[12] Astronomy is the science by which the movements of the heavenly bodies, including the earth, are measured. How can we thoroughly understand any terrestrial phenomena without considering the nature of the earth and its relation to the other units of the solar system?[13]

Terrestrial physics includes two fields: physics proper and chemistry. Material bodies may be regarded in either their physical or chemical aspects. Physics is more general than chemistry; it deals with masses rather than elements. Chemical phenomena depend upon the laws of physics, without being influenced by them in turn. Chemical action is conditioned by the laws of weight, heat, electricity. The study of inorganic phenomena thus falls under three scientific heads: astronomy, physics, and chemistry.

Organic phenomena include two types: individual

and group. The first refers to the function and structure of all individual forms in the plant and animal worlds. It is general physiology, or, in modern terms, biology. It involves the study of all life and the general laws pertaining to the individual units of life.

Biology rests on chemistry, because it is in chemistry that all reliable knowledge about nutrition or secretion is found. Biology is indebted to physics for knowledge concerning the weight of, temperature of, and related facts about living organisms. Biological laws are partially determined by astronomical factors. If the earth were to rotate faster than it does, the course of physiological phenomena would be accelerated, and the length of life would be shortened.[14] If the orbit of the earth were to become as eccentric as that of a comet, changes of a fatal nature would occur to all life on the earth. If there were no inclination of the earth's axis, the seasons would be unknown, and the geographical distribution of living species would be vastly different from the present situation. All accurate work in biological studies is mathematical in character. Thus biology, the science of organic phenomena, is dependent on all the preceding divisions on the scale of knowledge.

The study of gregarious or associative life is a special field. Comte called this science social physics, and for it invented the specific term, sociology. It rests in turn upon biological, chemical, physical, astronomical knowledge and uses mathematics as its tool. Comte virtually defines six sciences: mathematics, astronomy, physics, chemistry, biology, and sociology. He treats of transcendental biology, which is the basis of modern psychology. Comte urged that no science could be effectually studied without competent knowledge concerning the sciences on which it depends. It is necessary not only to have a general knowledge of all the sciences but that they should be studied in order—this is Comte's dictum to the student of sociology. Comte insisted that one general science could not develop beyond a given point until the preceding science has passed a given stage.

Each of the six general sciences has passed through the three stages of thought. Mathematics, which has advanced furthest into the positive stage, is still connected with superstition, such as that which hovers round the number 13. The other general sciences are less further along. Sociology, the latest science to develop, Comte hoped by his works to push over into the positive stage.

Comte divided sociology, or social physics, into social statics and social dynamics. Social statics is the study of the laws of action and reaction of the different parts of the social order, aside for the time being from the general social movements which are modifying them.[15] Social dynamics considers the laws of progress. Social statics inquires into the laws of co-existence of social phenomena;

social dynamics examines the laws of social succession. . Sociology is the study of social organization and of social progress.

Society is in a state of anarchy. Individuals with the best of purposes are continually weakening the efforts of each other. Powerful persons are crushing the weak. The defeated are conniving against the strong. Why all this social anarchy? To Comte the answer is clear. Behind moral and social anarchy there is intellectual anarchy. People do not have a knowledge of the fundamental laws of social order and social progress.

Moreover, people fail to appreciate the necessity of knowledge of social laws. They are insensible to the value of sound social theory. They want nothing but the "practical," unmindful of the fact that the "practical" is as likely to be based on incorrect social theory as upon sound social conceptions.

The necessity of fundamental concepts concerning society underlies social organization. In the absence of these general ideas, there is "no other daily resource for the maintenance of even a rough and precarious social order than an appeal, more or less immediate, to personal interests."[16] In the absence of a moral authority, the material order requires the use of either terror or corruption; the latter is less inconvenient and more in accordance with the nature of modern society.[17] Moreover, politicians and other public men work against the elaboration of the social theory which is necessary for the salvation of society. They sneer at the development of social science. Many of those who occupy the chief political stations regard with antipathy the true reorganization of society. Social principles are not even sought. On the other hand, social charlatanism attracts by the magnificence of its promises and dazzles by its transient successes. Comte deplored attempts to re-make society through institutionalism, regardless of social theory. He stressed the fundamental importance of social principles as the only means of guaranteeing a correct institutional procedure. As a practical principle of social adjustment, Comte endorsed the Catholic ideal: In necessary things, unity; in doubtful things, liberty; in all things, charity.

Comte protested vigorously against materialism. He pointed out that for three centuries the best minds had been devoted to material science and had neglected societary problems.[18] Material institutions should be modified and made to harmonize with the underlying laws of social evolution. A moral reorganization of society must precede and direct the material and political reorganization.[19]

Social improvement is a result of mental development. This development favors the preponderance of the noblest human tendencies. Prevision and science when applied to society will bring out the best phases of human nature, and thus result in social improvement. Although the lower instincts will continue to manifest themselves in modified action, their less sustained exercise will debilitate them by degrees.[20]

The three chief causes of social variation result from, first, race; second, climate; and third, political action in its whole scientific content. The first and second factors cannot be changed greatly, but the political influences are wide open to modification by social prevision. In this connection sociology finds its manifestation.

With the development of society, intellectual activity and gregariousness slowly overcome the preponderance of the affective over the intellectual phases of life. But even in the best natures the personally affective elements are more powerful than the social affections. Real intellectual development, however, will strengthen man's empire over his passions, refine his gregariousness, and release his energies for social activities.

Comte makes the family the social unit. Man cannot live in isolation, but the family can survive by itself.[21] The striking characteristic of domestic organization is its establishment of the elementary idea of social perpetuity, by directly and irresistibly connecting the future with the past.[22] Family life will always be the school of social life, both for obedience and for command.[32] Comte failed to escape the logic of the patriarchal family life. He did credit women, however, with being superior to men in the spontaneous expansion of sympathy and sociality, although inferior in understanding and reason.

The direction of social evolution is toward further development of the noblest dispositions and the most generous feelings, and away from the expression of the animal appetites and the material desires.[24] The trend is from the satisfaction of the selfish impulses to the habitual exercise of the social impulses. Happiness depends on the presence of new stimuli in one's form of activity. A life of labor that is full of constructive stimuli is after all the fittest to develop personality.

Comte was the friend of popular education.[25] He based his contention on the invariable homogeneity of the human mind. The minds of people of all races are potentially similar. All members of the race are capable of development to a common plane.

In his *Positive Polity,* Comte made important changes in his thinking. This work was the product of his later years, and shows the effects of deprivation and struggle. It is inferior in quality to his earlier treatise on *Positive Philosophy.* It is a question, therefore, how far his later ideas should be permitted to supersede his thinking when he was in his prime. In his later thought-life he receded from his emphasis upon the intellectual nature and stressed the importance of the affections. He made affection the central point of life and developed the concept of love. We tire of thinking and even of acting, he asserted, but we never tire of loving.[26]

The Comtean ideal became a disinterested love of mankind. Comte developed a religion of humanity. His contact with Christianity gave him the belief that it is chiefly ecclesiastical. He did not see in Christianity a social keynote. Hence, he attempted to create a purely social religion. He made mankind an end in itself; he failed to see that human society is probably an outcropping of universal purpose.

If we judge Comte by his own time and age, we shall see the importance of his contributions to social thought, which were as follows: 1. There is need for accurate thinking about society. Mathematics is the best tool for obtaining social accuracy. 2. Comte developed positivism with its emphasis upon observation and classification of social data. 3. Knowledge has scientific divisions, according to the principles of increasing dependence and decreasing generality. This scale begins with mathematics and astronomy, includes physics, chemistry, biology, in order, and ends with the social sciences, particularly sociology. 4. Sociology deals with the static and dynamic phases of human association. 5. Comte developed a humanitarian philosophy. 6. Comte insisted on an intellectual understanding of social processes as the only true basis for overcoming social anarchy and for solving the problems of society.

Chapter XIV

Marx and Socialistic Social Thought

Socialism proper had its beginning in the second and third decades of the nineteenth century. It developed primarily in continental Europe and in England. Although Plato's communism and More's utopianism were forerunners of socialism, the social unrest in Europe in the early years of the nineteenth century was the direct causal factor. Socialism also represented a reaction against the prevailing *laissez faire* thought regarding the evils of society and the suffering of the poorer classes.

Socialism began with the concepts and experiments of Saint Simon and Fourier in France, of Robert Owen in England, and of Rodbertus, Lassalle, Marx, and Engels in Germany. In France the movement was carried forward by Proudhon and Blanc; and in England by the Christian socialists, chiefly Maurice and Kingsley. In Germany, Marx maintained the position of leadership for many decades, and finally became the best known exponent of socialist thought in the world.

In his *New Christianity,* Saint Simon, who was referred to in the preceding chapter, made a unique contribution to social thought. His thinking was not deep, or systematic, but characterized by ingenuity. Saint Simon advocated a society in which only useful things are produced. In this industrial order, men of science will be in control. Saint Simon was greatly interested in the welfare of the poorest classes. His *New Christianity* was essentially a plea that the whole world devote itself to the improvment of the living conditions of the very poor. The influence which Saint Simon had upon Comte has already been mentioned.

Another important socialistic ideal was developed by Fourier (1772-1837), who worked out a social system in which the *phalange* is the chief instrument in securing a perfect society. The phalange is composed of from twenty-four to thirty-two groups of people. Each group comprises from seven to nine individuals. The unifying bond is natural attraction, or free elective love and sympathy. The members of each phalange live communistically in a large commodious structure called a *phalanstère*. The phalanges were to unite in one large world federation, with headquarters at Constantinople.

The people work according to their interests, frequently changing occupations. The products of labor are subdivided; a minimum goes equally to all, irrespective of any conditioning factors; of the remainder five-twelfths goes to labor, three-twelfths to special ability, and four-twelfths to capital. Difficult common labor is paid the most, on the assumption that he who does pleasant labor receives pay in mental ways. Every individual should have an opportunity to become a capitalist; and every woman should be enabled to become independent economically. These utopian plans of Fourier called for a sudden and complete transformation of human nature. They underestimated the force of human selfishness.

Socialistic thought was carried into politics by Louis Blanc (1811-1882). He declared that no genuine reformation of society could take place until political machinery was organized democratically. The democratic state would endow national workshops. These workshops would be operated by industrial associations composed of workingmen, who would elect their own officers, regulate their own industries, and provide for the distribution of the returns from industry. Once started by the state these industrial associations will expand and increase in number until the whole nation, and then the world, will be organized in this way.

Blanc participated in the French Revolution of 1848 and became a member of the provisional government. His national workshop idea failed in practice. His enemies were partly responsible for this defeat, because the essentials of productive work and guarantees of character which Blanc urged were disregarded. The fact, however, that these two essentials were considered necessary for the successful development of national workshops indicates that the system, under average conditions, might not be a success.

Nearly all the early socialists were evolutionists rather than revolutionists. They did not advocate class struggle theories. They developed bourgeois rather than proletariat ideas. An outstanding exception to these statements is found in the radical attitude of Babeuf (1760-1797), who was essentially a forerunner of Marxian socialism and also of the anarchistic philosophy of Proudhon and Bakunin. Babeuf vigorously proclaimed the sovereignty of the proletariat, and advocated the abolition of inheritance laws and of private property. He urged that the property of corporations be confiscated, and that a communistic state be established.

The well-known principles of justice, liberty, and equality were utilized by Proudhon (1809-1865), a philosophic anarchist. He would have the same wages paid to an unskilled workman as to a successful business or professional man. He predicted that equalization of opportunity would bring about an equalization of ability.

Proudhon attacked property rights. He declared that property is theft. In itself property is lifeless, but it nevertheless demands rent, interest, or profits, or all three. It protects itself behind law, and in order to guarantee its alleged rights, it calls out the militia, evicts families, and takes bread from the mouths of little children. It robs labor of its just returns.[1]

By unsatisfactory reasoning Proudhon urged the free development of individuals in society, whereby each individual would learn to govern himself so well in society that government would no longer be needed. This theory is Proudhon's concept of anarchy. In this doctrine Proudhon neglects to provide an adequate dynamic or to foresee the ultimate complexity of human relations.

In England, Robert Owen (1771-1858) became a founder of socialism. As a factory manager, Owen developed social ideas. Living in an age of long hours, woman and child labor of the worst forms, and deplorable housing conditions, Owen deserves the credit of inaugurating a twentieth century program of welfare work. It was Owen's theory that the workingman is so subject to his environment that even his character is determined for him. Owen attempted in theory and practice to prevent the impingement of the economic environment upon the workers. He believed in self-governing organizations of labor. He inaugurated the co-operative movement as a means of securing industrial justice and of giving the workingman a chance at the free development of his personality.

Owen objected to Malthus' doctrine of population on the ground that it failed to consider the marvelous increase in the means of subsistence which might come from the application of inventive genius to the sources of the food supply. He also protested against the Malthusian argument for the restriction of population, because this argument did not give due weight to the unjust distribution of wealth and to the enslaving social organization to which labor is subject.

Owen's experiments, particularly at New Harmony, Indiana, demonstrated that a communistic organization of society in itself cannot save society. The strength of Owen's social thought lay in its accentuation of the need for providing labor with opportunities of industrial initiative and co-operation.

During the middle of the nineteenth century in England, the Christian socialists flourished. The founders of this movement were Frederick Maurice and Charles Kingsley. These men were clergymen who became greatly interested in the welfare of the working classes. They made clear the evils of the prevailing economic order, the formality of the Manchester school of economics, and proposed to apply the principles of Christianity to the economic system of the day. They opposed economic competition. For this method they urged the substitution of the ethical and spiritual principles of co-operation and love in industrial relationships—for both employer and employee in all their dealings with each other. Their socialism is essentially a vigorous application of Christian love to every-day relationships.

The influence of Christian socialism strengthened

the experiment of the Rochdale weavers who in 1844 had organized a consumers' co-operative society. The concept of consumers' co-operation received its original impetus from the thought and practice of Robert Owen, achieved a measurable degree of concreteness under the efforts of the Rochdale weavers, and through Maurice and Kingsley won the assistance of Christianity.

In Germany, Rodbertus, Lassalle, Marx and Engels molded the thinking of socialists about the nature of human society. Rodbertus (1805-1875), the son of a university professor, was a quiet, deep thinker about social processes. According to his analysis of social development, three stages may be pointed out. The first was marked by slavery, or by private property in human beings. The second state is an indirect form of the first, namely, one of private property in land and capital. Through this type of ownership the economically fortunate or shrewd are able to exercise widespread power over the unfortunate and the uneducated. In the third state, toward which society is trending, the concept of service will rule, and private property as a dominant concept will be compelled to take a thoroughly subordinate place in human activities. The ultimate goal, according to Rodbertus, is a world communist society, with land and capital as national property, and with labor rewarded according to its productiveness.[3]

Rodbertus denied the validity of the wages fund

theory and argued that wages are not paid by capital; it is that part of the productive earnings of labor which labor receives. His fundamental thesis is that labor is the source and measure of all value. He advocated an evolutionary procedure whereby the state should pass legislation that would guarantee just returns to labor. This form of state socialism is to be gradually developed, until a scientific socialism is reached with its emphasis upon a government of labor, for labor, and by labor.

The founder of Social Democracy in Germany, Ferdinand Lassalle (1825-1864), wrote two significant treatises, the *Bastiat-Schulze* and the *Working Men's Programme*. Lassalle believed that natural conditions are productive of misery and vice, and that it is the chief business of the state to extricate men from this thraldom. The state should provide means for lifting the laboring man to a level of industrial freedom.

Lassalle objected to the theory known as the iron law of wages. He protested against the smallness of the share of his earnings which the laborer really receives. He advocated the establishment of productive associations wherein labor might perform the double function of workman and capitalist. In order that these productive associations might be started, the state should advance funds. After the productive associations have secured momentum they will continue by virtue of their own strength. Ultimately, industry will be conducted exclusively through productive associations; both industrial and social democracy will finally rule in political life. Lassalle became the founder of the Social Democratic party in Germany. Lassalle boldly denounced the reactionary classes that were in political power in his time and led the workers in a movement to overthrow the existing social order.[3]

The name of Karl Marx (1818-1883) is supreme on the list of socialists. Marx was born in Germany of Jewish parents, and educated at the universities of Bonn and Berlin. He became a journalist, but the paper which he edited was considered too liberal and was suppressed. Marx went to Paris in 1842, where he continued editorial work. At this time he was influenced by French socialism and its leader, Proudhon. In 1845, he was expelled from Paris at the request of the Prussian government. He went to Brussels. In the meantime a deep friendship with Friedrich Engels (1820-1895) had been established.

In 1847, Marx and Engels issued the Communist Manifesto.[4] This radical document was circulated widely and became extensively accepted by social revolutionists. Its doctrines were:

1. Abolition of property in lands; rents to be used for public purposes.
2. Abolition of all rights of inheritance.
3. Progressive income tax.
4. Nationalization of the means of transporta-

tion and commerce.

5. Extension of productive enterprises by the state.

6. Compulsory labor.

7. Free education; no child labor.

8. Elimination of the distrust between town and country.

Marx returned to Germany and established the *Neue Rheinische Zeitung* in Cologne in 1848. Engels served as editor. Because of revolutionary activity, Marx was forced to leave Germany in 1849. He went to Paris and then to London, where he became a newspaper correspondent and where he lived until his death in 1883.

In 1859, the *Kritik der politischen Oekonomie* was published. It contains the essential principles of Marx's system of thought. In 1864, Marx found the opportunity for which he had long been seeking, namely, to organize the workers of the world into one large association. On September 28, in St. Martin's Hall, Marx in the presence of a vast concourse of people, he initiated the "International Workingmen's Association." The fundamental idea was to organize the societies of workingmen which have a common purpose, namely, the emancipation of the working classes, into a world or international union for co-operative purposes, The International proposes that governments shall put the interests of the working classes to the forefront of national concern, and subordinate the present attention they give to war, diplomacy, and national jealousies.

In 1869, Marx, aided by Karl Liebknecht (1826-1900), Engels and others, organized in Germany the Social Democratic Labor Party. The movement which Lassalle had started became united with the Marxian movement, and in 1875 the German Social Democracy presented a united front to capitalism. Marx, Engels, Liebknecht, and Bebel are its best-known leaders. Bismarck was forced to acknowledge its power, and condescended to inaugurate a system of social insurance in order to appease its rank and file.

In 1867, 1885, and 1895, the three volumes of *Das Kapital* appeared, in chronological order.[5] By this work, *Capital,* Marx is known throughout the world. The style is laborious; the analyses are minute and in places difficult to follow. The method is historical. Marx analyzes social evolution. He traces the rise of capitalism from its humble beginnings to its autocratic fruition. In this development the instruments of capital showed a tendency to congregate in a decreasing number of hands. By this token it will be seen that the number of the propertyless ever increases. Likewise, their influence decreases. In this way, the proletariat is developed, a product of capitalism.

A definite class, the capitalist, acquires increasing industrial, political, and social power. The proletariat suffer increasing misery. They own nothing except their ability to labor. They are forced to throw this human quality on the commercial market and sell it to the highest bidder. But capitalism increases the number of the proletariat. This tendency, together with the increase in population, creates a superabundance of labor. Laborers are forced to compete in the labor market. The laborers who will sell their labor for the least wages will be employed. Capitalism thus forces wages to a mere subsistence level, with the result that the misery and suffering of the proletariat are greatly augmented. In this way the laborer is crushed by the operation of the iron law of wages.

By the operation of the iron law, the capitalist is enabled to appropriate to himself an increasing amount of the earnings of labor. This appropriated amount is called the surplus value. Marx developed at length the concept of surplus value. Capitalism exploits the laborer by taking possession of as large a proportion of the earnings of labor as it can obtain—through its might and its shrewdness.

The growth of capitalism, also, causes a class consciousness to develop among the members of the proletariat. This class consciousness is increasing. It produces labor organizations; these organizations are acquiring vast power. The struggles between them and the capitalistic classes go on. The two groups have little in common. By force of numbers the proletariat are bound finally to win, and to overthrow the capitalistic classes which are now in power. They will seize the means of production and manage them for the good of all.

Marx did not outline an utopia. He described the historical evolution of society as he saw it, and he participated in plans for the organization of all laborers for their common good. Inasmuch as Marx advocated compulsory labor, the laboring class under Marxian socialism would include all people. Marx advocated an equal distribution of wealth, not in the sense of the popular misconception of that term, but in the sense that the earnings from the industry shall be distributed to the workers in proportion to their achievements.

In Russia, Marxian socialism in 1918 came into power. The Bolsheviki represent the radical wing of the Marxian followers. They established essentially a dictatorship of the proletariat, substituting it for the dictatorship of capitalists which existed under the reign of the czars. Bolshevism substitutes occupation for geographic area as a basis of representative government. This program is deficient and sociologically untenable, because occupational groups do not encompass all phases of human personality. A government based on occupational group needs is representative of only a portion of the elements of human life. When seventy-five per cent of the people are illiterate, as has been the case in Russia, no form of government whether democratic or not can be other than a dictatorship.

Revolutionary socialism coincides, in part, with syndicalism, a movement which developed in France and England. Syndicalism is a radical form of trade unionism. It declares that workingmen cannot hope for genuine betterment through politics. They must organize and inaugurate a general strike. This universal strike will paralyze the present régime and render it helpless. As a result the workers will come into power. In the meantime, the workers must keep up a running warfare with capitalists and the government which supports capitalism. Sabotage is a common concept among syndicalists. It implies a program of destroying machinery, hindering the production of economic goods, and creating inefficiency in capitalistic industry. In both England and the United States, syndicalism has appeared. In the United States, the Industrial Workers of the World, or I. W. W., confess to doctrines similar to those which have been espoused in Europe under the name of syndicalism. The philosophic exponent of syndicalism has been George Sorel.

Revolutionary socialism has been paralleled in certain ways by anarchism. These teachings first acquired force through the writings of Proudhon. Another leading anarchist was the Russian nobleman and military officer, Michael Bakunin (1814-1876). Although of aristocratic birth, Bakunin became furious when he observed the human misery among the masses which Russian autocracy was producing. He became an agitator. He was confined in dungeons and exiled to Siberia. He escaped from Siberia, and by way of California went to England and then to Switzerland. His chief work is *God and the State.* Vital, vigorous, magnetic, fearless—these are the adjectives which describe the personality of Bakunin.

Bakunin scorned rank, birth, and fortune. He attacked external authority of all kinds. He denied the validity of concepts such as "God" and the "state"; they are parts of systems which enslave the free will of man. Classes must be abolished and the masses of individuals freed from all enslaving institutions, such as marriage, the church, the state.

In a related way Prince Kropotkin (1842-1921) developed anarchistic principles. Peter A. Kropotkin was of aristocratic Russian birth and a person of mild, courteous manners. His father was a serf owner; the son could not bear to see the sufferings which the serfs underwent. He threw away the privileges of rank and became a defender of the oppressed. He attempted to correlate the theories of anarchism with those of mutual aid, and fought socialism with the concept of centralized control on the ground that it would destroy individual liberty.[6] In Chapter XXII, Kropotkin's theory of mutual aid will be analyzed.

Anarchism and socialism make similar attacks upon the evils of capitalism. Both are determined to overthrow capitalism. Both believe in revolt. They part ways when they advocate a constructive program for the new order which shall follow the violent overthrow of capitalism. Unlike socialism, anarchism holds that all government is an evil and that industry can go on without organization. It advocates a free communism.

One of the essentials in the Communist Manifesto was the appropriation of rents for public purposes. Starting from a viewpoint distinctly different from that of Karl Marx, Henry George (1839-1897) became the founder of single tax propaganda. In early manhood Henry George came to San Francisco and established a struggling newspaper. At once he found himself practically overwhelmed by the brutal competition of the metropolitan press and telegraphic news service. George was crushed by monopoly. It was this defeat which gave him a new idea—an idea that was to command the attention of the world.

As George walked the streets of New York City he puzzled over the existence of indescribable destitution and suffering in the shadow of the princely rich with their ostentatious luxuries.[7] Why in a land blessed with generous natural resources should there be such poverty? Although discovery has followed discovery and invention has followed invention, neither has lessened the toil of those who most need respite. With material progress poverty takes on a larger aspect. Material progress may be likened to an immense wedge which is being forced, not underneath society, but through society. "Those who are above the point of separation are elevated, but those who are below are crushed down."[8] George set himself the task of finding out why poverty is associated with progress.

This cause George found in the land situation. As land increases in value, poverty increases. The price of land is an index of the disparity in the economic conditions of the people at the extremes of the social scale. Land is more valuable in New York City than in San Francisco, and there is more squalor and misery in New York City than in San Francisco. Land is more valuable in London than in New York City, and likewise there is more squalor and destitution in London than in New York City.

When increasing numbers of people live in a limited area under a system of private property in land, rents are raised and land values go up. The cost of living mounts, wages are kept to a minimum, overcongestion of population ensues; and again, rents and land values are increased.

Upon what does title to land rest? Where did it originate? In force. But has the first comer at a banquet the right to turn back all the chairs, and claim that none of the other guests shall partake of the food that has been provided? Does the first passenger who enters a railroad car thereby possess the right to keep out all other persons, or admit them only upon payment to him of sums of money? "We arrive and we depart, guests at a banquet continually spread, spectators and participants in an entertainment where there is room for all who come."[10] These illustrations are pertinent to the unjust elements in the present economic order.

As a result of private property in land, the owner possesses power over the tenant, a power which is tantamount to a system of slavery. There is nothing strange, therefore, in the poverty phenomena of the world. The Creator has not placed in the world the taint of injustice. The fact that amid our highest civilization men faint and die with want, is not because of the niggardliness of nature or the injustice of the Creator, but is due to the injustice of man.[11] Since the owner of land receives wealth without labor to an increasing degree, so there is an increasing robbery of earnings of those who labor.

George attacked Malthusianism, and pointed out the deficiencies in the proposed remedies for poverty, such as greater economy in government, diffusion of knowledge, and improved habits of industry. He then proceeded to give his own and well known solution, namely, making land common property through a system of taxation of land values alone. Since land, not labor, is the source of all wealth, it is just and necessary to make land common property.

The weakness of Henry George's argument lies in his single panacea for securing justice. He overemphasized the importance of one line of procedure. He neglects other important factors, such as a selfish human nature. He rendered, however, a splendid service in showing the weaknesses in the system of private property in land. In this connection he has been unequaled in his contribution to social thought.

In this discussion of the contributions of socialism to social thought, many types or expressions of socialism have not been presented. The educational propaganda of the Fabian socialists in England should be mentioned as being very effective. Although small in number this group of intellectuals, the best known being Sidney and Beatrice Webb, have exerted a constructive and practical influence upon social thought.

Socialism has assumed various phases. (1) It originated in utopianism and in a loose, broad type of communism. (2) It then took the form of associationism, urging the organization of groups of associated individuals, such as phalanges. As utopianism was in part the expression of a poetic imagination, so associationism represented a bourgeois philosophy. (3) In the next place socialism assumed political aspirations, and advocated a governmental program whereby the existing governments shall gradually extend their power until they exercise control over rent-producing land and interest-producing capital. (4) State socialism, however, was supplanted in many minds by ideas of more radical procedure. Marxian socialism holds that a class conflict is inevitable and that the workers must overthrow the capitalists, together with the governments which they control. (5) To the other radical extreme is philosophic anarchism, with its emphasis upon the abolition of all existing governments and the establishment of individual autonomy.

Socialism has made several contributions to social thought. (1) It has called the attention of civilized mankind, and particularly of the economically wealthy classes, to the needs of the weaker classes. It has introduced humanitarian concepts into the minds of the socially unthinking educated classes. (2) It has jolted many economic autocrats from their thrones of power. It has thrown the spot light of publicity upon the selfish and wicked ostentation of the hereditary leisure classes. (3) It has held social theory to a more practical course and to developing more immediate social solutions than it otherwise would have achieved. (4) It has developed a power equal to that held by individualism. It has helped to demonstrate the dualistic nature of social evolution, that is, that there are two poles to human life rather than one.

CHAPTER XV.

BUCKLE AND GEOGRAPHIC SOCIAL THOUGHT

It has long been observed that climate, fertility of soil, rainfall, and similar factors have had a powerful influence upon human nature and upon the development of civilization. The chief founders of this line of thought were Buckle and Ratzel. In recent years Semple and Huntington have become well-known authorities. Many other thinkers have contributed to the present knowledge concerning the interactions between geographic factors and human development.

One of the first writers to elaborate a climatic theory of social evolution was Bodin (1530-1596). Hot climates, he observed, further the rise of all kinds of superstitious beliefs. Cold climates produce brute will-power. Temperate climates constitute an essential basis for the development of reason. In the ideal commonwealth which Bodin described, all three types of climate are represented.[1] The northern zone furnishes the fighters and the workers. The southern zone produces poets, priests, and artists. The temperate zone is the parent of legislative, judicial, and scholarly leaders.

In the *Spirit of Laws* to which reference was

made in Chapter XI, Montesquieu accentuated the importance of environmental influences on social processes. He attempted to show the effects of climate upon social institutions. Montesquieu did important pioneer work in what is now known as the field of anthropo-geography.

By way of contrast, the attitude of Hume, whose contributions to social psychology have already been noted, stands out sharply. According to Hume, physical causes have no particular effect on the human mind. No geographic factors influence either the temperament, disposition, or ability of people. Hume was led to this extreme position by his staunch faith in the subjective and psychological factors of human nature.

The distinguished German scientist, Alexander von Humboldt (1769-1859), travelled extensively throughout the world, observing the physical geography of many lands in conjunction with the meteorological conditions of each. At the same time von Humboldt was a careful observer of the customs, manners, and standards of the various peoples with whom he came in contact. In these travels and studies, von Humboldt was careful to note relationships between soils and civilizations. His contributions to social thought were of this descriptive nature, based on first-hand observations in many parts of the world.

The writings of Henry Thomas Buckle (1821-1862) contain an extensive and detailed explanation of the ways in which geographic and natural factors modify human life. Buckle starts with a decidedly dualistic universe—a dualism which is disjunctive. The dualism consists of nature and mind, each subject more or less to its own laws. Rejecting both the doctrine of free will and of predestination, Buckle concludes that the actions of men are determined solely by their antecedents and that they have a character of uniformity.[2] Man modifies nature, and nature modifies man, but in the past in many parts of the world the thoughts and desires of men are more influenced by physical phenomena than they influence such phenomena. Because of this dominant activity of the physical forces, these should be studied as a basis for understanding the history of man.

The physical factors which have powerfully influenced men are four: climate, food, soil, and the general aspects of nature. By the fourth, Buckle refers to those appearances which are presented chiefly through the medium of sight and which produce their chief results by exciting the imagination and suggesting superstitions. The three first-mentioned factors do not operate on the mind directly.[3]

The first effect of climate, food, and soil upon man that may be noted is that they lead man to accumulate wealth. These accumulations permit that degree of leisure from "making a living" which enables some members of society to acquire knowledge. Upon these acquisitions of knowledge, particularly of socialized knowledge, civilization depends. This progress in the early stages of civilization rests on two circumstances: "First, on the energy and regularity with which labor is conducted, and second, on the returns made to that labor by the bounty of nature."[4] Both these causes are the results of physical antecedents. The returns which are made to labor are regulated by the fertility of the soil. Moreover, Buckle asserted, the energy and regularity with which labor is conducted will be entirely dependent on the influence of climate.[5] When heat is intense, men will be indisposed and partly unfitted for active industry. Climate also affects the regularity of the habits of laborers. In very cold climates, the weather interferes with regular habits and produces desultoriness. In southern countries regular labor is likewise prevented—this time by the heat. Thus, in the early stages of civilization the fundamental law may be stated: the soil regulates the returns made to any given amount of labor; the climate regulates the energy and constancy of labor itself.[6]

Of the two primary causes of primitive societary growth, the fertility of the soil is more important than the climatic influences. It is only where soil fertility exists that civilization can arise at all.[7] But in Europe, climate has been more effective than soil fertility. In Europe a climate has existed which has stimulated human activities.

Since the mental powers of man are unlimited

they are more important, once they get started, than the powers of nature, which are limited and stationary. Man has endless capacity, through his dynamic mental tendencies to develop the physical resources of the earth.

The birth rate depends on food supply. In hot countries, where less food per capita is required than in cold countries, and where an abundance of food exists, the birth rate is very high. In cold countries highly carbonized food is necessary, but this food is largely animal in origin and great risk is involved in procuring it. Hence the people of cold countries become adventuresome.[8]

By the study of physical laws it is possible to determine what the national food of a country will be. In India, for example, the physical conditions are decidedly favorable to the growth of rice, which is the most nutritive of all cereals, and which, consequently, is a causal factor in a high birth rate.

But where there is a cheap national food, the increase in population becomes very great. As a result, there are multitudes of people who are able to keep just above the subsistence level. A few individuals who understand the operation of these physical laws are able to manipulate the multitudes in such a way as to make themselves immensely wealthy. Since wealth, after intellect, is the most permanent source of power, a great inequality of wealth has been accompanied by a corresponding inequality of social and political power.[9] It produces classes and even castes. Poverty provokes contempt. Class conflict results. The poor are ground low, murmur, and are again subjected to ignominy. Under such conditions democracy has a hard struggle. When physical conditions favor one class, that class will constitute itself the government and bitterly oppose the extension of government to all other classes. In Europe there was no cheap national food, no blind multiplication of population, and hence no such disparity between classes as in India. In Europe it has been easier for democratic movements to spread.

Early civilization developed in the Euphrates valley, the Nile valley, and in the exceedingly fertile regions of Peru, Central America, and Mexico. Modern civilization is found largely in fertile river valleys, such as the Thames, Seine, Rhine, Po, Danube, Hudson, Mississippi. But in the Amazon valley, the fertility of soil has not invited the growth of a large population. The trade winds have brought in a superabundance of moisture, producing torrential rains, and a luxuriance of plant life and a complexity of virile animal life which thus far have defied the skill of man to overcome.

The fourth physical factor which Buckle presents is the general aspects of nature. Of these the first class excites the imagination and the second stimulates the rational operations of the intellect.[10] In regard to natural phenomena it may be said that whatever inspires feelings of terror, of the vague and uncontrollable, and of great wonder tends to inflame the imagination and to cause it to dominate the intellectual processes. Where nature is continually exhibiting its power, man feels his inferiority. He assumes a helpless attitude. He ceases to inquire or to think. His imagination, rather than his reason, reigns. On the other hand, where nature works smoothly and quietly, man begins to assert his individuality. He even essays to dominate nature and other men. His cognition develops and his volition expresses itself vigorously.

All early civilizations were located in the tropics or sub-tropics. In these regions nature is dangerous to man. Earthquakes, tempests, hurricanes, pestilences prevail. Consequently, the imagination of man takes exaggerated forms. The judgment is overbalanced; thought is paralyzed. The mind is continually thrown into a frantic state. These reactions throw human life into feeling molds, into poetic rather than scientific forms. Religious feelings are promoted. The leading religions of the world originated in the sub-tropical and tropical regions of the earth.

East Indian literature and thought illustrate the effect of nature upon the feelings and the imagination. The works of the East Indians on grammar, law, history, medicine, even on mathematics, geography, and metaphysics are nearly all poems.[11] Prose writing is despised. The Sanscrit language boasts of more numerous and more complicated metres than can any European tongue. The East Indian literature is even calculated to set the reason of man at defiance.[12]

The imagination, for example, in India has produced an exaggerated respect for the past; it is this situation which has led poets to describe a Golden Age in the remote past. In the literature of India there is recorded the statement that in ancient times the average length of life of common men was 80,000 years. There are instances of poets who lived to be half a million years old.

In Greece, on the other hand, nature is more quiet and the mind of man functioned in a reasoning way. In the North Temperate zone science developed. "The climate was more healthy; earthquakes were less frequent; hurricanes were less disastrous; wild beasts and noxious animals less abundant."[13] Buckle, in other words, insists that everywhere the hand of nature is upon the mind of man.

The work of Buckle, the chief exponent of the influence of physical nature upon mental man, accentuates important phases of the growth of civilization. Buckle over-emphasized his anthropo-geographic observations. However, they constitute a part of the whole picture of human progress, and when seen in the light of modern mental growth and control of environment they shrink into proper proportions.

The field which Buckle opened has been developed extensively by Friedrich Ratzel (1844-1904). This German scholar, traveler, and geographer is generally credited with putting anthropo-geography on a scientific basis. Miss Ellen Semple attempted to translate his work on *Anthropo-Geographie* into English, but found the German constructions so difficult to handle accurately that it was necessary for her to put Ratzel's observations into her own words. She also points out in Buckle a lack of system and an undue tendency to follow one generalization after another. Her own *Influences of Geographic Environment* has now become a standard work on the ways in which physical nature affects mankind.

Miss Semple, following but improving upon Ratzel, has shown in turn the influences of geographical location, area, and boundaries upon people. She indicates the various ways in which oceans, rivers, and coast lines have molded human minds; she distinguishes between mountain, steppe, and desert effects upon mankind. She describes man as a product of the earth's surface. She stresses unduly the physical influences; she considers nature the dominating force. Even where civilized man has developed inventive powers and spiritual prowess, nature is given the credit.[14] Nevertheless, Miss Semple has marshalled facts in powerful array and increased their force by literary skill. No student or teacher can afford to neglect Miss Semple's extensive survey of the interactions between physical nature and human progress.

Among the many other writers upon the relation of geographic factors to civilization the investigations of Ellsworth Huntington are significant.[15] He has described the climatic conditions that are most favorable to mental stimulation and growth, and then has classified all districts of the earth according to the degree in which they stimulate or arrest mental advance.

In this same connection William Z. Ripley has investigated the relation of climate to races.[16] After analyzing races and distinguishing between them and the geographic influences upon pigmentation, head, form, stature, and other traits, mainly structural, he classifies climatic elements in order of importance, as follows: humidity, heat, and monotony. A high humidity, excessive heat, and long series of sunshine or of cloudy weather produce mental enervation, stagnation, and retrogression.

Acclimatization of races is a very slow process, according to Ripley. It requires centuries. Perhaps the white race can never become truly acclimated in the tropics. Racial differences he shows are due to environmental factors far more than is ordinarily supposed.

In conclusion, it may be said that physical forces have operated strongly on man. But when man has developed modern mental tools, he has been able to escape a part of the enslaving environmental influences. The history of the relation of geographic factors to human progress indicates a fundamental but a proportionate decrease in those influences.

Chapter XVI

Spencer and Organic Social Thought

In the second half of the last century social thought passed under biological influence. Society was discussed in terms of biological analogies, that is, it was compared in its structure and functions to organic life. Herbert Spencer was the leader among those writers who attempted to analyze society in terms of biological figures of speech. He also stressed the structural nature of society, and in his *Principles of Sociology* he went into great detail in giving a historical description of social institutions.

The Greek writers, the Hebrews before them, the founder of Christianity made references to the likenesses between human society and plant and animal life. Mankind has often been compared to a tree or a plant with its manifold, evolving branches and fruit.

Spencer's famous organic analogies were preceded by the studies of biologists, such as Lamarck and Darwin. Lamarck (1744-1829) argued that by activity and use man could develop traits which would be transmitted by inheritance. Although this theory has been undermined by Weismann, it served as a basis for the further study of the biological laws of human evolution.

The thought of Charles Darwin (1809-1882) upon the nature of evolution was stimulated in part by Malthus' doctrine of surplus population and the consequent struggle for existence. He also based his ideas on the Lamarckian theory of transmission of acquired characters. He developed the concepts of the prodigality of nature and the struggle for existence, which led to the resultant concept of natural selection and survival of the fittest. The process of natural selection accounts for the instincts, imitation, imagination, reason as well as for self-consciousness, and the esthetic and religious impulses. In this way man, according to the Darwinian formula, has ascended by stages from the lower orders of life.

The fittest to survive, concluded Darwin, are those individuals who are best fitted to meet the conditions of their environment. If the environment be competitive, savage, brutal, then the fittest will be the strongest physically and the most vicious. If the environment be co-operative, then the fittest will be the individuals who co-operate best. With the development of intelligence and sagacity in early human society, individuals otherwise cruel learned to co-operate. A tribe of co-operating individuals would be victorious in a conflict with a tribe of non-co-operating members. Thus co-operation and a co-operating environment themselves are the result of natural selection.

Unfortunately, Darwin's concept of natural selection has been grossly distorted. Upon this misapprehension, a doctrine of "social Darwinism" has gained recognition. According to this false interpretation of Darwinism, the tooth and fang struggle for existence among animals is the normal procedure among human beings. The most brutal, cruel, and shrewd men are "fitted" to survive in an environment of physical and mental competition. Likewise, the nations which can marshal together the most powerful armies and navies are the "fittest" to survive in a world where each nation is accountable unto itself alone. Thus, it is seen that human society is simply an extension of the animal society and that the fundamental law of social progress is the law of force and might, first physical, and then physical and psychical.

But this interpretation is false to Darwin's own principles. While Darwin did describe and lay great emphasis upon the tooth and fang struggle for existence, he noted and stressed the fact that even among animals, modifying influences were at work. He made clear that co-operation exists among many species of animal life, and that this co-operative tendency is an important survival factor. He also saw that among the highest types of animals there were new and complex expressions of co-operation, and that the higher mental activity of these animal types seemed to be a correlate in some way of the greater co-operative spirit. The application of this principle to human progress implies that the co-operative spirit may ultimately become the chief survival force, and that some day the "fittest" to survive will be those individuals or groups of individuals who co-operate most wisely. This theory will be developed further in the chapter upon "Co-operation Theories in Sociology." The chief contributors have been Kropotkin and Novicow.

Darwin made another important contribution to social science in his theory of sexual selection. This idea is a phase of natural selection. Among the higher animals the females choose their mates. The males, for example, with the singing voice and beautiful plumage, are the most likely to be chosen. These males thus become the progenitors of the next generation of the given species; the less attractive males mate if at all with the inferior types of females. Thus signs of male attractiveness come to possess survival value.[1]

Among human beings the principle of sexual selection operates, but in a reversed sexual form. During the earlier centuries of human history the custom developed whereby the males took the initiative in choosing mates. As a result, the females resorted to all sorts of devices to make themselves "attractive" and to get themselves "selected."

The social theories of Herbert Spencer (1820-1903) have caused more controversy than those of any other writer in the sociological field. The fact that in these controversies the ideas of Spencer have usually been worsted will not blind the fair-minded seeker after truth to the important rôle which Spencer took in the field of social thought.

Spencer early developed the habit of causal thinking, that is, he believed in causes, and hence searched everywhere for causes. Because of the acrimonious discussions which took place between his father and mother, and because of his own independent nature, he repudiated the orthodox religious explanations of the universe. He was trained for the profession of civil engineering. His studies in mathematics and mechanics accentuated his precise and somewhat materialistic interpretation of the universe. His social theories are an outgrowth in part of his emphasis upon the laws of co-existence and sequences in the physical world.

In order to understand Spencer's social laws it is necessary first to consider his general law of evolution. He traced everything in the world back through causal chains to two fundamental factors, namely, matter and motion—two aspects of force. As a result of the operation of some First Cause, an integration of matter began to take place, accompanied by a concomitant dissipation of motion. As a result, matter passes from an indefinite, incoherent homogeneity to a definite, coherent heterogeneity. During this process the unexpended motion undergoes a similar change.[3]

The best explanation of this law of evolution can be found in its application to societary phenomena. Suppose that a modern city neighborhood undertakes to organize itself. It possesses physical resources and mental abilities. The "neighbors" are all more or less untrained in community organization activities. In this sense they are homogeneous. At first they are unable to work together; in fact they do not know what to do; thus, they form "an indefinite, incoherent homogeneity." But with experience in community organization activities, the individuals of the neighborhood learn to work together. Each finds the type of work which he can do best. All work toward a definite goal. Thus, a definite, coherent heterogeneity arises. Further, the unexpended energies of the people are influenced and transformed by the pattern ideas which experience in community organization measures has taught.[8]

This application of Spencer's law of evolution to human progress has weak as well as strong points. There is not always an original homogeneity. Upon close examination this homogeneity disappears before a variegated conglomeration of heterogeneous experiences and potentialities of all the individuals who are concerned. It is not necessary to point out additional errors. Spencer deserves credit, however, for developing the concept of social evolution as a phase of natural evolution and for stressing the idea of natural causation in societary matters.

Spencer began his *Principles of Sociology* with a very elaborate description of primitive man—the original societary unit corresponding to the biological cell. The physical, emotional, and intellectual life of primitive man is given prominence. An analysis is made of the behavior of man, the original social unit, when he is exposed to the various environing conditions—inorganic, organic, and super-organic. The emphasis upon "man" as the primary unit neglects the importance of the "group" in the social evolutionary process. Moreover, Spencer underrated the intellectual nature of primitive man; he denied to early man the qualities involving excursiveness of thought, imagination, and original ideas.[4]

Spencer's discussion of primitive ideas shows widespread reading of volumes of source materials. The "inductions" are often influenced by preconceived notions of human life, despite Spencer's sincere desire and effort to be scientific. While the horde, the family, and other groups are described, the influences which are the result of the interaction of individual minds and the interactions between the individual and his group are scarcely recognized.

In regard to the state, Spencer carried forward the theories which have already been noted, namely, of individual rights. He repudiated the state which is the product of the military organization of society. Such a régime is primordial and uncivilized. It is an organization of homogeneous units in which the units, or the individuals, are slaves to the organization.

Spencer believed in a new industrial development whereby individuals would become differentiated and developed, and whereby individuals would be shifted from an autocratic maximum to a democratic maximum. To Spencer, man is vastly superior to the state. In the coming industrial order Spencer foresaw an era in which the main business of society will be to defend the rights of individuals. Spencer forecasted an epoch of industrial states which have abolished war. In such a day the only conflicts that will take place between states will be natural. These will be only the competitions that arise naturally between states that are engaged in building up the best individuals, that is, those persons who develop their individuality most freely and harmoniously.

The rise of industrial states with a minimum emphasis upon government and a maximum emphasis upon individuality will produce a world order in which national barriers will slowly melt away and a planetary unity will develop. Spencer's industrialism, however, has fundamental weaknesses. It implies that social organization is more important than social process. It neglects to provide for inherent psychical changes. It assumes that an industrial society, *per se,* will be peaceful. It underestimates the importance of socializing motives.

In the changes from a military to an industrial organization of society, the six main sets of social institutions undergo deep-seated changes. Spencer describes at length these six institutional structures, namely, the domestic, ceremonial, political, ecclesiastical, professional, and industrial. Two, the political and industrial, have been mentioned on the preceding page. Spencer's treatment of the other four is accurate to a degree but at fundamental points is unreliable—judged by current conceptions and data.

Perhaps Spencer is best known for his treatment of the organic analogy. He set up the hypothesis that society is like a biological organism and then proceeded to defend his thesis against all objections with great logical force. But logic was his sociological downfall, for it overcame his scientific insight.

Spencer found four main ways in which society resembles an organism.[5] (1) In both cases growth is attended by augmentation of mass. (2) In each instance growth is accomplished by increasing complexity of structure. (3) In the organism and in society there is an interdependence of parts. (4) The life of society, like the life of an organism, is far longer than the life of any of the units or parts.

But there are ways in which society and an organism are unlike.[6] These were analyzed by Spencer and determined to be merely superficial differences. There are four of these main differences. (1) Unlike organisms, societies have no specific extensive form, such as a physical body with limbs or a face. (2) The elements of society do not form a continuous whole as in the case of an animal. The living units composing society are free, and not in contact, being more or less dispersed. (3) The parts of society are not stationary and fixed in their positions relative to the whole. (4) In an organism consciousness is concentrated in a small part of the aggregate, while in society consciousness is diffused. The alleged superficiality in this difference between society and an organism was difficult for Spencer to maintain.

In discussing the organic analogy further, Spencer compared the alimentary system of an organism to the productive industries, or the sustaining system in the body politic.[7] Furthermore, there is a strong parallelism between the circulatory system of an organism and the distributing system in society with its transportation lines; but more particularly, its commercial classes and media of exchange. Then, in both cases there has developed regulating systems. In an organism there is a dominant center and subordinate centers, the senses, and a neural apparatus. A similar structure appears in society in the form of an adjustive apparatus, or government, for the purpose of adjudicating the differences between the producers and the consumers. These parallelisms throw only a small measure of light upon the nature of society. They appear ridiculous when carried to an extreme, for example, to the extreme to which Spencer himself went when he compared the King's Council to the medulla oblongata, the House of Lords to the cerebellum, and the House of Commons to the cerebrum.

Spencer uses his analogies very extensively and vigorously, and later refers to them as merely a scaffolding for building a structure of deductions. This conclusion contains contradictory elements. When the scaffolding is removed, society is left standing as a more or less intangible affair. If a society is like an organism, it experiences a natural cycle of birth, maturity, old age, and death. But according to the telic concept of progress that was advanced by Lester F. Ward and developed by later writers, the death of society does not come with organic inevitableness, but depends on the vision, plans, courage, and activities of that society's members. A society need never die.

For many years it has been popular to criticise Spencer. Nearly all the criticisms are justified. Moreover, they have been so numerous that little of worth seems to be left in Spencer's writings. However, Spencer's contributions to social thought are not negligible for several reasons. (1) He emphasized the laws of evolution and natural causation. (2) He described social evolution as a phase of natural evolution. (3) He pointed out the likenesses between biological organisms and human society. (4) He made the rôle of social structures, or institutions, to stand out distinctly. (5) He stressed the importance of individuality. (6) He undermined the idea that the State is a master machine to which all the individual citizens must submit automatically.

In the United States, Spencer possessed an able and loyal friend in John Fiske (1842-1901). Fiske built his social thought upon the evolutionarily formulae of Darwin and Spencer. In his *Cosmic Philosophy,* or philosophy of the universe, Fiske contended that the evolution of man produced fundamental changes in the nature of cosmic evolution. With the development of man there appears a new force in the universe, the human spirit, or soul. The advent of this psychical entity has produced a subordination of the purely bodily, physical, material forces and established a control by spiritual forces. Moreover, in human evolution there has been a slowly increasing subordination of the selfish phases of spiritual life to the altruistic. With the apparent cessation in important bodily changes there have come unheralded and unanticipated psychical inventions, which have released man from the passive adaptation to environment which animals manifest, and given to him an increasingly positive control over the processes of adaptation. Humanity as the highest product of the evolutionary processes has the power to change the whole course of cosmic development. Fiske distinctly emphasized the psychical forces in evolution and the part which they are playing in making mankind purposeful and in organizing groups on social principles. Humanity is not a mere incident in evolution; it is the supreme factor.[9] The main purpose of man is not the perpetuation of the species, but the development of increasingly higher and more social purposes.

Following the ideas of Maine, Tylor, McLennan, and Lubbock, Fiske concluded that social evolution originated when families, "temporarily organized among all the higher gregarious mammals, became in the case of the highest mammal permanently organized."[10] Gregariousness developed into definite family relationships and responsibilities. Social evolution produced an increased complexity and specialty in intelligence, which in turn required a lengthening of the period "during which the nervous connections involved in ordinary adjustments are becoming organized." Such a transformation requires time, and hence the need for a period of infancy which is not common to the lower animals. Accompanying this period of infancy, there is the development of strong affection of relatively short duration among higher animals. Among mankind parental love takes on the characteristics not only of intensity and unselfishness but of duration and forgiveness. In this phase of evolution there is a correlative development of three factors, namely, the prolongation of infancy, the rise of parental affection, and increasing intelligence. The gradual prolongation of the period of infancy is partly a consequence of increasing intelligence, and in turn the prolongation of infancy affords the circumstances for the establishment of permanent relationships, of reciprocal behavior, of sociality.

Fiske was one of the first social philosophers to point out the significance of foresight as a phase of evolutionary development. Perhaps the chief way in which civilized man is distinguished from the barbarian is in his ability "to adapt his conduct to future events, whether contingent or certain to occur." Civilized man has the power to forego present enjoyment in order to safeguard himself against future disaster.[12] This quality is the essence of prudence and is due in large part to civilized man's superior power of self-restraint, one of the chief elements in moral progress. It is equally important as "an indispensable prerequisite to the accumulation of wealth in any community." It is the basic factor in civilized man's elaborate scientific provisions and in his numerous far-reaching philosophic and religious systems.

Paul von Lilienfeld (1829-1903) made the organic analogy a definite part of his theory of society. He compared the individual to the cells in an organism; the governmental and industrial organizations, to the neural system; and the cultural products of society, to the intercellular parts of an organism.[13]

Lilienfeld compared the stages of growth of the individual to the stages of racial development, namely, savage, barbarian, and civilized. This analogy was made use of by Fiske. Although somewhat true in a very general sense, this recapitulation theory cannot be carried into minute details.

The concept of social capitalization was originated by Lilienfeld. By it he meant the ability of society to store up useful ideas and methods and transmit them from generation to generation. In this way each generation becomes the inheritor of all the human experiences that have gone before.

Lilienfeld was one of the first sociological writers to develop the definite concept of social pathology.[14] His treatment of this theme, however, was exceedingly weak. He distinguished between a normal and diseased organism and then, by analogy, between a normal and diseased society. Social pathology, according to Lilienfeld, deals with three sets of diseases, namely, of industry, of justice, and of politics. Lilienfeld carried the organic analogy to a ridiculous and puerile extreme when he compared the diseases of industry to insanity; of justice, to delirium; of politics, to paralysis. He also elaborated a system of social therapeutics to correspond to the diseases.

In Albert Schaeffle (1831-1903), the organic analogy found another disciple, but a more worthy one than either Spencer or Lilienfeld. In the thought of Schaeffle, society is not primarily a large organism but a gigantic mind. Schaeffle presented a functional analogy rather than a biological analogy. Whereas Spencer was especially interested in social structures, Schaeffle set his attention upon social functions.

In his functional analogies Schaeffle compared the reason with the legislature in society; the will, with the executive officers; and the esthetic judgment, with the judiciary. Schaeffle's psychology is inaccurate and on the whole unscientific; his analogies add little to an understanding of society. Nevertheless, his thought on these subjects represents an advance over the ideas of Spencer.

In the *Bau und Leben des Socialen Körpers,* Schaeffle undertook to develop a complete sociological system. His teachings follow the principle that "function leads structure and structure limits function." Activities produce developments in bodily structure, and also cause the formation of new social institutions. Bodily structures and social institutions alike limit activities and usefulness. These propositions are a reversal of the emphasis which Spencer maintained. They are fundamentally correct.

Although Schaffle referred frequently to the "social body," he did not give the concept a specific meaning. He introduced the term "social process," but did not analyze its nature. He repudiated the idea that the individual is the social unit; he considered the group to be the all-important unit in society. Natural selection in social evolution manifests itself in conflicts between the ideals of different groups. René Worms, it may be added, has assumed the existence of a social consciousness apart from the consciousness of individuals, and argued that the chief difference between biological organisms and social organizations is one of degree.

Schaeffle considered that government justifies itself in protecting the weaker members of society, and in maintaining the highest welfare of all. He pointed out the social responsibility which rests upon the best educated and most fortunate members of society. Schaeffle wisely emphasized the development of purposeful activity on the part of both the individual and society.

The ideas of John Stuart Mackenzie differ from those of Spencer, Lilienfeld, and Schaeffle. Mackenzie does not use the figure of an organic analogy; he speaks in terms of homologies. According to Mackenzie, society is not like an organism; it is organic.

The organic nature of society is threefold. (1) There is an intrinsic relation between the parts of society and the whole. The individual reflects the culture of the group in which he has been trained. (2) The development of a group is by virtue of intrinsic processes. A group builds on ideas derived from both the past and from other groups, but it does not genuinely grow unless it takes these ideas and makes them over into a part of its own nature. (3) Society develops towards ends which are discoverable in society itself. By analysis of the ideals and motive forces of a group, it is possible to determine in what direction the group is moving.

Mackenzie argues for the inner principle of things and particularly of society. He believes, however, that knowledge concerning this inner principle and the essential unity of mankind cannot be reduced to a science, but will constitute the basis of a social philosophy. Social philosophy does not supply facts, but seeks to interpret the significance of the special aspects of human life with reference to the social unity of mankind.[15]

The family and the state are the two forms of association in which the most intimate bonds of union are nurtured. Language, if it can be called a social institution, is perhaps the most fundamental institution of all, because it produces that community of spirit whereby intimacy in social intercourse can take place and whereby the realization of a common good can be achieved.[16]

According to Mackenzie, there are three main lines of social progress, and hence three main types of social control to be encouraged.[17] (1) The control of natural forces by human agencies. (2) The control of individuals by the communal spirit. (3) Self control.

The road of social advance is beset with obstacles. The chief are these: (1) The dominance of vegetative needs. These economic factors are so universal and insistent that they are likely at any time to override all other human needs. (2) The insistence of animal impulses, chiefly love and strife. While love promotes unity, it generally produced a limited unity. Moreover, one mode of unity is apt to conflict with other types of unity, and thus lead to intense strife. (3) The mastery of mechanism. Life is easily crushed under the weight of organization; thought, by scholastic pedantry; industry, by economic systems; nationality, by soulless bureaucracy. (4) Anarchism. The remedy for over-organization is not anarchy, for life and society are composed of numbers of conflicting tendencies, which must be controlled by the power of thought. But the exercise of merely individual thought will not suffice. Individual thought is likely to be egocentric, to evade the problems of group life, or to solve them selfishly. (5) Conservatism. An established and successful civilization is in danger of relying too much on its past. It often carries within itself the canker of decay, and frequently lacks any clear vision of higher development.

Mackenzie is committed to internationalism. It is no longer fitting for anyone to think of his own country as an exclusive object of devotion. "The earth is our country, and all its inhabitants are our fellow-citizens; and it is only the recognition of this that entitles us to look for any lasting security."

Mackenzie advances beyond the organic analogists when he describes the ways in which society is organic. As a social philosopher he has contributed important pattern-ideas. He has escaped from the foibles of the organic analogy and at the same time indicated the values that lie beneath that concept.

This chapter deals with a significant period in the history of social thought. The biology of the time was very faulty and the sociological applications of biological knowledge were consequently of little merit. The early years of the present century were characterized by noteworthy improvements in biological thinking. The facts about the laws of heredity and variation increased in number; a science of heredity was established. The first decade of the present century also marks the rise of the science of eugenics. In a later chapter the contributions of recent scientific biology, and particularly of eugenics, to social thought will be presented.

CHAPTER XVII

THE SOCIOLOGY OF LESTER F. WARD

The name of Lester F. Ward (1841-1913) stands forth between the old and new eras of social thought. Ward belongs to both the old and new. He adopted Comtean positivism and built in part upon Spencer's evolutionary principles, but opposed Spencer's *laissez faire* ideas and his evolutionary determinism, especially in regard to education. Perhaps his most notable work was the way in which he shocked a Spencerian-tinged world of social thought into a new method of thinking.

Ward became the ardent advocate of social telesis. Man can modify, defeat, or hasten the processes of nature. Ward brought the concept of dynamic sociology to the attention of the world. Although he was interested in social statics, his primary concern was in the fact that man through the use of his intelligence can transform not only the natural world but the social world, and that he can harness not only the natural forces to social ends, but even the social forces to social purposes. Hence it is that Ward holds rank today, despite his monistic philosophy and his false psychological beliefs, as one of the world's leading sociologists.

Lester F. Ward was born in Joliet, Illinois. He received a limited schooling, and early went to work, first on a farm and then as a wheelwright. He manifested an unusual liking for books and to a great extent was self-educated. He entered the employment of the United States Government, where he remained for more than forty years, after he was honorably discharged from service in the Civil War. In the Government service he held the positions of geologist and paleontologist. Despite his strenuous and efficient work for the Government, he found time to think through and write out an elaborate sociological system of thought.

Ward's published works in sociology began with his *Dynamic Sociology* (1883) and ended with the *Glimpses of the Cosmos* (1913) in several volumes, which, with the exception of volume one, have been published posthumously. The intermediate books of importance in order were: *Pure Sociology, Applied Sociology,* and *Psychic Factors of Civilization.*

Ward was characterized by an impressive command of his subject and "a terrific mental drive." In 1906, he began the unique experiment of teaching sociology at the age of 65. As a professor of sociology he served Brown University until his death—for a period of seven years. He was supported by the indefatigable assistance of his wife, as shown by the many files which she kept of "Reviews and Press Notices," "Autograph Letters," and "Biography."

Ward was led to produce the *Dynamic Sociology* because of his observation that preceding 1875 there was an essential sterility in social science thinking. Ward observed that the prevalent teachings of Herbert Spencer were statical, and that the ideas of Spencer's American disciples were only passively dynamic. Ward believed that before the science of society could be truly established the active dynamic factors must be described. A science which fails to benefit mankind is lifeless. To save sociology from the lifelessness which it was manifesting, Ward wrote the *Dynamic Sociology*. He contemplated social phenomena "as capable of intelligent control by society itself in its own interest."[1] His main thesis in the *Dynamic Sociology* is "the necessity for universal education as the one clear, overshadowing, and immediate social duty to which all others are subordinate." He argued for a truly progressive system of popular scientific education.[2] He declared that not one-hundredth of the facts which original research has already brought forth are today obtainable by a one-hundredth of the members of society, and hence not one truth in ten thousand is fully apprehended.[3]

The prevailing doctrine in social thought, that of *laissez faire* as championed by Spencer, drew forth Ward's best intellectual efforts as a challenger. Ward protested against the teaching that natural forces are operating only as elements in the all-powerful evolutionary process. He pointed out that man is distinguished from animals by the development of his psychical nature, i. e., of his foresight and reason. He demonstrated that by this development man is able to master and regulate the operation of the blind evolutionary forces. Hence, the doctrine of *laissez faire* is not only false but pernicious. It defeats social progress. The truth is, said Ward, society is able to improve itself, and it should set itself scientifically at once to the opportunity.

Passive, or negative, progress is represented by the social forces operating in their natural freedom, subject only to general evolutionary laws.[4] Active, or positive, progress is represented by the social forces guided by conscious human purposes. Social statics deals with the nature of social order; social dynamics treats of the laws of social progress. Social dynamics concerns itself with two types of studies. One line analyzes and describes what is going on in society under the influence of natural laws—this is pure sociology. It is pure diagnosis; it has nothing to do with what society ought to be. It describes the phenomena and laws of society as they are.[5] The other procedure discusses the application of human purpose to the natural social forces—this is applied sociology. It studies the art of applying the active, or positive, forces to the natural evolution of society. This method is distinctly a human process and "depends wholly on the action of man himself." Applied sociology treats of social ends and purposes.

Pure sociology describes the spontaneous development of society; applied sociology deals with the artificial means of accelerating the spontaneous processes in society.[6] Pure sociology treats of achievement; applied sociology, of improvement. But applied sociology is not social reform; "it does not itself apply sociological principles, it seeks only to show how they may be applied." It lays down principles as guides to social action. The carrying of these principles into social and political practice is social reform.

The distinction is now clear between natural and artificial progress.[7] The former is a blind growth; the latter, a purposeful manufacture. One is a genetic process; the other, a teleological process. One is characterized by increasing differentiation; the other, by a process of calculation. Artificial progress is considered superior to natural progress.

Ward was a monist. He believed in the absolute unity of nature, from the revolutions of celestial orbs to the vicissitudes of social customs and laws.[8] He held that "life is a property of matter," and naïvely declared that "it is simply the result of the movements going on among the molecules composing a mass of protoplasm."[9] Psychic phenomena are "the relations which subsist among the material molecules of the brain and nervous system and between these and the material objects of the outside world. . . ." Since mind is relational, it is immaterial, but it has matter for its basis. Relations, however, constitute the properties of matter, and hence mind, as well as life, is a property of matter.[10] The logical length to which Ward goes in supporting his monistic doctrine is in itself a proof of his error.

Unlike Comte, Ward believed that man originally was anti-social and completely selfish. In the earliest stage of human existence, man lived a life almost solitary, or at least in small groups.[11] He was surrounded by destructive forces both inorganic and organic. Against the wild and ferocious beasts he found himself almost physically helpless. Some of his number overcame their physical defenselessness by using their "wits." Through sagacity and cunning they were able to withstand the attacks of the wild beasts, to survive, and to propagate their young. Along with increased cunning there went an increased brain size in proportion to size of body, and also an improved brain structure qualitatively.

This brain development is the essential prerequisite for perceiving the advantages of association.[12] Man early recognized the merits of association, and moved up from the solitary, or autarchic, stage of social life to the second, or constrained aggregate stage. This second stage does not contain the elements of permanency because of its forced nature. The tendencies toward association are often counteracted and at times destroyed by fierce contests for the limited natural foods. In contending that man's early ancestors were very irascible and quarrelsome beings, Ward went beyond the limits of scientific induction. In believing that altruism is an outgrowth of egoism, Ward again violates the best scientific thought. The probabilities are that both egoism and altruism have developed *pari passu,* and in part from different causes. During the second stage human speech became an art. It was a natural outgrowth of the associational life.

The rise of the rudiments of an established government marks the beginning of the third period in human society. For protection, tribes unified themselves under central controls. Through compulsion or interest, and for protective reasons, tribes united; the spheres of social organization thus were enlarged. But government, which was established for the purpose of securing peace, became one of the chief causes of external wars. Governments, autocratic control, and territory hunger led peoples into destructive war. The world is still in this third stage.

But some day, according to Ward, wars between nations will cease, national prejudices will soften, diversity of language will be overcome, and all governments probably will be consolidated into one. This picture represents the fourth, or ideal, level of societary life, and may never be attained. Ward cherishes the strong belief that the present national stage will be succeeded by the cosmopolitan, or pantarchic, age. Ward perceives an ultimate triumph of humanitarian sentiments, which will be also "a triumph of practical interests, that shall sweep away the present barriers of language, national pride, and natural uncongeniality, and unite all nations in one vast social aggregate with a single political organization."[13]

Ward's analysis of social evolution rests on his conception of the social forces. The primary social force is desire. Desire is the expression of any of the native impulses which, at the given moment, has not been gratified. This striving for gratification constitutes desire and the moving force in the societary world. "Desire is the essential basis of all actions."

The desires are numerous and complex, but upon examination lend themselves to classification. There are two fundamental and primary sets of desires, the nutritive and the reproductive. The end of the first is to preserve the individual; and of the second, to preserve and maintain the race.

"The first desire of all creatures is for nourishment." This desire remains dominant throughout life. The human race, Ward summarizes, spent its infancy—thousands of years—in the single pursuit of subsistence.[14] When the natural food supply failed, man was forced to be inventive and to labor or die. Too many individuals in one place meant either the migration of some individuals or that others must compel nature through labor to increase her normal yield of subsistence.[16]

The nutritive desire has led man to labor. Labor, however, is not the natural condition of man.[23] Work, according to Ward, is unnatural and irksome. The constant spur of hunger transformed man into a working man. To be useful, however, work must be continuous and applied steadily to a given object until that object is attained. This process is the essence of invention, the highest and most useful form of labor. Without wings, valuable weapons of offense and defense, claws for digging, man has had but one line of advance open to him, namely, invention, whereby he could overcome his limitations and master nature.

Ward overlooked what Veblen has called the instinct of workmanship. Man has a desire to do, to achieve, to be active—only so can he escape the terrors of ennui. He secures illimitable enjoyment from seeing the crude materials of nature change under the manipulations of his hand and mind into works of art.

Nevertheless, the need of nutrition was probably the chief factor in the invention of tools and in the storing of food against the hungry day. These tools and stores constituted property. Property at once represented power. The law of acquisition soon exerted a great force. Intense rivalries in acquiring property developed. "The grand rivalry was for the object, not the method; for the end regardless of the means."[16] Through the centuries and until the present hour, the morality of obtaining wealth has rarely risen to the morality of many other phases of life.

Deception early came into prominence. We deceive an animal, in order to catch and domesticate or kill him. We deceive a fellow human being and take his hard earned property away from him. Society, blindly, has praised deception even when used by one individual against the welfare of his fellows. Society has honored him who could "drive a bargain."

Ward declared that the desire to acquire property regardless of the method is as strong as ever.[17] The only changes that have come are a mitigation of the harshness of the method and the rise of compulsory laws and codes which force individuals to "drive their bargains" and to practice their deceptions within prescribed limits. The acquisitive impulses have created major social evils, as evidenced by "the exceeding indigence of the poor and the exceeding opulence of the rich," and by a relatively large proportion of non-producing rich people to the entire number of wealthy.[18] On the other hand, those who are poor because they are indolent are only a small proportion of those who are poor and industrious.

The evils of acquisitiveness cannot be overcome by softening the human heart. Ward would make it impossible for individuals to take away the property of others by making it to the interest of all individuals not to act in that way. And then he would teach them, through the social sciences, that such conduct is against their own highest development.

Ward pronounced the money-making tendency one of the most useful and at the same time "one of the coarsest and cheapest of all mental attributes."[19] It is useful because it is "the spur of all industry and commerce; it provides the leisure which makes intellectual pursuits possible; it encourages exploration, discovery, and invention; it is the basis of all large business undertakings; and it has been an essential force in the development of civilization. Since civilization is so exclusively artificial, money can buy a vast variety of objects of human desire; hence, the possession of money is strenuously sought.

On the other hand, money-making confers a pleasure which after all is sordid.[21] It often leads to avarice. It has produced a pecuniary inequality of mankind which socially admits of little justification. From a moral viewpoint the great struggle for pecuniary possession has been man's greatest curse.[22] Because of it, many infants have opened their eyes as millionaires in a world of boundless plenty; others (equally worthy) have opened their eyes as beggars in a world of abject poverty.

Society becomes divided into two main classes: the industrials and the non-industrials, or parasites. The non-industrials use their cunning in various ways.[24] The leading non-industrial modes of acquisition are these: robbery, theft, war, statecraft, priestcraft, and monopoly. This list represents the chronological order and history of non-industrial types of acquisition.

Robbery is the coarsest manner of acquisition. Theft represents the lowest order of cunning. Wars of conquest are robbery on so large a scale that they arouse group patriotism. Cunning and treachery in war have given way to strategy. Statecraft has often been characterized by the egoistic attempts of a few shrewd individuals, who have devised means for supplying the wants of the many, and appropriated rich rewards for themselves from "the befriended and grateful community." Priestcraft as represented by many of the priests of Brahma, Buddha, Osiris, Ormuzd, Mahomet and even Jesus have developed successful modes of acquisition. They have often stood at the gates of death, and for pay guaranteed to the stricken and fearful friends of a departed loved one a safe journey through the perils following death. Monopoly takes cunning advantage of a scarcity of the means of substance, or creates an artificial and false scarcity. Monopoly has organized the fields of transportation, exchange, finance, labor, manufacture.

The non-industrials co-operate better than the industrials and against the welfare of the latter. The industrials, unfortunately, do not understand the principles of co-operation very well and do not have the intelligence to carry them into practical operation. They receive less education than the non-industrials; the years of their industrial apprenticeship are taken from their school days. After their apprenticeship begins, the fatigue of their labor gives them little time or energy for intellectual improvement.[25] In pronouncing co-operation the product of superior intelligence Ward neglects the rôle played by the gregarious, parental, and related social instincts. Ward sees only part of the truth when he calls competition a natural law, and co-operation artificial. He wisely observes, however, that those who co-operate thrive at the expense of those who compete.[26] In the same way that individuals co-operate in order to secure their own gain, society must organize to secure the progress of all.

The second primary set of fundamental forces is the reproductive. These operate for the future and for the species. In animals they operate without arousing shame or modesty. Among human beings they are manipulated through the agencies of the reason and the imagination and give rise to the sentiments of shame and modesty.[27] They are so clouded in secrecy that they arouse dangerous forms of curiosity.

Among animals the choice of mates is largely determined by the females. In fact, among the lowest types of animals there are no males. Among certain higher forms of animal life the male appears as a mere adjunct. But among human beings, male sexual selection developed. This change in sexual selection is one of the differences between the brute and the human worlds. This transition is explained by the fact that the higher a being rises in the scale of development the more sensitive its organs become, and by the correlated fact that the male human being through his reason is able to arouse and satisfy a thousand desires within the female, and thus cause her to look to him for "that protection and those favors which he alone can confer."[28]

In the human world the reproductive forces have first produced a crude sexual love, animal in its nature, but far-reaching in its basic implications. Sexual love is an unconscious but dominant factor in courtship. In its refined form, and modified by the addition of genuine but often short-lived affective elements, it becomes romantic love. Romantic love, according to Ward, unfits lovers for the normal pursuits of life. While under its spell they are unable to enjoy anything but each other's presence. "The man is unfitted for business, the woman for social life, and both for intellectual pursuits. The only spur that can make either party pursue other things, is the sense of doing something that the other desires."[29]

In the sense that natural, or sexual, love becomes the basis of romantic love, so romantic love in turn represents the genesis of a still higher form of love, namely, conjugal love. The love of a man for his wife or of a woman for her husband is, however, fundamentally different from romantic love. It is more stable, less disturbing to the normal processes of life, and makes the home and the family socially productive institutions. It often reaches a high state of refinement and develops its beauty of content from the sharing together by husband and wife of great joys and sorrows.

Maternal love, an outgrowth of maternity, manifests startling degrees of courage even among animals. Under the spur of the need for defending her young, a mother will often perform miraculous deeds. In its highest form maternal love manifests a remarkable strength throughout life and an extra-human power of forgiveness.

Then there is consanguineal love, which according to Ward includes paternal and fraternal affections. It becomes the blood bond or feeling of attachment that exists among the members of a primitive kinship group, and it leads to feelings of race and world solidarity and attachment.

Ward also pointed out that for each of these forms of love there is a correlative hate. This force of repulsion is often greater than the correlative love. Jealousy often leads to violent and destructive actions. Race hatred frequently becomes a vicious, brutal, and widespread sentiment that paralyzes all tendencies toward world progress.

Marriage institutions have developed from the

operation of the reproductive forces. Polygamy, polyandry, and a score of other types of marriage have arisen, although monogamy has demonstrated itself to be the superior type of marriage institution.

The reproductive forces have led to numerous sexuo-social inequalities. Men and women have come to occupy separate spheres of activity, and to represent distinct social conditions.[80] Although the two sexes live together and appear to be companions, they are in fact dwelling in separate worlds and on different planes. There are several principal inequalities. (1) There is an inequality of dress, which has loaded woman with ornaments and caused her an enormous amount of disease and suffering. (2) There is an inequality of duties, which has kept woman confined to the house, and made a slave or a pampered pet of her. (3) There is an inequality of education. Society has shut woman in the past from all opportunities for gaining knowledge by experience. Moreover, society has seen fit to debar women from the knowledge that is acquired by instruction. (4) An inequality of rights has meant that women have been discriminated against before the law. Without direct representation in legislatures, women have suffered in proprietary matters. (5) A general sex inequality has at times made woman the property or the slave of man. In short, women have been denied, until with recent years, entrance to the higher intellectual forms of activity and at the same time denied social and political rights.

Reverting to Ward's classification of desires, we may now proceed to a discussion of the third set of forces, the sociogenetic. In contradistinction to the nutritive and the reproductive desires, or to the ontogenetic and the phylogenetic forces, respectively, the sociogenetic forces lead directly to race, or social, improvement. The ontogenetic forces guarantee individual preservation; the phylogenetic, race preservation; and the sociogenetic, race and social progress. Ward classified the sociogenetic forces as moral, esthetic, and intellectual.[31]

Morality is either racial or individual. Race morality is largely an outgrowth of custom. Duty, according to Ward, is conduct favorable to race safety, while virtue is "an attitude of life and character consistent with the preservation and continuance of man on earth."[32] Individual morality on the other hand, is based on altruism. Altruism is the expenditure of energy in behalf of other individuals, and involves the power of representing the psychic states of others to one's self. Morality leads to humanitarianism, whose aim is meliorism. Meliorism aims to reorganize society so that the minimum pain and the maximum enjoyment may be insured. Meliorism is a non-sentimental improvement or amelioration of the human or social state.[33]

Ward holds that the esthetic forces consist of a desire for open or deep-seated symmetrical forms.

Behind a landscape which at first appears irregular and jagged, there is a fundamental symmetry and balance. Sculpture, painting, and landscape-gardening are largely imitations of nature. Architecture, however, emphasizes straight lines, regular curves, and other symmetrical and geometrical figures.[34] Because of the invention of popular musical instruments, music is open to and enjoyed by the common people. No such invention, unfortunately, has taken place in the fields of painting and sculpture. These realms are limited to the highest geniuses and "their choicest productions appropriated by the few who combine wealth with taste."[35]

The intellectual forces are chiefly the desires to know. These desires are threefold: (1) to acquire knowledge, (2) to discover truth, and (3) to impart information.[36] The desire to acquire knowledge is perhaps strongest in the young. Youth will often learn anything, without exercising any powers of discrimination. The gratification of the desire to discover new truth yields almost divine thrills of satisfaction. There are four methods of imparting information to others, viz., (1) by conversing, (2) by teaching, (3) by lecturing, and (4) by writing.

In addition to the dynamic forces there is the directive agent in society, namely, the intellect. Ward makes a precarious distinction between the feelings and thought, or between intellect as a seat of emotion, appetite and motive power, and intellect as the organ or source of thought and ideas.[37] Ward's psychology is admittedly unscientific. The thought or ideational phase of the intellect Ward divorced almost absolutely from the affective aspects of consciousness. He failed to perceive the dynamic character of thought and ideas. He made thought simply the directive agent in society.

In thought, Ward found the hope of the race. Thought can restrain and control social energy. It can produce telic methods of progress which are immeasurably superior to the blind, ruthless methods of nature. The procedure of nature with unlimited resources is "to produce an enormously redundant supply, and to trust the environment to select the best.[38] Nature secures success through "the indefinite multiplication of chances." Hence the survival of the fittest results in a sacrifice of a great majority—a highly wasteful method. The method of mind is the reverse. Though prevision, mind utilizes all the dynamic forces of society, that is the human desires, in constructive, orderly ways. Social waste may be reduced, by telic methods, to a minimum. Mind can perceive the best social ends and pursue them, whereas nature works blindly. Thought has in its power the possibility of subjugating natural forces and turning them into contributors to human needs.

Ward developed essentially four leading principles of social dynamics and hence of societal progress. (1) The first law he called "difference of potential." This term, which he borrowed from physics, refers to the difference in potential possibilities of individuals. This difference is manifested, for example, in the crossing of cultures. It disturbs social stability, and creates social liability. Sex is a device whereby a difference of potential is maintained. While asexual reproduction is characterized chiefly by repetition of forms, sexual reproduction creates changes in the stock in countless directions. The difference of potential which is caused by a crossing of strains is highly dynamic, resulting in unnumbered variations, and hence in providing endless opportunities for progress. In a similar way a cross fertilization of cultures opens many opportunities for social advancement. "Progress results from the fusion of unlike elements."[40] Difference of potential, again, is illustrated in the friction of mind upon mind. Thoughts conflict, and the result is likely to be an invention.

Difference of potential may lead to creative synthesis.[41] When two elements are joined, the result is usually more than the sum of the parts. The combining of hydrogen and oxygen in given proportions produces water, which manifests characteristics that are not possessed by either of the constituents. Likewise, the combining of two ideas by the human mind may result in a new idea, and thus in progress.

(2) A second dynamic principle is innovation, which has its biological homologue in the sport, or mutant. Throughout nature and society, fortuitous variations occur. Life at times breaks over the bounds of pure heredity—the result is innovation. Variation, in the sense of mutation or innovation, appears to be due to the exuberance of life. At times nature appears to react against being bound by rigid laws of heredity, to defy her own rules, and to become rampant.

Social innovation is invention. New ideas often appear accidentally. The mind in its exuberance coins new phrases, catches new glimpses of reality, and creates ideas which are contrary to all that is established and supposedly true.

(3) Ward's third law of progress is called conation. This concept refers to social effort which is carried on naturally to satisfy desire, to preserve or continue life, to modify the surroundings. In satisfying normally the gregarious desires, the individual advances the cause of social progress. In preserving the life of the child, the mother presumably contributes to the welfare of the race. The sacrifices which parents make in behalf of children are efforts which further the welfare of society. Every constructive modification of either the physical or spiritual environment benefits mankind. Conation is thus a term which covers a multitude of activities that are performed in the or-

dinary course of daily life, and which unconsciously to the doers are adding to the sum total of human welfare.

(4) The fourth dynamic principle which Ward described has already been discussed, namely, the principle of social telesis. The possibilities in social telesis are illimitable. Social telesis can turn the passions and desires of men into socially useful channels. These passions are bad only when directed to wrong ends. They are like fire—they can destroy or they can refine. If individuals as members of society could develop prevision and work together for societary ends, they would be able to transform the world.

Ward believed that greatness does not rest so much in intellectual power as in emotional force. He had great faith in persons of average intellectual ability who are ambitious. It thus becomes the part of wisdom for society to educate wisely the average intelligence. Ward challenged the idea that only a very few persons are geniuses and that these individuals, by virtue of their superior abilities, will uniformly overcome their environments. He held that genius is largely a matter of focalization of psychic energy, and that by this process all individuals may have the honor of contributing something valuable to civilization.

Ward pointed out that geniuses are as likely to appear in one social stratum as in another, among the poor as among the healthy, in the hovel as in the palace. He also demonstrated how society allows genius and talent to be ruthlessly destroyed among the lower classes through denial of opportunity. As a solution for this problem, Ward advocated social distribution, that is, the distribution of all useful knowledge to all humanity everywhere. A scientific system needs to be perfected for the more thorough and equal distribution of the great volume of valuable knowledge which has already been discovered. Ward was a strong advocate of the socialization of education.

In an article which appeared in the month following his death, Ward discussed his idea of social progress under the terms, eugenics, euthenics, and eudemics.[42] He supplemented a theory of sound birth with a theory of sound environment. The practical result in society would be a state of eudemics, or a society of sound people.

Ward was an advocate of sociocracy. By sociocracy he did not mean a democracy or a rulership that is likely to be conducted selfishly by the individuals who exercise sovereign power. Sociocracy connotes a rulership of the people in which each individual is governed primarily not by his own interests but by the interests of society.

Achievement was a large concept in Ward's mind. He made "achievement" one of the chief goals of human life. By achievement in behalf of human progress individuals gain social immortality. The masses of humanity are achieving little or nothing in behalf of society.

In this treatment of Ward's sociological thought it has not been the aim of the writer to enter upon a dissertation regarding the abstract and philosophic implications that are involved in the subject matter. Neither has he attempted a polemic against the weaknesses in Ward's thinking, except to note the defective monistic philosophy and the erroneous "faculty" psychology. It has been his purpose to let the strong, constructive elements in Ward's system of sociology speak clearly and effectively for themselves.

CHAPTER XVIII

ANTHROPOLOGIC SOCIOLOGY

Additional light upon the nature of sociological thought may be secured by consulting the anthropologists, and particularly, the students of social origins. The last mentioned group of scholars have been unusually successful in making valuable contributions to sociological thought, because they have used the psychological approach.

For more than a century the anthropologists have been searching for materials and advancing theories concerning the origin of man, of conflict and co-operative tendencies, and of the early ideas and institutions of the human race. They have been aided by the investigations of the geologists and especially of the paleontologists. The ethnographers and ethnologists have also discovered important data. The findings of all these groups of investigators, as far as they relate to the main thread of this book, will be here treated essentially as a unitary contribution. There is not space to deal specifically with the work of anthropologists, such as Tylor, Morgan, Pitt-Rivers, Haddon, Frazer, Goldenweiser, Keane, and a number of other prominent authorities.

Anthropological social thought will be indicated here under several headings. As far as possible the controversial and technical theories in anthropology will be avoided. Certain of the ideas that have been advanced by Sumner, Westermarck, Hobhouse, Wundt, Boas, and Thomas will receive special attention, because they are unusually pertinent to the main theme of this volume.

1. There is common agreement among anthropologists that man is the descendant of a branch of higher animal life, and that the creation of man took place by a slow, evolutionary process. The slowness of this developmental process does not necessarily lessen the mysterious or miraculous character of it. It places the origin of the human race at a much earlier date than was once supposed—perhaps from 200,000 to 500,000 years ago. The animal inheritance of man need not lead anyone to deny the correlative fact that man possesses spiritual qualities not common to the highest developed animals.[1]

Even the psychic equipment of man can be traced in its origins to the primates with their individual and social instincts. The instinctive bases of human conduct are hundreds of thousands of years old. They are so intrinsically a part of human nature that no discussion of current social problems will neglect the imperiousness of the ancient instinct heritage of the human race.

2. There is extensive anthropologic evidence

that mankind had a common origin. The remains of the earliest human beings are found in a region which extends through India from Java to England. From these geographic centers primitive man seems to have migrated in various directions—northeast, southwest, and finally to the Western Hemisphere. Different climatic and environmental conditions affected the migrating groups in different ways. Those who migrated into the tropical regions were retarded because of the enervating climatic factors. Those who reached the frigid zone were also retarded, or subjected to recidivism for a different reason—a harshness of living conditions and an excess of environmental obstacles. The north temperate zone with its fertile lands and its invigorating climate afforded the proper *milieu* for the development of the race.

3. An important question relates to the alleged potential equality of all races. The common origin of races is admitted, but the question remains open whether, for example, the African races possess the same innate mental abilities as the Caucasian races. The controversy here is sharply drawn between the environmentalists and the eugenists. Each side of the debate has collected a large body of evidence. In reality, the question apparently boils down to this: Have the many centuries of living under the enervating torrid zone conditions effected the African races so deeply that under favorable cultural circumstances they have become incapable of de-

veloping beyond a certain mental level which is lower than that attained by the Caucasian races? In the past the answer to this question has been a strong affirmative. The bulk of the evidence that has been collected in recent years indicates that the affirmative answer is incorrect.

4. It is becoming clear that every race is a composite of several races. Ethnological data show that the five grand divisions of the human race may be sub-divided into racial stocks, and into races and sub-races, until more than 600 races may be described; and furthermore, that each of the 600 or more races represents an amalgamation of at least three or four races. It is evident that no clear line of racial demarcation can be drawn, and that purity of race may be a fictitious term.

5. Intermarriage of the representatives of races belonging to similar racial stocks seems advisable—according to the ethnologist. Pure bloods apparently die out. The strongest races today are those in which amalgamation has taken place recently—that is, within one thousand or two thousand years, for example, the English, or the Scotch-Irish.

A mooted question of world importance relates to the intermarriage of the representatives of races widely different, such as the white and the yellow races, or the white and the black races. No race has yet developed out of such combinations. Race prejudices and social distinctions have produced conflicts which thus far have prevented the formation of such a race. Very few scientific data are available regarding miscegenation.

Apparently, the interbreeding of whites and blacks leads ultimately to the elimination of the racial characteristics of the blacks and to the complete dominance of the whites. There are some writers who assert that this process takes place to the gain of the lower race and to the loss of the higher race. The last-mentioned point has not yet been proved. Miscegenation between whites and blacks occurs under such abnormal and vicious social conditions that the racial tendencies are definitely obscured.

6. Conflict between races is primordial; conflict between races today is illustrated in national wars and race persecutions. Weaker races have often combined against a stronger race; from these experiences there has come a growing sense of the value of co-operation. Nations with high moral principles have united against a powerful neighbor nation with bullying tendencies. Out of these temporary combinations there has arisen a sense of need for permanent forms of national co-operation. This common need will ultimately lead, undoubtedly, to a permanent association of nations.

The conflict between the grand divisions of the human race will probably continue for a long time to come. Sometimes it is concentrated in an antagonism between the white and yellow races; and again, it is expressed in the more fundamental struggle between Occidentalism and Orientalism.

7. The origin and development of primitive ways of doing constitute a well-cultivated field of study. Anthropologists have published an endless amount of materials on the origin of languages, religions, occupations, sex distinctions. A portion of this work has been done without an accurate understanding of the psychological principles that are involved, and hence has to be viewed with caution or neglected entirely.

W. G. Sumner, whose argument in favor of individualism and of a *laissez faire* governmental policy was given in Chapter XI, published in his *Folkways* a minute and extended account of the nature of primitive institutions.

In the development of his theories, Sumner began with the needs of primitive peoples and with the attempts to meet these needs. Repetition of these acts leads to established ways of doing, that is, to folkways. Folkways are "the widest, most fundamental, and most important operation by which the interests of men in groups are served."[2] Societal life consists chiefly in making folkways and applying them. Even the science of society might be defined as the study of folkways. Folkways are the product of the trial and failure method of meeting needs. They tend to become firmly established and to be passed on from generation to generation. They become traditional. They acquire all the authority which is attached to the memory of respected ancestors. Even the ghosts of ancestors stalk the earth keeping guard over the folkways. The folkways carry with them the conviction that they are essential to human welfare. It is this conviction which gives them the force of *mores*. Thus the folkways are not purposeful methods of securing progress but unconscious ways of meeting current exigencies; they are blindly and rigorously forced upon successive generations.

8. Races are guilty of ethnocentrism.[8] Each race considers itself the center of mankind. It judges all other races by its own standards, and not by a higher standard that is determined by data that are representative of the best interests of all races. Ethocentrism compels each race to exaggerate the importance of its own folkways and to depreciate the folkways of other races. For example, the Romans and Greeks called all outsiders "barbarians." The Jews considered themselves "the chosen people," and the Romans and Greeks as "pagans."

9. Sumner divided the chief motives of human action into four classes: Hunger, sex passion, vanity, and fear (of ghosts and spirits). Behind each of these motives there is a set of interests. (1) Hunger led primitive man to invent simple weapons and tools, such as arrows and hoes, and then to produce and hoard more complex forms of wealth. A strange peculiarity of wealth is its effect on its creator; it seems to be stronger than

its creator. It often bears him down to a slavish, materialistic, and even selfish existence. Labor in the struggle for existence is irksome and painful. Wealth and labor, however, are both commendatory when they are used to increase human welfare. In this statement Sumner overlooked the fact that wealth in order to be commendable must also be produced under constructively social conditions, and that labor in order to be praiseworthy must in its exercise be individually helpful. In other words, Sumner's test of the use to which wealth and labor are put is incomplete.

Sumner gave a new meaning to the term, slavery. He held that "men of talent are constantly forced to serve the rest. They make the discoveries and inventions, order the battles, write the books, and produce the art."[4] Sumner deplored the tendency to call whatever one does not like by the name of slavery. He felt that marriage slavery, rent slavery, sin slavery are terms which are coined by a too easily disgruntled people.

(2) The sex passion leads to sex *mores* which cover the relations of men and women to each other before marriage and in marriage, and the obligations of married persons to society. The sex *mores* determine the nature of marriage and of divorce. Sumner derided sex equality. Man has a more stable nervous system than woman, is more self-absorbed, more egoistic, less tactful. Since man has greater physical strength than woman,

woman was educated by circumstances in primitive days to adapt herself to the stronger sex, and to win by developing charms where her lack of comparative strength rendered her helpless. Resignation and endurance thus became acquired traits of women.

Neither renunciation nor license is the proper method of control of the sex passions. Both produce unnecessary agony. License, for example, "stimulates desire without limit, and ends in impotent agony." Sumner advocated temperance and regulation—a regulation which comes from knowledge and judgment.

Women by necessity must bear an unequal share in the responsibilities of sex and reproduction. Likewise, men must bear an unequal share of the responsibilities of property, war, and politics. For the latter types of duties women are hampered by a delicately adjusted and cumbersome generative system which men do not possess.[5]

Formerly women yielded to the will of men. Today, the marital state is one of endless discussion, a defeat for one party or the other, with unpleasant effects upon life and character. In ancient times women took pride in the supervision which their husbands exercised over them and valued themthemselves as hidden treasures.[6] This protected position was considered aristocratic. Under polygamy, women looked with pity and disgust upon the man who cannot, or is unwilling to, support more than one wife.

At this point it is interesting to note that W. I. Thomas has distinguished between the sexes on the basis of differences in metabolism—men being katabolic and women anabolic. Man consumes more energy than woman.[7] He is better fitted for bursts of energy, while woman possesses more endurance. Man's structural variability is toward motion; woman's, toward reproduction. Hence man seems to have been assigned in primitive society to tasks requiring violence and exertion, whereas to women fell the work requiring constant attention.

Civilization thus far has largely profited by the intelligence of man. If to this situation it will develop and add the intelligence of women, it will be supplanted by a higher type of civilization. Under these conditions a large percentage of marriages will represent "the true comradeship of like minds," instead of being frequently, as now, an arrangement in which woman is treated as a pet.

(3) The motive of vanity is all-powerful. "One likes to be separated from the crowd by what is admired, and dislikes to be distinguished for what is not admired."[8] To satisfy vanity, barbarian mothers "deform their babies toward an adopted type of bodily perfection." Aristocracies grow up out of appeals to vanity. An aristocracy is a group of persons closely united who define the possession of things for which they are admired and which the masses do not possess. Vanity leads to all types

of absurdities and indecencies in dress. Teeth are knocked out for the sake of appeasing vanity. An Indian woman puts a board on the forehead of her baby to make the forehead recede.

(4) Fear as a motive rules the lives of primitives. Fear of ghosts and spirits is peculiarly enslaving. Pestilence, defeat in war, bodily pain were all considered the result of the wrath of the gods.

The mass phenomena of fear are especially pitiful. Manias of various types rule whole masses. Witchcraft thrived for centuries on the strength of fear. Pilgrimages and crusades were partly due to fear; demonism was a product of fear. When fear became firmly established in the folkways, it acted as an ever-ruling tyrant. In the *mores* it became firmly entrenched and was a leading factor in moulding character. Through religious practices and dogmas it defined a "hell" and ruled with a fearful hand.

10. Upon simplest analyses, according to Sumner, four societal values stand out with clearness: intellectual, moral, economic, and physical.[9] Each of these, however, is composite. The highest societal value seems to result from a harmonious combination of the four values enumerated. The best member of society is he in whom the intellectual, moral, economic, and physical values are more or less equally and harmoniously represented.

11. Sumner divided society into five main classes.[10] (1) The masses represent social medi-

ocrity. They are of average social usefulness. (2) Then there are the dependent and defective classes —a drag upon society but not harmful or vicious. (3) The delinquent classes are grossly harmful. They are anti-social and a grievous burden. (4) Above the masses there are the people of talent, and (5) above the talented are the geniuses. "A man of talent, practical sense, industry, perseverance, and moral principle is worth more to society than a genius who is not morally responsible, or not industrious."[11]

It is a mistake to think of the masses as being at the base of society; they are located at the core. They are traditional, conservative, and the bearers of the *mores*. The lowest sections of the masses are a dead weight of ignorance, disease, and crime.

12. A social institution is composed of an idea, notion, or interest, and a resultant structure. The primary institutions are property, marriage, and religion.[12] These began as folkways; they became customs. Social institutions can be modified only when the *mores* are changed; they develop rituals, which are ceremonious, solemn, and strongest when perfunctory and when exciting no thought.[13]

Sumner boldly asserted that nothing but might has ever made right, and that nothing but might makes right now.[14] The fact that property began in force is not proof that property is an unjust institution. Marriage and religion also began in force, but the element of justice in the existence of these institutions is not seriously questioned today. Sumner, however, did not discriminate between force as an agent or a tool, and force as a primary cause. He did not distinguish clearly between hate and love as the dynamic factors behind action that is decisive. He did not set forth the distinction between harsh, material, immutable force and a kindly, spiritual, attracting love.

13. The persistency of folkways and *mores* is illustrated in a thousand ways by Sumner. He described (1) their slow variability under changed life conditions, (2) their sudden variability under revolutionary conditions, (3) the possibility of changing them by intelligent action, (4) the problems involved in adjusting one's self to the *mores* of another group, (5) the conflicts between the *mores* of different groups.[15]

The *mores* are powerful engines of societal selection. The most important fact about the *mores* is the power which they exert over the individual. He does not know their source. He is born into them. He accepts them in his early years uncritically. His habits and character are moulded by them. If in adult life he challenges them, he is ostracized by his group, labeled unpatriotic, and even trodden under foot.[16] The *mores* develop powerful watchwords, slogans, and even epithets of contempt and disapproval which only the most independent and courageous individuals dare to face.

14. Ideals are entirely unscientific, declared

Sumner.[17] They are phantasies little connected with fact. They are often formed to pacify the restless, or to escape settling a question justly in the present. The "poor" are told to look to the next life for their rewards. The radicals are urged to accept the Christian virtues of meekness and lowliness. Ideals are useful, chiefly, in homiletics, in self-education *via* auto-suggestion, in satisfying vanity, in marriage. In these observations, Sumner undoubtedly pointed out genuine weaknesses in ideals. He underestimated the psychological fact that they spring from the very real affective phases of consciousness, and that they can be projected rationally. He was right, however, in deploring the chasm which exists between ideals and practices, and in showing how ideals may become encysted in literature although not in the *mores*. "The Greeks proved that people could sink very low while talking very nobly."

Immorality is conduct contrary to the *mores* of the time and place.[18] Chastity is conformity to the current taboo on the sex relation. "Modesty is reserve of behavior and sentiment." Even "nakedness is never shameful when it is unconscious," that is, when there is no consciousness of a difference between fact and the rule set by the *mores*.

Sumner deduced an important principle when he asserted that the "*mores* can make anything right." The *mores* give usages a certain order and form, and cover them with a protecting mantle of propriety. The sanction of the *mores* is utilized by the class in power in order to maintain the established régime, even though it be one of injustice.

Sumner decried the importance which is ordinarily attached to book learning,[19] because it is addressed to the intellect rather than to the feelings which are the springs of action. The real education is that which comes through personal influence and example. It is derived from "the habits and atmosphere of a school, not from the school text-books."

15. Despite Sumner's failure to appreciate the significance of a thoroughgoing psychological approach to an analysis of folkways, his description of these societal phenomena constitutes a unique and valuable contribution to social thought. Sumner's rigorous attitude toward social life did not permit him to enter into an extensive interpretation of the folkways in the light of folk ideals. He dealt with what *is* to the exclusion of what *ought to be.* He saw the past so clearly, and the present so much as a reflection of the past, that no enheartening forward look was possible. He rested his theories on the inexorable work of the laws of biological evolution, modified chiefly by his belief in a strong individualism.

Sumner's fundamental theses have been developed and modified by A. G. Kellor. Professor Kellor has projected the Darwinian principles of variation, selection, transmission, and adaptation into societal concepts. In fact, he has done this so well that he has given the Darwinian principles full sway, not allowing sufficiently for the rise and operation of complex psychic principles. He has made the folkways the connecting link between organic and societal evolution, but has not noted fully the new, countless, and often intangible but powerful factors by which societal evolution is characterized.

16. The rôle that concepts of conduct have played in the evolution of society, has been analyzed by E. A. Westermarck and L. T. Hobhouse. The former is usually known as an anthropologist, and the latter as a sociologist. Professor Westermarck has shown that, strictly speaking, a custom is not merely the habit of a certain group of people; it also involves a rule of conduct.[21] It possesses two characteristics—habitualness and obligatoriness.

Not every public habit, however, is a custom, involving an obligation.[22] There may be certain practices which are more or less common in society, but which at the same time are generally condemned. The disapproval of these is as a rule not very deep or genuine.

Dr. Westermarck has indicated that there is a close similarity between the conscience of a community and of an individual.[23] If a group commits a sin twice, it is likely to be considered allowable. In order to get at the real nature of societal life, the "bad habits" as well as the professed opinions of groups must be examined.

"Society," says Dr. Westermarck, "is the birthplace of the moral consciousness."[24] Emotions which are felt by the community at large tend to take the form of conduct standards. The moral emotions lead to a variety of moral concepts. These fall into two main classes: concepts of disapproval, such as the concepts, bad, vice, wrong; and concepts of approval, such as good, virtue, and merit.

Professor Westermarck is convinced of the tremendous influence that religious beliefs have exerted upon the moral ideas of mankind.[25] This influence has been exceedingly varied. Religion has taught the principles of love and yet has indulged in cruel persecutions. It has condemned murder and yet been a party to child sacrifice. "It has emphasized the duty of truth-speaking, and has itself been a cause of pious fraud." Professor Westermarck has contributed to social thought not only in his valuable descriptions of the rise and evolution of moral ideas, but also in his *History of Human Marriage,* to which reference will be made in Chapter XXIV.

The writings of L. T. Hobhouse reveal a thorough, comparative study of the conduct rules of mankind. Professor Hobhouse has described the evolution of ethical consciousness as displayed in the habits, customs, and principles that have arisen in human history for the regulation of human conduct. He has shown how, in the lowest forms of the organic world, behavior is regulated, and directed to some purpose.[27] This behavior is somewhat definitely determined by the structure of the organism itself.[28]

There are three forces which may be called social, or which tend to keep society together. These social bonds are: (1) the principle of kinship, (2) the principle of authority, and (3) the principle of citizenship.[29] Kinship is the moving force in primitive society. The principle of authority becomes prominent when one tribe captures and enslaves a weaker group. This principle is also invoked in order to secure an integration of openly diverse attitudes within the group, even of modern national groups. It is exemplified in the various forms of absolutism in government. The principle of citizenship finds expression when certain individuals within the group are delegated to perform as servants and ministers of the public as a whole.[30] Personal rights and the common good are the two reigning ideals. Every individual is recognized as having a right to the conditions requisite for the full development of his social personality. The good in life consists "in the bringing out into full bloom of those capacities of each individual which help to maintain the common life."[31] The third principle, that of citizenship, when carried to its conclusion reveals the possibility of a world state.[32]

It is the contention of Professor Hobhouse that there is a close connection between the growth of law and justice and the prevalent forms of social organization. Organized law has developed out of a sense of community responsibility, which, however, has expressed itself as a rule in crude ways, and without distinguishing between accident and design. This sense of community responsibility in primitive groups tends to hold in check the spirit of anarchy and of self-redress. Sooner or later, the method of community self-redress yields to the authority of a chief or of a council representing the whole community.[33] Ultimately the community develops a special social organ for adjusting disputes and preventing crime. It is then that the ethical idea becomes separated from the conflicting passions of the collectivity. Thus, the foundations are laid for true judicial inquiry by evidence and genuine proof, and for a system of scientific public justice.

17. In applying the principles of folk psychology to the anthropologic field, William Wundt has developed a new method and new theories. Folk psychology is the study of "the relations which the intellectual, moral, and other mental characteristics of peoples sustain to one another."[34] The term was originated by Lazarus and Steinthal, whose works will be referred to again in Chapter XXII. In the masterpiece on the *Elements of Folk Psychology,* Wundt has given a psychological description of the main processes and institutions in society, tracing them from their beginnings in

the processes of nature; he has made a survey of human progress. His study opens with a discussion of the processes which produced the digging stick, the club, and the hammer; it ends with an analysis of world empire, world culture, world religions, and world history. The intervening ages are the totemic and the age of heroes and gods.

World empire affected primarily the material aspects of the life of peoples. It led to world intercourse, which in turn multiplied the needs of peoples. These multiplied needs were followed by exchanges of the means of satisfying the needs. The external and material phases of culture are survived by the spiritual phases—thus world culture is a sequence of world empire. It may be said that the vicissitudes of peoples under the rule of the world empire idea brings forth a unified history. World culture in turn creates a common mental heritage for mankind.[36]

In the establishment of a world culture, world religions are the leading forces. They have been foremost in creating the idea of a universal human community. In particular, Christianity is based on a belief in a God who makes no distinction between race or class or occupation. Consequently, "it has regarded missionary activity among heathen peoples as a task whose purpose it is finally to unite the whole of mankind beneath the cross of Christ."[37]

For a long time in human history, religious development was considered to be the main connecting link—such was the contention of St. Augustine. In 1725, Vico argued that the development of language and jurisprudence is of universal import.[38] Finally, world history has become an account of the mental life of peoples—"a psychological account of the development of mankind."

18. The work of Professor Wundt is similar in many ways, although characterized by a distinctive starting point and by many differences, to the contributions of Franz Boas and W. I. Thomas. Professor Boas has declared his belief in man's ability to dominate the laws of organic evolution as expressed in human life. He has brought forward a large amount of evidence in support of the theory that environment has caused differences between races. He has pointed out that race prejudice is largely a product of social environment, and that under changed conditions of life it has little place in the world. Boas is a strong advocate of the theory, already advanced in this chapter, that all races are potentially equal in ability, and that they would demonstrate the truth of this statement, if given a common cultural background and social opportunities. He has advanced the idea that "the organization of mind is practically identical among all races of men."[39]

Professor Boas has amassed considerable evidence to show that in the matter of inhibition of impulses, of power of attention, of ability to do original thinking, primitive man compares favorably with civilized man. Inasmuch as the social environment is powerful and education is effective in making over social environments, education can raise all races to the same high level, and at the same time unify them upon the same knowledge bases. This contention is similar to the position that Professor Hobhouse has made clear, namely: "While race has been relatively stagnant, society has rapidly developed." Moreover, social progress is determined not by alterations or racial type, but by modifications of social cultures.[40] These modifications are caused primarily by the interactions of social causes.

19. Noteworthy pioneering in the field of social anthropology and social origins has been done by W. I. Thomas. He has developed the theory that progress results from "crises."[41] As long as life runs along smoothly, a lack of interest is likely to ensue. The result is ennui. But a crisis in any of the life processes arouses the attention, that is, produces a concentration of psychic energy. A disturbance of any habit is a crisis. When the exigences of the crisis are solved through a focalization of consciousness, the situation is said to be controlled by the individual, who again lapses into a state of disinterestedness until another disturbance of habit occurs. The new method of control will be imitated. If imitated widely, it will mark a rise in the level of civilization.

It will be observed at once that the power of attention to meet crises is largely an individual matter and that the rôle of the individual is very important. The group level of culture limits the power of the mind to meet crises and to make adjustments.[42] The mind is limited by the psychic fund which the group already possesses. If there is no knowledge of mathematics in the group, then a large banking system is impossible. Crises, attention, control—these are the three leading concepts in Thomas' theory of social origins.

Control is the object of all purposeful activity.[43] It is the end, and attention is the means. An animal differs from a plant in that it has a superior control over a larger environment than does the plant. "It does not wait for food, but goes after it." Man differs from an animal partly in the fact that his fore limbs are free to secure new and varied forms of control. Moreover, man through his mind has a superior instrument of control. By the use of knowledge, mind is effective in controlling factors that are present in neither time nor space. Through its inventions, such as language, religious creeds, mechanical appliances, forms of government, man has risen to a high level of civilization.

Thomas has analyzed the social process in terms of social attitude and social values. An attitude is a process of individual consciousness that determines "the real or possible activity of the individual in the social world."[45] A social value, on the other hand, is any datum that has an empirical content accessible to the members of a social group and a meaning which may make it an object of activity. Activity is thus the bond between a social attitude and a social value. The value is the meaning which a material or spiritual datum may have. An attitude is a real or implied going out after value. Social psychology is the science of social attitudes. At this point anthropologic social thought has merged into social psychology.

Until twenty-five years ago, anthropology interpreted societary origins pretty largely in terms of the individual. With the use of a social psychology such as Cooley represents, "anthropology has given more accurate explanations and become essentially a social anthropology."

Before we discuss the different phases of psycho-sociologic thought, it will be well to make clear the recent advances that have been made in the biologic phases of social thought. The center of attention in this field is the relation of the laws of heredity to human progress, which constitutes the problem in eugenics. A discussion of eugenic social thought will bring forward in a scientific way the chief elements of an intellectual situation that was left, in Chapter XVI, in the unsatisfactory Spencerian formulae. A presentation of eugenic social thought will give a valuable background to the discussion which follows concerning psycho-sociologic thought.

Chapter XIX

Eugenic Sociology

Eugenic social thought is the child of biological discoveries. Eugenics, the science of good breeding, which did not achieve scientific standing until the closing years of the last century, may be traced back in its incipient forms to Plato, who advocated that strength should mate only with strength, and that imperfect children should be eliminated from society. In its scientific origins eugenics dates from 1859, when Darwin's *Origin of Species* was first published. Its beginning as a distinct field of human thinking is found in the articles by Francis Galton on "Hereditary Talent and Genius," which appeared in 1865; and in 1869, in book form under the title, *Hereditary Genius*.[1]

Eugenic social thought deals with the operation of the laws of heredity in society. It was a part of this field which Francis Galton made world-known by his treatises on *Hereditary Genius* and *Inquiries into the Human Faculty*.[2] In 1904, Galton wrote a paper entitled: "Eugenics; Its Definition, Scope and Aims." In this dissertation the new science of eugenics was formally introduced to the world. Galton's analysis of eugenics became its leading interpretation.[3]

The mantle of the founder fell upon Professor Karl Pearson, whose work at times has assumed a distinctly statistical nature. Professor Pearson's leaning toward biometry has brought severe criticism upon him. The statistical approach, while exact and thought-provoking, is subject to various errors in interpretation of data. The viewpoint from which Professor Pearson writes, however, is not one-sided. For example, he states that "it may require years to replace a great leader of man, but a stable and efficient society can only be the outcome of centuries of development."[4] He holds that group conscience ought for the sake of social welfare to be stronger than private interest, and that the ideal citizen should be able to form a judgment free from personal bias.[5]

C. W. Saleeby, another English writer, has developed an independent reputation as a eugenist.[6] In the United States, such men as C. B. Davenport[7] and Paul Popenoe have made important eugenic contributions. The recent tendency has been to be wary of purely statistical studies of heredity and to rely more definitely upon case studies. However, since eugenics is directly indebted to the studies of heredity and since heredity must be investigated for several generations, eugenic social thought has not yet developed far.

Galton defined eugenics as the science of good breeding. Its aim as a pure science is to study the agencies under social control "that may improve or impair the racial qualities of future generations, either physically or mentally." Galton's program, as outlined by the founder shortly before his death, insisted upon (1) a study of the laws of heredity, (2) a dissemination of knowledge about heredity, (3) a study of the factors underlying marriage, (4) a study of birth rates, and (5) a case study of individual families.

Eugenic social thought holds that heredity among human beings operates according to the same laws that govern heredity among animals. The theory of Mendelian units becomes in practice the theory of multiple factors. The unit characters, upon analysis, appear to be complex and to be inherited in complex ways. Multiple factors are inherited from generation to generation directly when pure factors are united with pure factors. But when the pure is united with the hybrid, then the laws of dominance and recessiveness operate. In such combinations certain factors tend to express themselves in greater proportion than do other elements. This failure to secure expression in a given generation, however, means that the specific factor is recessive for the time being. Later, it will likely appear.

Galton stated another important eugenic law, the law of regression. Each peculiarity is inherited by the offspring on the average in a slightly less degree than it is found in the parent. Hence, according to Galton, good traits and poor traits alike are inherited in a degree nearer mediocrity by the offspring than by the parents. This law partially explains why gifted men rarely have sons who are equally gifted. The law seems to hold good for large numbers, but not when considered in relation to single families. It serves as a check upon variation and mutation.

Galton and Pearson advanced another statistical law, the law of ancestral inheritance. Galton supposed that the parents contribute to the child one-half of his inherited factors, the grandparents one-fourth, and so on. Pearson has secured statistical evidence which shows that Galton's geometric series is incorrect, and that on the average in a large number of cases the parents together contribute to the child .624 of his traits; the four grandparents, .198; the eight great grandparents, .063; and so on.

The law of mutation, described by de Vries and other geneticists, refers to the appearance of mutants, or individuals who do not reproduce to form but represent a new line of heredity. In this way the appearance of genius may often be accounted for. However, the factors which explain the appearance of mutants have not yet been analyzed.

Another fundamental genetic consideration is the law of selection. If individuals with worthy traits mate only with individuals who possess worthy traits, a superior stock will be produced. This tendency is very important, since it points the way to a potent method of securing social progress.

Eugenic social thought has been developed in part on the basis of the Weismann theory of no or slight transmission of acquired traits. The germ-plasm is transmitted from individual to offspring in a direct line of descent. Injuries to the parent rarely change the nature of the germ-plasm. Only extreme malnutrition or excessive use of alcohol apparently exerts a definite influence on the germ cells. Nature has thus made provision for the protection of germ-plasm, whether strong or defective. Society, then, may encourage the mating of individuals who possess strong physical and mental traits, and discourages the mating of individuals who are defective—thus securing its own positive improvement.

Eugenic social thought follows two courses. Restrictive eugenics advocates the segregation of the so-called dysgenic classes, such as the feebleminded, the insane, and the grossly defective criminal. Public opinion reacts against sterilization; injustice that cannot be remedied may be done through the use of sterilization. Segregation by sexes, while involving expense, is a satisfactory eugenic method of safeguarding society against the reproduction of dysgenic persons.

The other trend of eugenic thought supports the raising of the standards of choice in mating. Constructive eugenics, as distinguished from restrictive eugenics, urges a program of education whereby young people will habitually rate one another by physical and mental standards rather than by wealth and class standards.

Eugenics disapproves of random mating. It favors assortative mating, because, for example, the "marriage of representatives of two long-lived strains ensures that the offspring will inherit more longevity than does the ordinary man."[9] Eugenics thus stresses the importance of teaching young people eugenic ideas, and of training them to be guided by these ideals rather than by caprice and passion.[10] Eugenic ideals include health, paternity and maternity, and pleasing disposition. Education and character are secondary eugenic ideals of importance.

A study of the birth rate shows that the inferior stocks and classes of individuals produce many more children than do the superior groups. Many cultured people do not marry, or if they marry they keep the birth rate very low. As a result, the racial character of a whole people may change within a few generations. The superior strains may be lost and the inferior furnish the entire population.

The low birth rate of the superior stocks is due to several fatcors: (1) The lengthening period of education and of professional training calls for the postponement of marriage. (2) The desire to give children the best advantages limits the birth rate. (3) The increasing spirit of independence on the part of women causes a postponement of marriage and a limitation of the number of children. These and other causes have produced a differential birth rate in favor of the inferior strains. Eugenic thought urges that the differential be reversed in favor of the superior strains. This conclusion implies that the dysgenic classes must be prevented from producing children, that the poor must be raised to higher educational and economic levels and taught to limit the birth rate, and that the eugenically superior be taught to increase the birth rate.

Eugenics pronounces war to be both dysgenic and eugenic.[11] (1) It is dysgenic in that the bravest and the physically best are killed first. In the case of a long war only the weakest men physically and mentally are left alive to propagate the race. (2) War is dysgenic in that it produces a large number of hurried marriages. Rational choices of mates are supplanted by sudden emotional reactions. (3) War is dysgenic in that sex immorality greatly increases. Prostitution flourishes in the neighborhood of military encampments, unless rigid means of control are established. (4) Again, the dysgenic effect of war is seen in the period of sociomental unrest which always follows war, and which among other things undermines rational sexual selection.

The chief eugenic effect of war is manifested during the period of training. This preparation period accents the importance of a strong physique and health measures. An insipid, stoop-shouldered population of city young men may be transformed into an army of fit soldiers. However, the conclusions are obvious that the dysgenic effects of war are far more potent than the eugenic gains, and that the eugenic advantages may be acquired in other ways than by promulgating war.

Eugenics looks askance at the feminism movement. Feminism once meant the development of the womanly traits of the sex. It now refers to the elimination as far as possible of sex differences. It would make women as nearly as possible like men. Eugenics objects to this trend, since it underestimates the importance of the fact that women physically are built to be mothers. To the extent that women enter into all the occupations, they will become men-like; and their efficiency as mothers of the race will decrease, and the race will suffer.

The economic equality of the sexes is a satisfactory doctrine to the eugenist if the doctrine is extended to make motherhood a salaried occupation, like mill work or stenography.[12] "Child-bearing should be recognized as being as worthy of remuneration as any occupation which men enter, and should be paid for (by the state) on the same basis."[13]

Eugenics would throw every possible safeguard around motherhood, especially in the period immediately before and after the birth of the child. The mother, even the expectant mother, "is doing our business, indispensable and exacting business, and we must take care of her accordingly. She is not only a worker but the foremost of all workers."[14]

Eugenic thought as represented in the writings of C. W. Saleeby has denominated alcohol, venereal disease, and tuberculosis as "racial poisons." While there is some doubt regarding the eugenic effects of taking small amounts of alcohol into the human body, eugenists are agreed that alcohol, when taken in excess quantities, affects the germ-plasm and produces a neurotic taint. It appears that alcoholism may be a cause in producing defective children. The verdicts of hygiene and economics that alcoholism is injurious to the race is supported by eugenics.

Venereal disease, another so-called racial poison, produces toxins which apparently affect the germ-plasm indirectly if not directly. It lowers the physical and moral tone and causes unfavorable racial tendencies. Venereal disease tends to destroy the generative organs and to cut off the birth rate entirely. It is a result of sex immorality which in itself tends to produce children under such abnormal conditions of vice that it becomes an anti-social, if not a dysgenic factor, in society. To the extent of course, that venereal disease kills off the racially useless, it may be considered eugenic.[15] Such a point of view, however, fails to rate properly the invasions which venereal disease is continually making upon normal and superior types of germ-plasm.

Tuberculosis weakens the membranous tissues

and probably leads in a few generations to an unusual degree of susceptibility to the invasion of tubercle bacilli. It is still a question, however, to what extent tuberculosis may be counted a racial poison. Professor Hobhouse has argued that, by the development of scientific hygiene, it will be possible to center attention not upon eliminating a tubercular stock but upon eliminating the tubercle bacilli.[16]

In regard to race questions the social anthropologist and the eugenist represent different poles of thought. As was indicated in the preceding chapter, the social anthropologists, such as Boas and Thomas, support the theory of potential race equality. The eugenist, on the other hand, contends that there are inherently superior and inferior racial stocks, and that the marriages of representatives of inferior stocks with representatives of superior stocks will produce children of a stock distinctly lower than that of the superior stocks. The eugenists in the United States hold that the immigration of the southern and eastern peoples of Europe will not only supplant through a higher birth rate the native stock of Nordic origin but, where marriages between natives and southern and eastern European immigrants occur, it will lower the racial quality of the population. While eugenic thought in this matter deserves a complete and respectful hearing, it must be considered along with the findings of social anthropology.

Eugenic thought opposes the miscegenation of

the Caucasian and African. The Negro, it is contended, is not only different from the Caucasian but as a rule is eugenically inferior, judged by the achievements of the Negro. Moreover, the eugenist interprets the anthropological tests to show that the innate ability of a colored man "is proportionate to the amount of white blood he has." The conclusion of eugenics is that "in general the white race loses and the Negro gains from miscegenation,"[17]—as far as the germinal natures of the two races are concerned. The eugenist would forbid all intermarriage between the races, and urge that the taboo against sexual intercourse between the races be extended.

In the light of eugenic thought genealogy may become scientific, in fact, it may become a valuable source of scientific materials for eugenics. Heretofore genealogy has been the concern of a few leisure-class people, who have taken pleasure and pride in recounting the fact that some one of a possible thousand or more ancestors several generations back was distinguished in some way or other, and who would have friends or the public believe that they inherited from this ancestor of note the characteristics which made him great. Eugenics points out a nobler purpose to which genealogy may be put. It urges that mental and physical traits of every individual in all families be carefully analyzed and accurately and systematically recorded. In this way it will be possible in a generation to have available a large amount of eugenic materials, and in a few generations a reliable body of data for studying racial heredity.

The debate regarding the comparative influences of nature and nurture has been long and bitter. It may be said here that both heredity and environment are more or less equally essential in the development of human personality. Without inherited factors in the individual the environment has nothing upon which to work. Without a stimulating environment the inherited traits will remain dormant. Each human being has inherited factors which, if played upon by certain environmental factors, may lead the individual to try to wreck society or himself or both. Every person, also, has traits which, if stimulated by the proper environmental elements may cause him to develop into a useful member of society. While the environment cannot change the inherited potentialities very much, if any, it is a prime factor of vast importance in determining which inherited tendencies will never find expression, which will be expressed in modified ways, and which will reach full fruition. Eugenics insists with increasing force that educational programs shall provide that every child be not only well reared but also well born. A weakness in eugenic thought is that it implies that sound racial stock is sufficient to guarantee progress; it tends at times to overstress an aristocracy of racial stock. It sometimes detracts from the importance of character and moral discipline as essential elements in social progress.

Chapter XX

Conflict Theories in Sociology

The concept of social conflict has already been introduced to the reader. In the chapter on Individualistic Social Thought the prolonged struggle between individual rights and genuine social control was analyzed. Malthus described the conflict between population and the means of subsistence. Comte insisted that man is not naturally a social being. Hence this unsocial nature of mankind is a fruitful source of human conflict. Marx pictured the class struggle; and Darwin elaborated the doctrine of the survival of the fittest.

The slightest grasp of social thought reveals the fact that human association is characterized at times by deep-seated and subtle conflicts; and at other times by a fundamental co-operative spirit. Some sociological writers have seen only or chiefly the conflicts of life; others have sought out the co-operative activities; still others have tried to discover the relationships between conflict and co-operation in societal development. This chapter will deal with the concept of social conflict, while the next chapter will be centered on the ideal of social co-operation and upon the relationship of conflict to co-operation in group processes.

One of the outstanding believers in the theory that conflict dominates societal life was Ludwig Gumplowicz (1838-1910). His system of thought begins with the assertion that primitive hordes were the original units of society. Gumplowicz dissented from Herbert Spencer's belief in the individual as the original societary unit, although he accepted the determinism that is inherent in Spencer's theory of evolution. Gumplowicz also repudiated Comte's belief in social amelioration through prevision, but subscribed to Comte's positivism.

According to Gumplowicz, society began with a large number of primitive groups, which were self-sustaining and self-conscious units. Each one of these hordes was a warring group, possessing an instinctive hatred of all other hordes.[1] As these hordes increased in size, the general food supply failed to meet the needs. Consequently, inter-group struggle resulted and the members of the weaker hordes were either destroyed or enslaved. The existence of slaves led to situations of intra-group inequality, which in turn created problems involving justice and injustice.

As a result of continual conflicts between groups, there are frequent changes taking place in their personnel. The vanquished are continually being absorbed by victorious groups. In a given successful group two classes are at once established, namely, the victors and the vanquished. Classes are thus continually arising out of new juxtapositions of heterogeneous racial elements.[2]

It was in an intense form of group self-interest that Gumplowicz found the mainspring of social progress. This self-interest leads to an exaggerated group appraisement, a strong degree of group unity, a state of warfare between groups—and perhaps progress. Basic to this group self-interest, there are the material needs of the members of the group; the economic desires and the occupational interests; and the moral and spiritual tendencies. The group is bound together by various factors, such as a common social life, a common language, religion, and culture.

Gumplowicz advocated a theory of potential race equality. He argued against innate racial superiority and racial inferiority. He doubted the existence of any pure races. Each race is a compound of other races, and hence races are potentially similar in fundamental respects. National progress, therefore, holds no connection with race purity.

Gumplowicz minimized the importance of the individual. Society rules. Centuries of traditions dominate. The thoughts of the individual are almost, if not entirely, a mere reflection of the social environment. The group develops group pride or group disloyalty in the minds of its members. The distinguished leader is largely the man who expresses the will of the group during the group crisis. Gumplowicz makes only a brief reference to the process of interaction between the individual and the group.[8] An underlying theory of natural determinism vitiates much of Gumplowicz's ideas concerning the individual.

Inasmuch as society, like individuals, passes through a cycle of growth and decay, subject to unchangeable natural and societary laws, there is no justification for individual interference with social processes. In fact, this theory led Gumplowicz into pessimistic conclusions concerning life. He failed to see that societal life is not necessarily a series of hopeless cyclical conflicts, and that social processes are becoming increasingly subject to human control—for good or ill. He did not appreciate the fact that groups are not subject to laws of cyclical growth and decay after the manner of individuals. Hence, his conflict theory of societal life ended in confusion and pessimism.

A reference was made in Chapter XI to the theories of Friedrich Nietzsche (1844-1900). This German philosopher developed the idea of social conflict, basing it on the concept of the "will to power." Leaders desire power. They enjoy to exercise power and they thrive under that exercise. Jealousy of the leaders arises. The weaker members of society join together against the possessors of power. They develop a will to power, but of a weaker type than that of the leaders. Conflicts ensue between the will to power of the superior and the will to power of the inferior.

The superior and the inferior types each possess a distinctive code of morality.[4] The supermen develop a harsh and rigorous attitude toward themselves and others. They gird and prepare themselves for the crises of life. They strive to augment their power. They become self-contained. They take pride in crushing weakness and in deifying strength. Their morality stresses those factors in life which create power. They feel a condescending pity for the weak. They experience no sense of responsibility for the inferior classes. Since supermen are the supreme goal of nature, supermen feel that all persons and things should contribute to increasing the power of supermen.[5] It is a waste of energy for supermen to give their lives in behalf of inferior persons. They are interested only in the welfare of other supermen.

The morality of the inferior is of a type which furthers weakness. It accents sympathy. It emphasizes gregariousness. The inferior create a slavish, cringing, meek morality. They sacrifice themselves readily and humbly in behalf of others who may be inferior to themselves.

Nietzsche believed in a eugenics program. He declared that marriages should be arranged with a view to producing supermen. Nietzsche's deterministic view of natural evolution led him to believe, however, that equality of privileges is unattainable. He opposed democracy because its theory of equal opportunities contradicts the tendencies of nature. He was no socialist. He asserted that an aristocracy of power is the only true goal for society. He carried forward the ruthless biological laws of tooth and fang into his conception of the highest types of civilization.

Moreover, the superman is a biological mutant. He appears sporadically. At this point Nietzsche's inconsistency becomes obvious. For example, if geniuses appear sporadically and without reference to biological laws, why attempt to arrange marriages so as to produce supermen? To get himself out of the dilemma, Nietzsche postulated cyclical returns of supermen and lost his bearings in trying to interpret an endless circular movement in social evolution, endlessly repeating itself. In an applied form Nietzsche's philosophy has appeared in German political life, but to the defeat of Germany.

In starting points, Nietzsche and Gumplowicz were widely different. Nietzsche began with an apotheosis of the man of power and extolled the achievements of supermen. Gumplowicz had little place for the individual, even for the most powerful. Both sets of theories ended in a deterministic philosophy of individual and social despair.

An unusually fundamental delineation of social conflict has been advanced by Simon N. Patten in his *Theory of Social Forces*.[6] Human society is the product largely of a pain economy in which the requisites for survival are determined "by the enemies and pains to be avoided." In a like manner a pain morality and a pain religion develop. The purpose of the pain morality is "to keep persons from committing acts and putting themselves in situations which lead to destruction." The pain-religion, likewise, aims to invoke the aid of higher powers in the human conflict with enemies and death. The social forces in a pain economy have been builded up in the form of sets of ideals, instincts, and habits.

Society, however, is now in a transition stage—entering a pleasure economy. A large number of the sources of pain have been eliminated through the inventive and administrative phases of civilization. Dangerous beasts and reptiles, barbarous invasions, and superstitious interpretations are uncommon among the advanced human groups.

No nation, unfortunately, has been able to live under a pleasure economy. Its members have not built up sets of instincts, habits, and ideals that withstand the effects of a pleasure economy. Consequently, individuals and nations have fallen into lethargy, vice, and decay. The enemies in a pleasure economy are found within the individual; these are as yet unconquered under the allurements of a pleasure environment. In discussing the conflicts between these habits and ideals, Dr. Patten may err in implying that the race once was not in a pain economy and hence did not originally develop out of such an environment, but he nevertheless has analyzed an important societal fact in his pain-pleasure transition concept.

Another type of conflict theory of society is advanced by Thomas Nixon Carver. Professor Carver begins his analysis with a discussion of the conflict of human interests. Originally all conflicts were settled on the basis of might. But conflicts between persons who are beginning to think, sometimes lead one or each of the contending parties to a consideration of adjusting the conflict by other than physical strife. At this point the concept of justice begins to take form.

Justice, according to Dr. Carver, is "that system of adjusting conflicting interests which makes the group strong and progressive."[7] Virtue and strength are pronounced identical, and strength is defined "according to its ability to make itself universal."

Conflict arises out of scarcity. Where two men want the same thing, conflict ensues. It is this antagonism of interests which produces moral problems and furnishes a basis of determining justice and injustice. One reason for the lack of supply of things which people seek is that in society human wants are unduly expended. If wants could be kept low and production high, an adaptation of people to things would take place which would greatly lessen conflict.

Conflicts take place in three different fields: (1) between man and nature, (2) between man and man, and (3) between the different interests of the same man.[8] If there were no such conflicts, there would be no moral problems. The result would be paradise.

The institutions of property, the family, and the state have developed out of antagonism of interests, which in turn, as has been said, is the result of scarcity. If things were not scarce, no one would think of claiming property in anything. In a similar way the kinship group becomes desirous of possessing property and hence acquires unity. In asserting that *the* unifying principle in the family is an economic one, Dr. Carver espouses a theory of economic determinism. In fact, he holds that "the economic problem is the fundamental one, out of which all other social and moral problems have grown."[9]

Dr. Carver somewhat softens his rigorous social theories when he admits that there may be a few people in the world whose feeling of humanity is strong enough to overbalance an antagonism of interests and to lead them to treat the world as a normal individual treats his family.[10] A world of such people would make a world of communism. But such a world is unthinkable, because world-loving people are social aberrations. The individual whose altruism is such that he gladly gives his body to a tiger, is not helping to transform the world into a world of saints but into a world of tigers.[11] Extreme forms of benevolence and meekness constitute the very food upon which selfishness fattens.[12]

Professor Carver, therefore, points out two sources of conflict, namely, scarcity of desirable things and self-centered appreciation. These two bases of conflict are fundamentally natural and normal. Conflicts appear, however, in a great variety of forms. This classification of the methods of struggling for existence is fourfold.[18]

(1) There is a group of conflicts which are primarily destructive, such as war, robbery, dueling, sabotage, brawling. These conflicts are all crude, primitive, brutal. They represent man at his lowest ebb. They are militant in character, depending upon the individual's power to destroy, to harm, or to inflict pain and injury.[14]

(2) Deceptive conflicts are of an order slightly higher than the militant. They include thieving, swindling, adulteration of goods, false advertising. They imply a greater degree of intelligence than the purely destructive types of conflict.

(3) Another form of conflict is persuasive in character, for example, political, erotic, commercial, and legal conflicts. Political competition includes seeking governmental appointments, running for office, campaigning for a political party. Erotic conflicts are in the main different forms of courtship. Commercial persuasion utilizes the agencies of advertising and salesmanship. Legal conflicts include litigations in the courts. In all these illustrations the individual strives to further his own interests by his persuative ability. Oftentimes

resort is made to cheap persuasive methods, such as demagogy or political claptrap. Sometimes the persuasion falls to the level of deception and, occasionally, to destructive depths.

(4) The highest form of conflicts are the productive types. Some productive conflicts refer to rivalries in producing economic goods; others to rivalries in rendering service. In his *Essays in Social Justice,* Professor Carver discusses three forms of economic competition at length. Here he includes competitive production, competitive bargaining, and competitive consumption of economic goods. The second class has already been referred to as commercial persuasion. Competitive production increases the supply of economic goods and "always works well." Competitive consumption, however, "always works badly." It means "rivalry in display, in ostentation, in the effort to outshine or to outdress all one's neighbors, or at least not to be outshone or outdressed by them." It is usually deceptive; it has no productive features about it. It may even assume a form of waste and destruction. The highest type of conflict is friendly rivalry in rendering service to other people.

Professor Carver would have self-interest direct its efforts toward the welfare of the nation. Since neither law nor government can eliminate self-interest, the next best thing is to connect it with national well-being. Nearly all useful things that are done in a community are undertaken through self-interest.[15] Even co-operation is a form of competition.[16] The purpose of co-operation is to enable groups of individuals to compete more effectively against opposing groups.

Competition is not an evil in itself. The spirit which dominates competition is the important thing. Some people are motivated by the pig-trough philosophy, which emphasizes struggle for the sake of possession and consumption of goods. The work-bench philosophy accents "action and not possession, production and not consumption."

These theories, excellent in many particulars, apparently do not rate at full value the fact that education and love can and do modify the self-interest of the individual, and at the same time direct the attention of the individual toward unselfish service. In stressing service through achievement and production, they neglect to emphasize achievement through service. Competition in rendering unselfish service is underrated.

It was Novicow, the Russian sociologist, who laid bare the alleged benefits of war, showing that the gains which come from war may be obtained through other methods of social interaction.[17] Novicow argued forcefully that the real enemies of a group of people are disease germs and death, not the best people of other nationality groups. Novicow's vision enabled him to perceive the foolishnes of men who lock themselves together in destructive conflict, when the real enemies are microscopic disease bacteria and the gaunt black specter of death.

Conflict bulks large in the sociology of Edward A. Ross. Any interference with the carrying out of the individual's plans and with the satisfying of his interests creates opposition. The best characteristic of the phenomenon of opposition is that it awakens and stimulates.[18] Competition operates according to psychologic laws; for example, the intensity of competition varies according (1) to the degree of personal liberty, (2) to the rate of social change, and (3) inversely as the efficiency of the selective agents.[19]

One of the most important forms of competition is found in industrialism. The invention and adoption of the power-driven machine has created an industrialism which is moulding and transforming society in startling ways, and which is causing "its members more and more to cluster at opposite poles of the social spindle."[20] Professor Ross expresses slight hope that the ownership of industrial capital will be disseminated through the working class according to the conflict rules of the present economic system.

Other conflict theories will be presented in the following chapters; for example, the conflict theories of Gustav Ratzenhofer and Albion W. Small will be noted in the chapter on co-operation concepts, and Gabriel Tarde's analysis of conflict will be taken up in the discussion of psycho-sociological thought.

In general, the social conflict doctrines, when carried to the extreme, fail to recognize that conflict and co-operation are correlative social processes. Humanly speaking, one is as old as the other. Both spring from the deepest types of human needs. While the earliest types of associative life may have been characterized by a predominance of conflict, the highest stages are ruled by the co-operative spirit. This transition together with the leading co-operation theories of social progress will be taken up in the chapter which follows.

Suffice it to say here that conflict and competition are essential to social advance. They are both highly useful when operating in the fields of production and service.

CHAPTER XXI

CO-OPERATION THEORIES IN SOCIOLOGY

One of the first persons to work out a systematic interpretation of co-operation was Giovanni Vico (1668-1744), an Italian philosopher.[1] Vico rejected the social contract idea because he believed that it was a false interpretation of the true principle of co-operation. The concept of a social contract embodied an artificial and metaphysical notion of social life.

In his chief work, *Principles of a New Science Concerning the Common Nature of Nations,* Vico inaugurated a study of actual social phenomena. He sought to discover possible social laws. He attempted to cast aside the accidental social elements and to organize the regularities of social phenomena into laws. He searched for the laws governing the growth and decay of societies. He undertook to analyze the history of human society.

Although Vico's important treatise was not known outside of Italy until a century and a half after it was originally published, it contained a statement of the factor which is basic to any sound co-operation theory of social progress. Vico was one of the first writers to describe the principle that all human groups have a common nature. His comparative studies of human institutions everywhere, led him always to the belief in the common mind of mankind, a concept which in recent years has been ably elaborated by D. G. Brinton. For this contribution Vico has been called "the father of sociology."

According to Vico, the fundamental social movement is a gradual unfolding or evolution of social institutions in response to the common needs of people. Society owes its development in part to the reflections of the wise, as the social contract theorists have said, but also to the human feelings even of the brutish. This natural sociability of man has furnished the chief basis for the rise and development of the spirit of co-operation.

The natural sociability of human beings has led, more or less unconsciously on the part of man, to the establishment of necessary social relations and institutions. The purpose of social organization is to produce perfect human personalities. Vico outlined the evolutionary character of society according to the spiral theory, namely, that society does return upon itself but that, when it completes a cycle, it is upon a higher plane of co-operation than when the given cycle began. Vico also made religion a necessary principle of progress. Although in adjusting himself to the prevailing theological dogmas of his time, Vico committed serious scientific errors, he nevertheless is deserving of special credit for his emphasis upon the common nature and natural sociability of mankind.

Hugo Grotius (1583-1645), the celebrated Dutch scholar, gave to social thought the international concept. He advanced the idea of the coming co-operation among the nations—nations which in his time were moved primarily by jealousy and hatred in their relations with one another. Grotius was the originator of a definite set of principles and laws for international co-operation. His work in this regard accentuated the importance of like-mindedness in matters of international polity.

Spinoza, whose contributions regarding the concept of sovereignty have already been stated, declared that the instinct to acquire is naturally stronger than the tendency to share. Hence, man must be educated to perceive the advantages of co-operative living. When this appreciation occurs, when the advantages of co-operation become clear, then man will sublimate his egoistic and self-seeking desires to altruistic communal living. As man comes to understand, step by step, the values of co-operative conduct, he will overcome, degree by degree, his selfish impulses.

The references which were made in Chapter XIV to the work and writings of certain socialists, such as Robert Owen, form another link in this discussion of the development of the co-operation concept. While the experiments in consumers' co-operation, such as the activities of the Rochdale Pioneers, have had splendid success in many countries, they have demonstrated that they can flourish only in an environment where the co-operative spirit rules. While the experiments in producers' co-operation have often failed and have not yet as a class been successful, they have testified to the absence of a developed co-operative spirit rather than to the failure of the principle upon which they are based.

Peter Kropotkin, whose opposition to socialism was indicated in Chapter XIV, rendered a useful service in writing his *Mutual Aid; a Factor in Evolution.* Kropotkin, a loyal Darwinian, protested against the falsely labeled "social Darwinianism."[8] Kropotkin made plain that Darwin's interpretation of evolution, while stressing the struggle for existence, also pointed out that there is in evolution a powerful tide of co-operation. The logical conclusion of this treatment of evolution, according to Kropotkin, is not a phase of "social Darwinianism" with its emphasis upon a biological struggle in the highest human realms, but a world of human association in which the co-operative spirit has risen to a position of control over physical force and selfish desire.

Kropotkin studied animal life extensively and concluded that, although there was among animals a severe struggle against a heartless Nature, there was essentially no bitter struggle for existence "among animals belonging to the same species."[8] There is no pitiless inner war for life within this species, and moreover, this alleged war is not a condition of progress. War, declared Kropotkin, is not a condition of social progress.

Kropotkin considered the clan and the tribe rather than the individual or even the family the starting point of society. The tribe itself developed a morale on the basis of beliefs in its common origin and in the worship of common ancestors. Then the possession in common of certain lands served to arouse new tribal loyalties. These loyalties expressed themselves in the form of "con-jurations," sworn agreements, and ultimately in fraternities and guilds for mutual support. Kropotkin believed that primitive man was naturally peaceful, and that he fought from necessity rather than from ferocity.

In primitive communal organization the judge and military chief united for "mutual insurance of domination," drawing to their support the slavish loyalty of the witch-doctor or priest. In the twelfth century, however, the old communal spirit broke forth with "striking spontaneity all over Europe;" it stopped for a time the growth of the despotic monarchies of Europe; it produced endless numbers of communes.

The free cities developed under the shelter of communal liberties, and in them art and invention flourished, producing the beauty of Raphael, the vigor of Michaelangelo, the poetry of Dante, and "the discoveries which have been made by modern science,—the compass, the clock, the watch, printing, gunpowder, the maritime discoveries, the law of gravitation."[4]

Then, there came the modern State formed by a triple alliance of the military chief, the Roman judge, and the priest. The industrial revolution and the rise of capitalism furthered the interests of the military-legal-priestly triumvirate. When the State and Church were separated, the money baron took the place of the priest in the triumvirate. With the overthrow of militarism the power of the triumvirate is broken, and the old communal co-operative feelings of man again begin to express themselves. Kropotkin led the way in defining the law of co-operative individualism. He urged decentralization in social control, and attacked monopolies of all types, public as well as private. Although he exaggerated the rôle of mutual aid in primitive society, considering it the main social factor, he nevertheless rendered a valuable service in giving the world a vigorous presentation of a significant concept.

The social process was analyzed in terms of both conflict and co-operation by Gustav Ratzenhofer (1842-1904). It is characterized by a continuous reappearance of the phenomena of individualization of structures already extant.[5] Both differentiation and socialization arise out of the operation of human interests. Both are implicit in the nature of man. Certain human interests lead to individualization and some to communitization.

At this point we encounter Ratzenhofer's theory of force. Force and interest are made the two primordial principles. These two factors work together in order to secure for the individual the largest possible degree of self development.

The struggle of pre-primitive men against the harsh phases of nature established a pre-primitive sociality. Struggle has always led to co-operation in the interests of preservation. Similarly, war leads to co-operation. In primitive society institutions arose in response to community needs. Among barbarians the increase in numbers produced an increasing emphasis upon conflict, which was expressed in robberies, wars, and enslavements. Warfare led to the formation of classes and class conflicts. Class interests, as distinguished from individual interests, then began to secure definition. With the rise of capitalism, the interests of capital were asserted; and at once the interests of labor, in apposition, assumed tangible expression. A stage, however, of stable social conditions is coming, in which the whole world will be organized on the basis of a single system of economic and noncompeting production and of free international exchange.[6]

Throughout this analysis Ratzenhofer gives force a leading place.[7] He also develops a theory of a ruling aristocracy of supermen. Despite these unfortunate emphases, Ratzenhofer's contribution to social thought in his theory of interests as dominating human factors, and his accent upon the rise of an increasing degree of co-operation, is noteworthy.

Professor Albion Small, whose methodology will be indicated in Chapter XXVII, has modified, corrected, and refined Ratzenhofer's theory of interests. "In the beginning were interests," says Professor Small.[8] An "interest" is defined as an unsatisfied capacity, an unrealized condition of the organism, a tendency securing satisfaction of an unsatisfied capacity.[9] In its subjective phase an interest is a desire, and in its objective phase, a want. An interest is developed when the individual knows something, feels something, or wills something. Consequently, the whole individual or social process consists in developing, adjusting, and satisfying interests.

The six groups into which Professor Small divides all interests are as follows: (1) The health interest arises from the sheer interest in keeping alive. It is expressed in the food interest, the sex interest, the work interest and includes all the desires which find satisfaction in the exercise of the powers of the body. (2) The wealth interest is encompassed in the desire for mastery over things. (3) The sociability interest is represented at its best by the appetite for personal interchanges of stimulus of a purely spiritual nature. (4) The knowledge interest arises from the curiosity impulses. The limits of its possibilities are expressed in the terms, nescience and omniscience. (5) The beauty interest secures satisfaction through an appreciation of the symmetrical phases of material and spiritual phenomena. (6) The rightness interest traverses the gamut of all other interests. It results in enjoyment when it secures the sanction of the individual's ideal self or of his whole self.

Each of these interests tends to be absolute.[10] Each seeks satisfaction regardless of the others. In consequence, there is a universal conflict of interests. Moreover, there is a universal conjunction of interests. The conflict, however, is more spectacular than the conjunction. In the history of mankind this conflict has been the predominating relationship. The social process has resolved itself into a series of reactions between persons some of whose interests comport, but others of which conflict. Furthermore, the social process is a continual formation of groups and institutions around interests. It is a perpetual equating and adjusting of interests;[11] it is a rhythm of differentiations and integrations.

Professor Small points out that struggle and co-operation are always to a certain extent functions of each other.[12] Moreover, in the social process viewed historically, there is a movement "from a maximum toward a minimum of conflict, from a minimum toward a maximum of helpful reciprocity." The social process, thus, is a perpetual readjustment between the forces which "tend backward toward more struggle, and those that tend forward toward more socialization." By a minimum of conflict, Professor Small does not mean absence of conflict, for he recognizes that stagnation would result in a society in which conflict was eliminated. By a maximum of co-operation he does not refer to a state of complete social solidification, which in turn would mean stagnation and death.

The fundamental social problem is to give free scope to those interests which require the fullest rational development of all other interests. The social problem is to intellectualize all the interests, and moreover, to intellectualize the conflict of interests. Hence the fundamental conflict today is between the knowledge interest and all other interests.[13] Socialization, then, becomes the process of transforming conflict into co-operation.

Sociology may be said to be the study of human interests, together with their conflicts and reciprocities. It is an interpretation of human association in terms of the effective interests of man. It focalizes within one field of vision all human activities so that the persons who have the benefit of this outlook may rate their own activities in relation to the whole.

In a concrete, specific way Professor Small has presented his theory of the social process in the book, *Between Eras, From Capitalism to Democracy*. Here is a vivid picture of the conflict between labor and capital, with the resultant misunderstandings and injustices. A young lady, Hector, observes the essential activities of labor and capital, and as a representative of capital perceives the relationship which actually exists between herself and one of the working girls. She receives large dividends, for which she puts nothing into the productive activities of the corporation. The working girl is paid low wages, but is giving her life to the industrial concern from which Hector's liberal dividends are pouring forth. The main end of the discussion is an argument for the establishment of the principle of industrial democracy. Professor Small urges that the employees, *per se,* be given representation on boards of directors. While this representation at first will necessarily be a minority one, it will serve the useful purpose of providing for regular meetings of the representatives of the employees around the same council table. These council meetings will enable the representatives of either party in the bitter labor-capital conflict to become acquainted with the problems which the opposing group faces. In this interchange Professor Small sees the rise of a spirit of co-operation which will melt many of the difficulties that have sprung up in the controversy between capital and labor.[14] Although Dr. Small's *Between Eras* was published in 1913, the idea of industrial representation was not considered seriously in the United States until about 1918. The initial steps which have thus far been taken toward industrial representation in the management of business and in the determination of wages, hours, and conditions of labor, have produced noteworthy co-operative results and have fully justified Professor Small's prophetic recommendation for the solution of a world-disturbing social situation.

The primordial social group, according to Professor E. A. Ross, is a band of mothers and their children. In such groupings preliminary socialization took place. In earliest societies definite principles of human action made themselves evident.[15] Domination was one of the ruling principles. Note for example the domination (1) by parents over offspring, (2) by old over young, (3) by husband over wife, (4) by men over women, (5) by the military over the industrial classes, (6) by the wealthy over the poor. The chief purpose in dominating is to exploit, that is, to use other individuals as means to one's own ends.[16]

Socialization, or social adaptation, runs the gamut of toleration, compromise, accommodation, and amalgamation. The simplest form of co-operation is mutual aid, which, however, is more popular among the lower classes than among the higher. Socialization, it may be noted here, has been shown by E. W. Burgess to be the fundamental process in the determination of social progress.[17]

Organization of effort is a specific societal method, which has developed in society, for getting things done. Organization results (1) in the accomplishment of ends which are unattainable otherwise, (2) in arousing a common interest intermittently in all, (3) in dividing a task into its natural parts, (4) in securing a degree of expertness, (5) in producing a co-ordinated, intelligent plan, (6) in eliminating needless duplication of effort.[18] On the other hand, organization leads to wastes and abuses, which are: (1) overhead expenses; (2) undue time devoted to making out reports and similar routine work; (3) a loss in personal contacts; (4) a tendency to formalism and red tape; (5) an inflexibility of machinery; (6) a misapplication of power to personal ends; (7) too much specialization; (8) the organization becomes an end in itself.

Socialization, in content, is the development of a we-feeling in a number of persons, and "their growth in capacity and will to act together."[19] A very simple causal factor of this process is the age-long custom of giving a banquet, that is, in eating and drinking together. A consciousness of kind arises which, as Professor Ross believes, is not the perception of a general resemblance but "an awareness of likeness or agreement in specific matters."[20] Nationalism, or the process of creating a spirit of national patriotism, illustrates the meaning of the socialization concept.

The sociology of L. T. Hobhouse, discussed in part in Chapter XVIII, is largely an interpretation of society in terms of increasing co-operation. Professor Hobhouse has defined social progress as the development of the principle of union, order, co-operation, and harmony among individuals. He has described a certain mutual interest, similar to Giddings' consciousness of kind, which has served to keep individuals together, from the lowest groups of savages to the highest civilized groups.[21]

The social process, as Professor Cooley analyzes it, is not a series of futile repetitions or brutal and wasteful conflicts, but an eternal, onward growth which produces increasingly humane, rational, and co-operative beings. While the element of conflict is useful in that it awakens and directs human attention and thus leads to activity, it is limited by a superintending factor of co-operation and organization to which the contestants must adjust themselves if they would succeed.[22]

The discussions in this and the preceding chapter have shown that the natural trend of evolution is away from a pitiless competitive and destructive social process, and toward a tempered, productive, and co-operative process. Of course, there are reactionary movements from time to time which halt the co-operative trend. On the other hand, the development of reason gradually eliminates the more brutal effects of conflict. Conflict, however, will always remain, as far as can now be seen, an essential factor in the processes of individual and societal growth. Through rational controls, it will operate in the direction and interest of the co-operative spirit. In the old social order, hate and the spirit of conflict have ruled. The spirit of co-operation has often been utilized only for selfish purposes. In the coming social order love and the co-operative spirit will direct, while the spirit of conflict will play a vital but secondary rôle.

CHAPTER XXII

PSYCHO-SOCIOLOGIC THOUGHT

A large number of references have already been made to psycho-sociologic thought. In origin it may be traced to the primitive days of the race. The folkways reveal keen psycho-sociologic observations. Undoubtedly, many phases of the psychic nature of group activities were known to the leaders of ancient civilizations. Plato wrote on the importance of custom and custom imitation as a societal force. Aristotle understood the socio-psychic nature of man when he observed that property which is owned in common is least taken care of, and when he declared that a fundamental test of good government may be found in the attitude of a people toward public service. In his theory of social attitudes Aristotle made a distinct contribution to psycho-sociologic thought.

Thomas More analyzed the causes of human actions. He was a worthy social psychologist when he protested against heaping punishment upon human beings, without attempting to understand the causes of criminal conduct and without seeking to remove the societal causes of such conduct. Bodin postulated a theory of interests in his explanation of social evolution. He made the common economic, religious, and other interests of man the basis of social organization. These interests, according to Bodin, led primitive families to form a commonality of organization or government.

It was Hobbes who believed that man originally was a being of entirely selfish interests. Man's interest in others was based on their ability to cater to his own good. This theory still has strong support; there are large numbers of individuals who today apparently are living according to this rule. Nations oftentimes still seem to be motivated by no higher principle. On the basis of an introspective psychology, Hobbes made the scientific observation that "he that is going to be a whole man must read in himself—mankind." Such a person must not simply find in himself this or that man's interests, but the interests of all mankind.

George Berkeley (1685-1753), bishop of Cloyne and eminent philosopher, in his *Principles of Moral Attraction* attempted to point out the analogies between the physical and social universe. His work was stimulated by the discoveries of Isaac Newton. He tried to apply the Newtonian formulas to society. While his "physical analogies" are of little value, they represent a stage in the rise of psychosociologic thought. He made the social instinct, or the gregarious instinct, in society the analogue of the force of gravitation. The centrifugal force in society is selfishness; and the centripetal, sociability. As the attractive force of one mass for another varies directly in relation to the distance between them, so the attraction of individuals for one another varies directly in proportion to their resemblances. The physical analogies, however, could not be carried far without being lost in the realm of absurdity.

The Scotch philosopher, David Hume, has been called the father of social psychology because of his splendid analysis of sympathy as a social force. "Let all the powers and elements of nature conspire to serve and obey one man, . . . he will still be miserable, till you give him some one person at least with whom he may share his happiness, and whose esteem and friendship he may enjoy."[1] "Whatever other passions we may be actuated by, pride, ambition, avarice, curiosity, revenge or lust,—the soul or animating principle of them is sympathy."[2]

But sympathy is not always limited in its operation to the present moment. Through sympathy we may put ourselves in the future situation of any person whose present condition arouses our interest in him. Moreover, if we see a stranger in danger, we will run to his assistance.

Vice was defined by Hume as everything which gives uneasiness in human actions. By sympathy, we become uneasy when we become aware of injustice anywhere. "Self-interest is the original motive to the establishment of justice; but a sympathy with public interest is the source of the moral approbation which attends that virtue."[3] There is a continual conflict between self-interest and sympathy, both in the individual and between individuals in society. Although at times this self-interest seems to predominate, "it does not entirely abolish the more generous and noble intercourse of friendship and good offices."[4]

Sympathy causes people to be interested in the good of mankind.[5] But whatever human factor is contiguous either in space or time has a proportional effect on the will, passions, and imagination.[6] It commonly operates with greater force than any human factor that lies in a distant and more obscure light. This principle explains why people often act in contradiction to their interests, and "why they prefer any trivial advantage that is present to the maintenance of order in society."

In accordance with the analysis of sympathy by Hume, Adam Smith made sympathy a leading concept in his theory of political economy. Smith also carried the concept of self-interest, with the resultant conflict between self-interest and social interest, into nearly all his economic theories.

According to Adam Smith there are four classes of people in modern life. (1) There are those who live by taking rent. They have social interests but are not socially productive; they grow listless and careless. (2) There is the class which takes wages. This group is large, productive, and socially interested, but their widespread lack of education makes them subject to the passions of the day, and hence socially useless or even harmful. (3) Those who take profit have interests at direct variance with the welfare of society. Their selfish interests become unduly developed; their public attitudes are usually dangerous to all except themselves. (4) The fourth group is composed of all who derive a living from serving one or more of the three aforementioned classes. The interests of the three first-mentioned groups often clash, leading to destructive social conflicts. Despite this conclusion, Adam Smith was an advocate of *laissez faire*. He urged that natural laws be allowed to express themselves normally.

In 1859, Moritz Lazarus and Heymann Steinthal began to contribute to social thought in the *Zeitschrift für Völker-Psychologie und Sprachwissenschaft*. They applied psychological methods to the study of primitive society. In this journal they made notable contributions concerning the social customs and mental traits of early mankind. It is in this field, which was discussed in Chapter XVIII, that the original work of such men as Franz Boas, W. G. Sumner, W. I. Thomas, and L. T. Hobhouse belongs. Fundamental pioneering in psycho-sociologic thought was done by Lester F. Ward (see Chapter XVII). Ward opposed the prevailing belief of his time, and particularly of Herbert Spencer, that society must continue as it now is going on, namely, an exhibition of a blind struggle of competitive forces. He not only perceived the rise of mind out of the obscure processes of social evolution, but more important still, he noted the part that mind may play in modifying the course of social forces. Although he considered the human desires to be the dynamic social elements, he gave to mind, through its power of prevision, the prerogative of directing the desires of mankind. Moreover, he pointed out the direction in which mind could best guide the desires. He urged a sociocracy in which the desires of the individual are so controlled that they operate only when in harmony with the welfare of other individuals. For establishing these fundamental considerations, Ward ranks high in the history of psycho-sociologic thought.

The chief founder of social psychology was Gabriel Tarde (1843-1904). He wrote the first important treatise in the field of the psychology of society. The *Lois de l'imitation* established Tarde's reputation as a social psychologist, and at the same time aroused the world of thought to the existence of a new phase of social science. Tarde was a jurist who inquired into the causes of anti-social conduct. He was greatly impressed by the observation that criminal acts are committed in waves. Upon examination of this fact he found imitation to be a potent factor, and began to analyze the laws of imitation. This study soon showed that not all is imitation but that much human conduct arises out of opposition. His analysis of the laws of opposition led him to the conclusion that imitation and opposition are the bases of a third social factor, invention. The social process, as he observed it, is characterized (1) by an ever-widening imitation of inventions, (2) by the opposition of conflicting circles of imitation, and (3) by the rise of new inventions (out of these oppositions), which in turn become the centers of new imitations. Thus, the social process goes on, endlessly and unconsciously or consciously. To understand society, Tarde believed that one must understand how minds act and interact.

Tarde's work, first presented is *Les Lois de l'imitation,* was formally developed in his *Logique sociale,* and summarized in his *Lois sociale* (English translation, *Social Laws*). Together, these books constitute a unique social theory. Although Tarde's approach to the psychology of society was objective and sociological, and although he did not give serious attention to the purely psychological nature of the mind nor to the instinctive bases of conduct, he nevertheless made a contribution to social thought which is valid and enlightening.

Society, according to Tarde, is a group of people "who display many resemblances, produced either by imitation or by counter-imitation."[7] Again, he says that society is "a group of distinct individuals who render one another mutual services."[8] Societies are groups of people who are organized because of agreement or disagreement of beliefs.[9] "Society is imitation."[10] The outstanding element in social life is a psychological process in which inventions are followed by imitations, which when coming into inevitable oppositions produce new inventions.

To the degree that a person is social he is imitative. In the way that vital, or biological, resemblances are due to heredity, so human resemblances are caused by imitation. The closer the human resemblances between individuals, even though they be occupational competitors, the larger will be the proportion of imitations and the closer the social relationships. The father will always be the son's first model.[11] A beloved ruler will so fascinate his people that they will imitate blindly, yea, even be thrown into a state of catalepsy by him. In such a case imitation becomes a kind of somnambulism.[12]

Imitations are characterized by inclines, plateaus, and declines.[13] The incline refers to the period of time which an imitation requires for adoption The plateau is the length of time during which an imitation is in force. The decline, of course, has to do with the passing away of an imitation. Each of these phases are of varying lengths—dependent upon the operation of almost countless socio-psychical factors. It is this career through which all imitations must pass that is the important phase of history.[14]

There are two causal factors determining the nature of imitation: logical, and non-logical.[15] Logical causes operate when the imitator adopts an innovation that is in line with the principles that have already found a place in his own mind. Extra-logical, or non-logical, imitations are those which are determined by the adventitious factors of place, date, or birth of the individual.

The fundamental law of imitation, stated in simplest terms, is that the superior are imitated by the inferior, for example: the patrician by the plebeian; the nobleman by the commoner; the beloved by the lover.[16] A more accurate statement of the law of imitation is that "the thing that is most imitated is the most superior one of those that are nearest." The term "superior" in all these cases must be used in the subjective sense, that is to say, that which seems to the specific individual to be superior, not necessarily that which actually is the superior, is imitated.

A country or period of time is democratic if the distance between the highest and lowest classes is lessened enough so that the highest may be imitated freely by the lowest.[17] Democracy will keep the distance between classes reduced to that minimum where imitation may operate.

An important phase of sociology involves the knowledge and control of imitations.[18] Sociological statistics should determine (1) "the imitative power which inheres in every invention at any given time and place;" and (2) "the beneficial or harmful effects which result from the imitation of given inventions."

Imitation is divided into sets of complementary tendencies; custom imitation and fashion imitation; sympathy imitation and obedience imitation; naïve imitation and deliberate imitation.[19] Everywhere custom imitation and fashion imitation are embodied in two parties, divisions, or organizations—the conservative and the liberal.[20]

Through custom imitation, usages acquire autocratic power. They control habit, regulate private conduct, and define morals and manners with imperial authority. Usages are frequently extra-logical imitations. Usages are commonly accepted first by the upper classes. They usually are related primarily to objects of luxury; they stick tenaciously to the leisure-time phases of life. Their most favorable *milieu* is a social and individual status of ignorance.

Fashion imitation rules by epochs, for example: Athens under Solon, Rome under the Scipios, Florence in the fifteenth century.[21] These epochs of fashion produce great individualities—illustrious legislators, and founders of empire. Whenever the currents of fashions are set free, the inventive imagination is excited and ambitions are stimulated.

Fashion imitation has a democratizing influence. A prolonged process of fashion imitation ends "by putting pupil-peoples upon the same level, both in their armaments and in their arts and sciences, with their master people."[22] In fact, the very desire to be like the superior is a latent democratizing force.

The counterpart of imitation is opposition. Opposition, however, may be a very special kind of repetition. There are two types of opposition: interference-combinations and interference-conflicts.[23] The first type refers to the coming together of two psychological quantities of desire and belief with the result that combination takes place and a total gain is made. The second type refers to the opposition resulting from incompatible forces. In this case an individual or social loss is registered.

From another standpoint, opposition appears in one of three forms, namely, war, competition, and discussion.[24] Conflicts often pass through these three forms, which are obedient to the same law of development, but in order are characterized by ever-widening areas of pacification, alternating however with renewals of discord. As war is the lowest, most brutal form of conflict, discussion is the highest, most rational form.

Opposition in human life is society's logical duel.[25] This duel sometimes ends abruptly when one of the adversaries is summarily suppressed by force. Sometimes a resort to arms brings a military victory. Sometimes a new invention or discovery expels one of the adversaries from the social scene.

The logical result of opposition is invention or adaptation. "Invention is a question followed by an answer."[26] Invention, or adaptation, at its best is "the felicitous interference of two imitations, occurring first in one single mind."[27] Inventions grow in two ways: (1) in extension—by imitative diffusion; and (2) in comprehension—by a series of logical combinations, such as the combination of the wheel and the horse in the inventions of the horse-cart.[28].

Inventions partially determine the nature of new inventions and new discoveries. A new invention makes possible other inventions, and so on. Each invention is the possible parent of a thousand offspring inventions.

To be inventive, one must be wide-awake, inquiring, incredulous, not docile and dreamy, or living in a social sleep. The inventor is one who escapes, for the time being, from his social surroundings.[29] Inventing develops from wanting. A man experiences some want, and in order to satisfy this want he invents. Inventiveness is contrary in nature to sheepishness.

Since an invention is the answer to a problem, inventions are the real objective factors which mark the stage of progress. But invention, according to Tarde, becomes increasingly difficult. Problems naturally grow increasingly complex as the simpler ones are mastered. Unfortunately, the mind of man is not capable of indefinite development, and therefore will reach a limit in solving problems.[30] At this point, Tarde is on doubtful ground. His argument can neither be proved nor disproved. Apparently, man's ability to solve problems increases with his training and experience in that connection. Moreover, man appears to be at the very dawn of his possibilities in the field of invention. He is only beginning to gather together systematically the materials for inventing, and to understand slightly the principles of inventing.

Inventors are imitative.[31] This statement is but another way of saying that inventions are cumulative, that they come in droves, that they are gregarious. A new discovery will arouse the ambition of many wide-awake persons to make similar discoveries. "There is in every period a current of inventions which is in a certain general sense religious or architectural or sculptural or musical or philosophical."[32]

Invention and imitation represent the chief forces in society.[33] Invention is "intermittent, rare, and eruptive only at certain infrequent intervals." It explains "the source of privileges, monopolies, and aristocratic inequalities." Imitation, on the other hand, is democratic, leveling, and "incessant like the stream deposition of the Nile or Euphrates." At times the eruptions of invention take place faster than they can be imitated. At other times imitations flow in a monotonous circular current.

The contributions of Tarde to social thought have stimulated numerous investigators to enter the field of social psychology. While Tarde's thinking has been severely criticised by the psychologists and modified by the sociologists, it has opened mines of valuable social ores. Not the least important consideration was the impetus which the Tardian thought gave to American writers, such as E. A. Ross.[84] Tarde's name, however, will be long revered for the penetrating way in which he developed the concept of imitation. Although Walter Bagehot, an English publicist, in an epoch-stirring book, *Physics and Politics,* published an important chapter on "Imitation" as early as 1872, it was Tarde's *Lois de l'imitation* in 1890 which at once became the authority on the subject. In the United States, Michael M. Davis, Jr., has written an excellent summary of Tarde's socio-psychologic thought.[85] As a critical digest of Tardian thought, Dr. Davis' *Psychological Interpretations of Society* is unsurpassed.

In 1892, Profesor H. Schmidkunz published an elaborate work on the *Psychologie der Suggestion.* This book is an important pioneer work. In the English language, the writings of Boris Sidis on the psychology of suggestion are well-known. Professor E. A. Ross has given an intensive treatment of the theme in his *Social Psychology.* In these various discussions, however, the fact is not made clear that suggestion and imitation are correlative phases of the same phenomenon. The point, also, is not developed that suggestion-imitation phenomena are natural products of social situations in which like stimuli normally produce like responses.

In 1895, the first book by Gustave Le Bon on crowd psychology was published. Le Bon has also written on the psychology of revolutions, of war, and of peoples. He gave a limited definition to the term, crowds, and then applied the term to nearly all types of group life. He conceived of crowds as "feeling phenomena." They are more or less pathological. Since the proletariat are subject to crowd psychology, they are untrustworthy and to be rewarded perpetually with suspicion. A sounder, more synthetic, and historical position concerning the psychology of groups and of society is taken by G. L. Duprat in *La Psychologie sociale.*

Italian contributions in the field of crowd and group psychology are represented by Paolo Orano's *Psicologia sociale,* which includes only a partial treatment of the subject that is indicated by the title; and by Scipio Sighele's *La foule criminelle* and *Psychologie des sectes.* Permanent groups, according to Sighele (following Tarde), are either sects, castes, classes, or states.[36] The sect is a group of individuals which possesses a common ideal and faith, such as a religious denomination or a political party. The caste arises from identity of profession. The class is characterized by a strong unity of interests. States possess common bonds of language, national values, and national prestige.

The concept of "consciousness of kind" was developed by Franklin H. Giddings in his *Principles of Sociology* (1896). Consciousness of kind is the original and elementary subjective fact in society.[37] Professor Giddings defines this term to mean "a state of consciousness in which any being, whether low or high in the scale of life, recognizes another conscious being as of like kind with itself." In its widest meaning, consciousness of kind marks the difference between the animate and the inanimate. Among human beings it distinguishes "social conduct" from purely economic or purely religious activity. Around consciousness of kind, as a determining principle, all other human motives organize themselves.

People group together according to the development of the consciousness of kind in them. Roughly speaking, there are four such groupings.[38] (1) The non-social are persons in whom the consciousness of kind has not yet developed — in whom it finds imperfect but not degenerate expression, and from whom the other classes arise. (2) The anti-social, or criminal, classes include those persons in whom the consciousness of kind is approaching extinction. They detest society. (3) The pseudo-social, or pauper, classes are characterized by a degeneration of the genuine consciousness of kind. (4) The social classes are noted for a high development of the consciousness of kind; they constitute the positive and constructive elements in society. At the head of the list are the pre-eminently social. These people devote their lives and means to the amelioration of society; they are called the natural aristocracy of the race, the true social élite.

Consciousness of kind is made possible in part by the operation of physical factors. Fertility of soil is one of the sources of human aggregation. Favorable climate makes aggregation possible. Aggregation of population is either genetic (due to the birth rate) or congregate (due to immigration). Aggregation leads to association—the proper *milieu* for the growth of consciousness of kind.

Aggregation guarantees social intercourse, which is a mode of conflict. Conflict, according to Professor Giddings, becomes the basis of social growth.[39] Primary conflicts are those in which one adversary is completely outdone, and hence likely to be crushed, by the other. Secondary conflict refers to the contests between more or less evenly balanced forces. Primary conflict is conquest; secondary conflict is growth. Among people secondary conflict leads to the development of consciousness kind through the successive steps of commur tion, imitation, toleration, co-operation, alli- The supreme result is the production of ors, nently social classes. Of these variou tion. Professor Giddings particularly stress that "It is the factor of imitation in th gradually assimilates and harmoniz Produces

Association reacts upon individ social self- self-consciousness, which in tur self. Social consciousness, or group awar rational dis- self-consciousness is charac cussion. With the rise of discussion, social memory, or traditions, becomes possible. Moreover, a sense of social values arises. Public opinion springs from the passing of judgment by the members of the group upon any matters of general interest.[41]

Social memory, or traditions, becomes highly differentiated.[42] It consists of impressions concerning the tangible world, the intangible world, and the conceptional world. The traditions in any field, plus current opinion in that field, form the standards, ideals, faiths, "isms" of the time. For example, the integration of economic traditions with current economic opinions is the general standard of living of the time and place. The integration of the aesthetic tradition with current criticism is taste, and the modification of a traditional religious belief by current religious ideas is a faith.

Inasmuch as consciousness of kind is the psychological basis of social phenomena, it is natural that the chief social value is the kind itself, or the ...pe of conscious life that is characteristic of the ...ety.[43] The social cohesion is another important ...a value. Social cohesion is vital to the unity of ...to oup; therefore the group is usually willing ...dis many sacrifices in its own behalf. The ...mun possessions and properties of the com- ...hero as territory, sacred or historic places, ...social onies, constitute the third class of ...eral pr A fourth group is found in the gen- ...which promote the growth of the group; for example, the principles of liberty, equality, and fraternity. The social values largely determine the social choices of groups and the nature of social organizations.

Professor Giddings develops an interesting theory of the dualism in social structures. Civilization is marked by the contemporaneous existence of public and private associations. Civilized society affords four main sets of dualistic associations: political, juristic, economic, and cultural. In the political field there are private political parties and the public association, namely, the government, or the political party in power. Among juristic associations there are the privately-organized vigilance committees and the public associations, such as the police, the courts, the prisons. In the realm of economics there are private individual entrepreneurs, partnerships, corporations; and on the other hand, there are the governmentally-owned railroads, postal service, the water systems, the coinage systems. In regard to cultural associations we may note the privately endowed universities and state universities, privately organized churches and state churches, private charities and public charities. This dualism in social structure is supported by Professor Giddings on the grounds that private associations are needed for purposes of initiation, experimentation, and stimulation; and the public associations serve the useful purposes of regulation and maintenance of balance among various contending factors.

The highest test of social organization is the development of social personality. An efficient social organization is one which makes its members "more rational, more sympathetic, with an ever-broadening consciousness of kind." [44]

In recent works Professor Giddings has developed the concept of pluralistic behavior. "Any one or any combination of behavior inciting stimuli may on occasion be reacted to by more than one individual." [45] The character of pluralistic reactions, whether similar or dissimilar, simultaneous or not, equal or unequal, is determined by two variables: (1) the strength of the stimulation; (2) the similarity or dissimilarity of the reacting mechanisms.[46] Thus Professor Giddings considers pluralistic behavior the subject matter of the psychology of society, or sociology.

In 1897, *Social and Ethical Interpretations,* by J. Mark Baldwin, was printed; it bears the subtitle of "A Study in Social Psychology." This was the first time that the term, social psychology, had appeared in the title of a book in America, though three years earlier, in 1894, one of the leading parts of Small and Vincent's *Introduction to the Study of Society* was designated "social psychology" and included a discussion of social consciousness, social intelligence, and social volition. Baldwin's *Social and Ethical Interpretations* and Giddings' *Principles of Sociology* appeared almost simultaneously, one by a psychologist and the other by a sociologist. One was written from the genetic viewpoint, and the other from the objective viewpoint; one dealt primarily with social psychology, and the other with a psychology of society; one was built around the concept of the social self, and the other around the concept of a consciousness of kind. They both hastened the development of an organic social psychology.

Professor Baldwin demonstrated that the self is largely a product of the give-and-take of social life. A child becomes aware of his self by setting himself off from other selves. It is in group life, that is, in contact with other selves, that the child develops a self consciousness.

Moreover, the self is bi-polar. One end of the self-pole is characterized by what one thinks of himself, and the other end by what he thinks of other persons.[47] "The ego and the alter are to our thought one and the same thing."[48]

People are so much alike because they are imitative. It is imitation which keeps people alike. Imitation integrates individuals. Imitation is either (1) a process whereby one individual consciously or unconsciously copies another individual, or (2) the copying of a model, that is, adopting a model which arises in one's own mind.[49]

Baldwin found the law of social growth in the particularization by the individual of society's store of material, and by the generalization on the part of society of the individual's particularizations. The essence of the first phase of this process is invention and of the second, imitation. Baldwin considered invention and imitation the two fundamental processes of social growth.

In this chapter the strength of the psychological approach to an understanding of societary processes has been demonstrated. In the chapter which follows the reader will find further materials, showing the tremendous vitality of psycho-sociologic thought.

CHAPTER XXIII

PSYCHO-SOCIOLOGIC THOUGHT

(CONTINUED)

In 1902, *Human Nature and the Social Order* by Professor Charles H. Cooley was published. This book was at once accepted as an authority on the integral relationship of the individual self and the social process. It was followed in 1909 by *Social Organization*, and in 1918 by *Social Process*. The three books constitute a chronological development of a logical system of psycho-sociologic thought.

The first volume treats of the self in its reactions to group life; the second explains the nature of primary groups, such as the family, playground, and neighborhood, of the democratic mind, and of social classes; the third analyzes the many elements in the processes by which society is characterized. The chief thesis of the three volumes is that the individual and society are aspects of the same phenomenon, and that the individual and society are twin-born and twin-developed. [1]

An individual has no separate existence. Through the hereditary and social elements in his life he is inseparately bound up with society.[2] He cannot be considered apart from individuals. Even the phenomena which are called individualistic "are always socialistic in the sense that they are expressive of tendencies growing out of the general life."[3] It is not only true that individuals make society, but equally true that society makes individuals.

Professor Cooley has given an excellent presentation of what he calls the looking-glass self. There are three distinct psychic elements in this phenomenon: (1) the imagination of one's appearance to another person; (2) the imagined estimation of that appearance by the other person; and (3) a sense of pride or chagrin that is felt by the first person. The looking-glass self affects the daily life of all individuals. "We are ashamed to seem evasive in the presence of a straightforward man, cowardly in the presence of a brave one, gross in the eyes of a refined one, and so on."[4] Even a person's consciousness of himself is largely a direct reflection of the opinions and estimates which he believes that others hold of him.[5]

Professor Cooley makes a lucid distinction between self consciousness, social consciousness, and public consciousness. The first is what I think of myself; the second, what I think of other people; and the third, a collective view of the self and the social consciousness of all the members of a group organized and integrated into a communicating group.[6] Moreover, all three types of consciousness are parts of an organic whole. Even the moral life of individuals is a part of the organic unity of society. Social knowledge is the basis of morality. An upward endeavor is the essence of moral progress.

The three groups which Professor Cooley has called primary are so labeled because through them the individual gets "his earliest and completest experience of social unity."[7] The family, play groups, and neighborhoods remain throughout life as the experience bases from which the more complex phases of life receive their interpretation.

An unbounded faith in human nature is enjoyed by Professor Cooley. Human nature comprises those sentiments and impulses which are distinctly superior to those of the higher animals, such as sympathy, love, resentment, ambition, the feeling of right and wrong.[8] The improvement of society, according to Professor Cooley, does not involve any essential change in human nature but rather "a larger and higher application of its familiar impulses."[9]

Communication is a fundamental concept in Professor Cooley's system of social thought. Communication is "the mechanism through which human relations exist and develop."[10] Professor Cooley has pointed out that not only does language constitute the symbols of the mind, but that in a sense all objects and actions are mental symbols. Communication is the means whereby the mind develops a true human nature. The symbols of our social environment "supply the stimulus and framework for all our growth." Thus the communication concept furnishes a substantial basis for understanding the psycho-sociologic phenomena which are ordinarily called suggestion and imitation.

Personality has its origin partly in heredity and partly "in the stream of communication, both of which flow from the corporate life of the race." A study of communication shows that the individual mind is not a separate growth, but an integral development of the general mind.

The means of communication developed remarkably in the nineteenth century, chiefly in the following ways: (1) in expressiveness, that is, in the range of ideas and feelings they are competent to carry; (2) in the permanence in recording; (3) in swiftness of communication; and (4) in diffusion to all classes of people.[12] Thus society can be organized on the bases of intelligence and of rationalized and systematized feelings rather than on authority, autocracy, and caste.

A free intercourse of ideas, that is, free and unimpeded communication, will not produce uniformity. Self feeling will find enlarged opportunities for expression. An increased degree of communication furnishes the bases for making the individual conscious of the unique part he can and should play in improving the quality of the social whole. On the other hand, freedom of communication is tending to produce "the disease of the century," namely, the disease of excess, of overwork, of prolonged worry, of a competitive race for which men are not fully equipped.[13]

Public opinion, according to Professor Cooley, is not merely an aggregate of opinions of individuals, but "a co-operative product of communication and reciprocal influence."[14] It is a crystalization of diverse opinion, resulting in a certain stability of thought. It is produced by discussion. Public opinion is usually superior, in the sense of being more effective, than the average opinion of the members of the public.

The masses make fundamental contributions to public opinion, not through formulated ideas but through their sentiments. The masses in their daily experiences are close to the salient facts of human nature. They are not troubled with that preoccupation with ideas which hinders them from immediate fellowship. Neither are they limited by that attention to the hoarding of private property which prevents the wealthy from keeping in touch with the common things of life.

The striking result of the social process is the development of personalities. The social process affords opportunities which individuals, ambitious and properly stimulated, may accept. Education may perform a useful function in adjusting individuals to opportunities. But education often fails because it requires too much and inspires too little; it accents formal knowledge at the expense of kindling the spirit.[15]

Social stratification hinders.[16] It cuts off communication. It throws social ascendancy into the hands of a stable, communicating minority. The majority are submerged in the morass of ignorance. Degrading neighborhood associations, vicious parents, despised racial connections—these all serve to produce stratification and to hinder progress.

Professor Cooley holds that in the social process the institutional element is as essential as the personal.[17] Institutions bequeath the standard gifts of the past to the individual; they give stability. At the same time, if rationally controlled they leave energy free for new conquests. Vigor in the individual commonly leads to dissatisfaction on his part with institutions. Disorganization thus arises from the reaction against institutional formalism manifested by energetic individuals. It may be regarded as a lack of communication between the individual and the institution. Formalism indicates that in certain particulars there has been an excess of communication.

The economic concept of value has long been analyzed in individualistic terms—the economic desires arise out of "the inscrutable depths of the private mind." To this explanation Professor Cooley replies that economic wants, interests, and values are primarily of institutional origin; they are socially created. Pecuniary valuations are largely the products of group conditions and activities.

It is in a rational public will that Professor Cooley sees the salvation of the social process. While he repeatedly expresses a large degree of faith in human nature as it is, he looks forward to a day, rather remote, when communication and education will enable all individuals to take a large grasp of human situations and on the basis of this grasp to express effectual social purposes. Unconscious adaptation will be superseded by the deliberate self-direction of every group along lines of broadening sympathy and widening intellectual reaches.

Professor Cooley has earned the title of a sound, sane, and deep sociological thinker. His contributions to social thought are found in his lucid descriptions of the social process from which personalities and social organizations arise, in his keen analysis of communication as the fundamental element in progress, and in his emphasis upon rational control through standards.

The year 1908 is a red letter year in the history of socio-psychologic thought. In that year two important treatises appeared, one written by William McDougall and the other by Edward Alsworth Ross. The former was developed from the psychological standpoint; the latter, from the sociological point of view.

Mr. McDougall considers social psychology largely as a study of the social instincts of individuals; Professor Ross concentrates attention upon the suggestion and imitation phases of societal life. In a sense Professor Ross begins his analysis where Mr. McDougall concludes.

Mr. McDougall treats the instincts as the bases of social life. He makes them the foundation of nearly all individual and social activities.[18] Instincts are biologically inherited; they cannot be eradicated by the individual. Instincts constitute the materials out of which habits are made. Consciousness arises only when an instinct or a habit (that is, a modified instinct) fails to meet human needs.

The primary instincts are the sex and parental, the gregarious, curiosity, flight, repulsion. Each is accompanied by its peculiar emotion, for example, the instinct of flight by the emotion of fear, the instinct of curiosity by the emotion of wonder. This instinct-emotion theory is, however, drawn out until it seems to become academic rather than actual in its details.

Professor McDougall points out that the instincts are the basic elements upon which all social institutions are built.[19] For example, the sex and parental instincts are the foundations of the family; the acquisitive instinct is an essential condition of the accumulation of material wealth and of the rise of private property as an institution. Pugnaciousness leads to war.

This emphasis upon the instincts reaches an extreme form in W. Trotter's *Instincts of the Herd in Peace and War,* where the herd instinct is made all-dominant. According to Mr. Trotter the herd instinct arouses fear in the individual and rules him through rigorous conventional means—in a large percentages of cases to his detriment.

In conjunction with his theory of instincts, Professor McDougall has advanced a noteworthy conception of the sentiments. The three leading expressions of sentiment are love, hate, and respect. Sympathy is regarded as an elemental sentiment, in fact, as an emotion in its simplest form. A sentiment is "an organized system of emotional tendencies centered about some object." The sentiments comprise an important phase of the self, and function powerfully in determining social conduct.

It was in 1901 that Professor E. A. Ross made his initial contribution to psycho-sociologic thought —seven years before his *Social Psychology* was published. His first great work was *Social Control.* In this excursus he defined social psychology as the study of "the psychic interplay petween man and his environing society."[20] This interplay is twofold: the domination of society over the individual (social ascendancy); and the domination of the individual over society (individual ascendancy). Social ascendancy may be either purposeless (social influence) or purposeful (social control). Social psychology, according to Professor Ross, deals with psychic planes and currents; it does not treat of groups, which is a part of the preserve of psychological sociology.

The psycho-sociologic grounds of control are found in such factors as sympathy, sociability, an elemental sense of justice, and particularly in group needs. There are individuals whose conduct exasperates the group. "In this common wrath and common vengeance lies the germ of a social control of the person."[21]

Perhaps the best part of Professor Ross' discussion of social control is his analysis of the agents of control.[22] Public opinion and law are the two most important means of controlling individuals. The weakness of one, in this connection, is its fitfulness; of the other, its rigidity. Personal beliefs and ideals function widely and effectively because of their subjective character. An individual may escape the operation of law; he can hide away from the winds of public opinion; but he cannot get away from his own ideas and conscience. It is for this reason that religious convictions are powerful. Art as a means of social control is commonly underrated. It arouses the passions, kindles sympathies, creates a sense of the beautiful and perfects social symbols, such as Columbia, La Belle France, Britannia.[23]

Systems of social control are political or moral.[24] The political form is more or less objective, is likely to be in the hands of a few, is apt to be used for class benefit. The ethical arises from sentiment rather than from utility; it is more or less subjective; it permeates the hidden recesses of life. The ethical system is usually mild, enlightening and suasive "rather than bold and fear-engendering." Individuals are ordinarily aware of political control, but the far-reaching influences of ethical control they little suspect.

The two most difficult problems for society to solve in connection with social control are these: (1) what measures of control may be best imposed; and (2) how these measures should be imposed.[25] The variety of disciplines which society may use varies from epithets to capital punishment. The methods vary from the democratic one of social self-infliction to the direct autocratic procedure. Too much control produces either stagnation or revolution, depending on the amount of energy the rank and file may possess. Too little control leads to anarchy, or at least to a reign of selfishness. A paternal social control may cause resentment or a crushing of self-respect.

Suggestion and imitation are social elements that Professor Ross has described in detail.[26] He has demonstrated that the more gregarious species are more suggestible than the species whose members are more or less solitary; that southern races are more suggestible than northern races, because of the different climatic effects upon temperament; that children are more suggestible than adults, because children possess a small store of facts and an undeveloped ability to criticize; that people of a nervous temperament are more suggestible than persons who are phlegmatic, because of difference in sensibility; that women are more suggestible than men, because they have not had the broadening influences which men have enjoyed, such as "higher education, travel, self-direction, professional pursuits, participation in intellectual and public life."[27]

The laws of imitation, particularly of fashion imitation and rational imitation, which M. Tarde was the first to outline, have been elucidated and illustrated by Professor Ross. He has cut boldly into the shams of fashion, convention, and custom, and made a strong plea for rationality in these fields. He has shown how mob mind, the craze, and the fad sweep not simply the foolish and light-headed individuals off their feet, but also the persons who are counted as sane and acquainted with common sense. In fact, he has made clear that even the most level-headed are blindly or slavishly governed by custom or fashion or both. He does not develop, however, the fact that imitation is largely a result of like-mindedness and common social stimuli. He implies an individual rather than a group origin of suggestion-imitation phenomena.

It is in discussion that Professor Ross sees one of the main hopes of progress.[28] Discussion brings conflicts to a head, and leads to group progress. Discussion changes a person's opinions. Adequate discussion leads to the settlement of a conflict and the creation of an established public opinion, which remains in force until a new invention occurs, a resultant conflict ensues, and a new public opinion comes into power.

In 1920, Professor Ross made his largest and most important contribution to social thought in his *Principles of Sociology*. This work, however, is essentially a treatise in social psychology. The original social forces are the human instincts, notably the fighting instinct, the gregarious instinct, the parental instinct, the curiosity instinct. The derivative social forces are societal complexes which tend to satisfy instinctive cravings. Professor Ross' classification of the derivative social forces, or interests, is primarily fourfold. These fundamental interests are wealth, government, religion, and knowledge. This classification contains only two, or at best three, of the six groups of interests which are found in Professor Small's exhibit.[29]

Professor Ross' analysis of the process of socialization has been indicated in Chapter XXI. This phenomena is to be sharply distinguished from ossification, which is the hardening of social life into rigid forms.[30] Groups often become unduly solidified. The salvation of such a situation lies in individuation, which is a process of pulverizing social lumps and releasing the action of their members.[31] Any movement that develops that spirit of personal liberty leads to individuation.

"Commercialization is the increasing subjection of any calling or function to the profits motive."[32] The various factors which hold the profits motive in check are: (1) pleasure in creative activity; (2) pride in the perfection of one's product; (3) the desire to live up to accepted standards of excellence; (4) abhorrence of sham in one's work; (5) interest in the welfare of the customer; (6) the social service motive. The profits motive, however, receives support from many social tendencies, notably: (1) the increasing distance between producer and consumer; (2) the growing differentiation between principals and subordinates; (3) the increasing importance of capital in the practice of an art or occupation.

Professor Ross has set forth a valuable exhibit of the canons of social reconstruction.[33] (1) Reforms must not do violence to human nature. (2) They must square with essential realities. (3) They should be preceded by a close sociological study of the situation which it is planned to change. (4) Reforms should be tried out on a small scale before being adopted on a large scale. (5) A reform should be the outcome of a social movement. (6) Under a popular government, reforms should move according to legal and constitutional methods.

In regard to the improvement of social institutions, Professor Ross rests his argument on the importance of standards. "Standards are, perhaps, the most important things in society."[34] Although invisible and intangible they reveal, better than anything else, the quality of a society.

The current standards of the family may be improved through imparting sound ideals of marriage, through fixing these ideals everywhere in social tradition, and through making "the social atmosphere frosty toward foolish and frivolous ideals of marriage."[35] Young people may well be taught to look upon divorce as a moral shipwreck. Loyalty to the state or society has its origin in the obedience of children to parents in the family. A sound family life, thus, is rated by our author as the bulwark of society.

In regard to industry, it is pointed out that the principle of the sovyet is associated in an entirely accidental way with Bolshevism.[36] The sovyet may well be judged on its own merits. The principle upon which citizens may be grouped for purposes of securing representation in government is not yet settled. Is a given geographical area a better unit for securing representation than occupational areas?

State socialism is objected to by Professor Ross on the grounds that it leaves the citizens so remote "from that which most vitally concerns him, viz., the regulation of the industry in which he works, that his yearly vote may be a mere fribble and he little better than a state serf."[38] Guild socialism, on the other hand, urges that each branch of industry shall organize itself democratically, and that the state shall be organized not with provinces and localities as semi-autonomies but with industries exercising a degree of autonomy. Our author endorses the general shift which is occurring at the present time from the coercive side to the service side of industrial life.

Professor Ross has deduced several important sociological principles of general import. These he calls the principle of anticipation, the principle of simulation, the principle of individualization, and the principle of balance.

By the principle of anticipation, he means that a known policy of an institution will come to be anticipated by the members of the institution and will result in modifying behavior.[38] Unfair advantage is often taken of people on the basis of this principle. For example, children frequently count on favor and leniency. The false beggar's whine is often effective. It is in this connection that genuine social reform differs from a common conception of charity, for the former method fits people to run, clears their course, and incites them to make the race,[39] while the latter fails to render assistance of permanent value.

The principle of simulation refers to the common tendency of "the unworthy to simulate every type or trait which has won social approval, in order to steal prestige from it."[40] Commercial competition has produced adulterations, misbrandings, counterfeiting. There is the professional athlete, who sometimes poses as a sincere enthusiast for physical development. Politicians are often expert dissemblers.

The principle of individualization refers to giving individuality a reasonable chance for growth. As society grows more complex, institutions more ossified, and life more standardized, the average individual is increasingly in danger of being crushed; at least, his opportunities for self-expression grow more slim. There is need of constant vigilance in education in allowing for individual differences, in industry for safeguarding the laborer in expressing his personality in his work, in government in permitting free discussion.

The principle of balance is stated by Professor Ross as follows: In the guidance of society each social element should share according to the intelligence and public spirit of its members and none should predominate."[41] There has been in the past, and even now there is in all countries, a bitter struggle taking place between classes apparently on the basis that some one class should rule all the other classes. Society has suffered immeasurably in this way. Sometimes society has been the victim of the rulership of the dead, of the rulership of masculinism, of clericalism, of militarism, of commercialism, of legalism, of leisure class ascendancy, of intellectualism, of proletarianism, but always by one class lording it over the weaker classes until some one of the weaker classes acquires strength enough to overthrow the class in power.

The socio-psychological thought of Professor Ross has penetrated the farthermost reaches of human life. It has been stated in lucid, stimulating language. It has commanded the attention of socially-thinking persons in many lands. It has defined the field of sociology, giving the psychological approach.

Special attention may be given to the concept of "the great society" as used by Graham Wallas. The Great Society is a name for current human society, the product of mechanical inventions, industrial production, commercial expansion, democratic evolution—highly organized and intricately complex. It is ruled, in the main, by men "who direct enormous social power without attempting to form a social purpose," and it is composed to a surpassing degree of individuals who recognize the power of society but dimly and who often treat society with distrust and dislike.[42]

Mr. Wallas substitutes organization for organism as a fundamental social concept. He makes a distinction between thought organizations, will organizations, and happiness organizations. Thought organizations are those institutions in society whose main function is the organization of thought, such as discussion groups, ranging from a philosophical club to an ordinary committee that is called together to plan new legislation. At this point Mr. Wallas asserts that he has attended perhaps 3000 meetings of municipal committees, of different sizes and for different purposes, and that he is sure that at least half of the men and women with whom he has sat "were entirely unaware that any conscious mental effort on their part was called for."[43] They attended in the same spirit that many persons attend church, namely, in the spirit that if they merely attend they are doing their duty, and that some good must come of it.

Will organization comes into existence because of imperfect social machinery. In industry three types of will organizations are striving for mastery —the institution of private property, represented by the individualists; the state, represented by collectivists; labor organizations, represented perhaps by syndicalists. There is urgent need for "the invention of means of organizing the conflicting wills of individuals and classes within each nation more effective than reliance upon any single 'principle,' whether representation, property, or professionalism."[44]

The organization of happiness has not proceeded far. Efficiency has supplanted happiness as a modern god. The ideal of making money has shadowed the ideal of making people happy. A social system organized on the basis of happiness avoids both destitution and superfluity, employs the Mean as the standard for the representation of all social interests as well as for all faculties of individuals, avoids the Extreme in all things.[45]

The writings of Charles A. Ellwood deal particularly with that part of sociological thought which rests upon psychological theory. Professor Ellwood defines a society as "a group of individuals carrying on a collective life by means of mental interactions."[46] As a result of mental interactions, co-ordination or co-adaptation of the activities of the members is effected.

The psychological basis of social interactions is found in such characteristics of the individual as spontaneity, instincts, emotions, consciousness, mind. Organisms possess spontaneity, that is, movements are set up in them without the apparent aid of external causes.[47] The organism, however, is dependent largely upon the environment for the development of its potentialities, "but the essential ground for the beginning of its activities lies within—in its own organic needs." Instincts, the product of natural selection, represent preformed neurological pathways that developed "in response to the demands of previous life conditions." The emotions, also hereditary, are complexes of feelings and sensations. The desires are complex combinations of feelings and impulses which are accompanied by an awareness of the objects that will satisfy the impulse.[48] Consciousness develops to solve problems which the instincts cannot meet. At first, consciousness is largely a selective activity. It develops, however, into a highly complex agency for mastering the problems of life and the universe.

Mind is a product of the social life-process. It has arisen under conditions of association.

One of the most fundamental phases of the associational process is communication. The need of acting together has given rise to intercommunicative symbols.

Professor George H. Mead has given a thoroughgoing discussion of communication, language, and the consciousness of meaning.[49] He begins with a social situation, where the actions of one person serve as stimulations to other persons, whose responses in turn act as stimulations to the first person. Thus life is a series of actions, stimulations, responses, resultant stimulations — these activities constitute gestures or symbols with meanings. Symbols and the consciousness of meaning of these symbols are the main elements in communication.

Communication, says Professor Ellwood, is "a device to carry on a common life-process among several distinct, though psychically interacting, individual units."[50] This definition probably emphasizes unduly the "individual units," which are doubtless a product, in part, of the stream of social life. Suggestion is an elemental, but quick form of communication, related in its simpler phases to sympathetic emotion. Imitation is a common mechanism whereby actions and ideas spread. Communication in the form of oral and written language is the chief mechanistic factor in securing social change.

The contention of Ward that primitive man was anti-social is refuted by Professor Ellwood, who points out that according to social anthropology the so-called anti-social traits of earliest man are not found fully developed among "savages" but among people of later ages. Primitives were characterized by a narrow sociality, confined largely to the family and small groups.[51]

Professor Ellwood's theory of social change is of a two-fold character: unconscious and conscious,—the former being characteristic of the lower stages of social evolution, and the latter, increasingly characteristic of the higher stages.[52] The forms of unconscious social change are manifold.

Natural selection tends to crush and destroy the weaker individuals and the weaker groups. Another type of unconscious social change is that which comes through a gradual disuse of certain cultural elements. One generation fails to copy the preceding in all particulars. Another set of sources of unconscious social change is found in the shifting relationships between individuals that is produced by "the increase of population, a new physical environment, a new cultural contact, a new discovery or a new invention." In fact, Professor Ellwood states that all social changes start in an unconscious way.[53]

Conscious change begins with the awareness on the part of one or more individuals that some social habit is not functioning well. Through communication, this awareness spreads from individual to individual. Discussion ensues. At first, discussion is largely critical of the unsatisfactory social situation. The useless or harmful elements in the situation receive first attention. As discussion proceeds, it takes on a more constructive nature, that is, it becomes projective, planful, positive. It suggests a change to be made. It becomes transformed into a more or less stable public opinion, demanding a substitution of a proposed way of doing for the old. The chief elements in guaranteeing conscious readjustments are free communication, "free public criticism, free discussion, untrammeled formation of public opinion, free selection of social policies and social leaders."[54] The selective process in conscious social change is public opinion, whose social function it is to mediate in the transition from one social habit to another.

Conscious social change in Western Civilization is endangered on one hand by an excessive individualism, and on the other by a socialism which threatens to suppress individual initiative and to underemphasize the rôle of mental and moral character. Professor Ellwood urges the importance of an education which will socialize the individual and at the same time develop a high type of personal character.

Social change, also, takes place under socially abnormal conditions, so long as societies fail to keep "a high degree of flexibility in their habits and institutions."[55] Autocratic rulers, propertied classes, ecclesiastical classes, special groups in power, a general intellectual stagnation, are factors which tend to resist institutional flexibility. If this adaptability does not exist, then social conditions will produce revolutions. If the ruling autocracy is so powerful that the lives of all objectors are snuffed out, then revolution is indefinitely postponed. If the energetic forces within a society are hampered greatly in securing constructive opportunities for expression, they become forces of discontent and agents of revolt. If a revolution comes, then much that is worthy in social organization will be obliterated along with the unworthy, confusion will reign and a reversion to the brutal stages of societal life is easily possible.

In his discussion of "the social problem," Professor Ellwood points out that the good fruits of the World War are in danger of being destroyed by "the blindness and selfishness of some in our socially privileged classes, the fanatic radicalism and class hatred of some of the leaders of the non-privileged."[56] The forces which are combining against making the world safe for democracy today are national imperialism, commercialism, materialistic standards of life, class conflicts, religious agnosticism, and a reckless attitude toward marriage and the family.[57] The social problem, from one angle, becomes the problem of training people to live together justly, constructively, and cooperatingly.

As Turgot indicated, the only way to avert social revolution is through suitable and well-timed reforms. Today, the reforms most urgently needed are three-fold: the substitution of an unselfish internationalism for a selfish nationalism, of a spiritual civilization for a rampant materialism, and of a socialized human race for individualized peoples. To bring about these changes is a gigantic task, namely *the* social problem.

Civilization is a complex of social values. Professor Ellwood's classification of values is widely different from the analysis that Professor Giddings has made (given in the preceding chapter). According to Professor Ellwood, western civilization is represented by the following groups of social values historically derived: (1) a set of spiritual and ethical values, described by the ancient Hebrews; (2) a set of esthetic and philosophic concepts from the Greeks; (3) a set of administrative and legal forms of Roman origin; (4) a set of personal liberty beliefs of early Teutonic derivation; (5) a scientific spirit and technique, originating during the Renaissance; (6) economic efficiency, born of the industrial revolution; and (7) an extensive group of humanitarian values, the product of the nineteenth century. This vast and complicated Western Civilization needs, however, to remove from its structure the three "rotten pillars" of hyper-individualism, materialism, and selfish nationalism, substituting for each its spiritualized and socialized counterpart.

The nature of social control, according to the analysis by Professor E. C. Hayes, is "to secure the completed and most harmonious realization of good human experience, regarded as an end in itself."[58] Social control should prevent activities which do not bear the test of reason, and should elicit those which stand that test, when judged by their own intrinsic value and by their effect upon other values. This statement of the purpose of social control is similar to that of other standard interpretations of the matter.

There are two types of social control.[59] The first is control by sanctions, and the second by social suggestion, sympathetic radiation, and imitation. Social sanctions refer to proffered rewards and threatened punishments. Professor Hayes, however, makes not law but personality the ultimate basis of social order. Repression of crime is a correct social procedure but of a distinctly lower grade than the movement to raise the moral character of those who never go to prison. *The* problem of social control is to take the instinctive tendencies of each individual when he is young and make them over into a disposition that is characterized by the four following traits: (1) reliability, or honesty; (2) controlled animalism, or temperance regarding eating, drinking, and other animal propensities; (3) steadiness in endeavor; (4) the social spirit, or justice.[60]

Professor Hayes' statement on the agencies of social control is similar in purport to the list that Professor Ross has given. Education is considered the chief agency of social control. Education can determine the direction of ambition; education can shift the emphasis in social valuations. Professor Hayes recognizes the import of heredity and how the degree of individual achievement is "more dependent upon heredity than upon the directions of effort." Society, however, has the power to decide which of its members shall develop as far as their potential abilities will permit, and also the power to determine the direction the activities of its members shall take.[61]

Among educational agencies of control the family ranks first.[62] The power of the family at its best in building personality is comparable to the influence in this connection of all other agencies combined. The profession of mother-work is more important to society than any other profession.

The social psychology of business enterprise, of the leisure classes, of the machine process, of industry and workmanship have been indicated by Thorstein Veblen. The unique, incisive work of Mr. Veblen is presented in several books, chief of which are his *Theory of the Leisure Class, Theory of Business Enterprise,* and *Instinct of Workmanship.* Mr. Veblen's ideas can best be illustrated by referring to his "canons."

The Canon of Pecuniary Emulation describes the restless straining of certain individuals in society to outdo one another in the possession of wealth.[63] Such possession is interpreted as conferring honor on its possessor. Wealth becomes intrinsically honorable. The Canon of Pecuniary Beauty refers to the impression that things are beautiful in proportion as they are costly.[64] The marks of expensiveness come to be regarded as beautiful features.

The Canon of Conspicuous Consumption is a term which describes a method of showing off one's wealth by an elaborate consumption of goods.[65] Conspicuous consumption is seen more in matters of dress than in any other line of consumption. The Canon of Conspicuous Leisure is the rule which some people are following when they live a life of leisure as the readiest and most conclusive evidence of pecuniary strength.[66] Sometimes a man keeps his wife frittering her time away in a doll's house in order to show his wealth status.

The Canon of Leisure Class Conservatism is Veblen's label for the conservative tendencies of the wealthy. Those whom fortune has greatly favored are likely to be content with things as they are. Such people are averse to social change, for social innovation might upset their comfortable existence. They have a dominant material interest in letting things alone.

Mr. Veblen's Canon of Pecuniary Efficiency means that many persons conceive of efficiency largely in terms of price. The person who can induce his fellows to pay him well is accounted efficient and serviceable.[67] The man who gains much wealth at little cost is rated high in his neighbor's esteem. The investor who at the turn of his hand reaps $100,000 in a stock or bond deal is praised widely. In other words, there is a common tendency to rate people high in direct proportion to the amount of money that they are able to extract from the aggregate product.

The Canon of Bellicoseness refers to the enthusiasm for war which the hereditary leisure class displays. The very wealthy, not being obliged to work for a living, find that time drags. Therefore, they seek excitement and relief from ennui, and find these conditions in various things, especially in war.

The Canon of Pecuniary Education covers the tendency to demand "practical" education, which, upon examination, is education that will guarantee individual success. "Success," for which education is to fit young people, turns out to be, in the eyes of the practical man, a pecuniary success. "Practical" means useful for private gain. The test that many persons would give to a course in education is this: Will it help one to get an income? The Canon of Pecuniary Thinking denotes that many occupations lead to habits of pecuniary thought. For numbers of people the beginning and end of their more serious thought is of a pecuniary nature.

The Canon of Machine Process Thinking is that mechanical employments produce a type of thinking that is based more or less on material cause and effect. The Machine knows neither morality nor dignity nor prescriptive right. The machine process laborers, working in a world of impersonal cause and effect, "are in danger of losing the point of view of sin."

Professor Veblen has developed the concept of the instinct of workmanship at considerable length. According to this contention, it is natural for individuals to do, to construct, to achieve, to work. Through activity the individual expresses himself and, in so doing, develops, and attains happiness. Every individual is a center of unfolding impulsive activity; he is possessed of a taste for effective work.[68] Labor acquires a character of irksomeness by virtue of the indignity that is falsely imputed to it by a hereditary leisure class.[69] It was the instinct of workmanship which brought the life of mankind from the brute to the human plan.

The contributions of Mr. Veblen to social thought are always of a thought-provoking nature. Sometimes they give rise to invidious comparisons, often they antagonize, but as a rule, they are unique. No brief reference such as is given in the foregoing paragraphs can do justice to Mr. Veblen's pungent criticisms of societal foibles.

It would be a decidedly incomplete treatment of the nature of psycho-sociologic thought that did not make reference to the work of George Elliott Howard, political scientist, historian, sociologist, but above all, social psychologist. In each of the fields in which Dr. Howard has achieved fame, his method of approach is psychological. He has prepared an excellent outline of the field of social psychology, together with a scholarly bibliography of the same. Perhaps the best way to treat Professor Howard's socio-psychologic thought, is to give a sample of it, as found in his address before the American Sociological Society when he was president of that body. The theme was, "Ideals as a Factor in the Future Control of International Society." This *magnum opus* served as an excellent introduction to the series of papers on the subject of social control which were read at the annual meeting of the Sociological Society in 1918, and which have been published together with the presidential address as Volume XII of the Publications of the Society.

By social control, Professor Howard means the standard conception of the "ascendency of the social consciousness."[70] In the same volume, however, Professor Carl Kelsey interprets social control as "the organization and utilization of our wealth and citizens for private purposes."[71] Professor Hutton Webster is inclined to believe that the main feature of primitive social control is "the superstitious fear of the new."[72] Professor F. Stuart Chapin sees the essential element of primitive social ascendency in the pressure upon the individual of social conditions, customs, and conventions."[73] Without giving additional interpretations of social control, the reader will be referred directly to Volume XII of the Publications as the best symposium that is available on the subject.

In discussing ideals as a phase of international control, Professor Howard makes clear that certa ideals exert a baneful influence. The ideal of the nation-state appears to be unmoral if not immoral.[74] Of four prevailing standards of ethics, namely, personal morality, business morality, national morality for home consumption, and "standards of international morality for use with outlanders," the scale is descending, and the fourth type is the lowest. Nationalisms have been overdeveloped—at the expense of a needed internationalism.

Another false ideal of which society needs to rid itself is its conception of the function of war and militarism. War is not a good in itself. War as war is not heroic. Race values constitute a third false ideal. "Every race deems itself superior to every other race and every race is mistaken."[75] Race conceit is contrary to the Christian ideal and has steadily been supplanted by the new doctrine of the potential equality of all races.

The ideal of democracy, on the other hand, rings true to the needs of progress. It makes for peace. Democracy, however, must rid itself of blemishes. Hereditary and class privilege must be abolished;

political corruption and race riots must be defeated; woman, "the original social builder, the mother of industry, the first inventor of the arts of peace," must be granted a full voice in social control.

The ideal of education is exceedingly delicate, for it involves the process of the changing of ideals. Education may prepare a people to admire autocracy or to build a self-governing democracy.

Dr. Howard enters a strong plea for social idealism—the most effective that has yet been written.[76] "The idealist is the inspired social architect, who dreams a plan for the sanitary or moral cleansing of a great city; the campaign for purging politics of graft; a law for saving little children from the tigerish man of the factory or the sweatshop; a referendum for banishing from the commonwealth the saloon, that chief breeder of pauperism, sin, and crime; a conference for the rescuing from the hands of predacious greed, for the use of the whole people, of the remnant of our country's natural wealth. The idealist is the statesman—the head of a nation—who dreams a scheme for safeguarding democracy and guaranteeing peace throughout the world."

It is evident from the introduction to the history of psycho-sociologic thought that has been given in this and the preceding chapter, supported by the materials in the chapters on social conflict and social co-operation concepts, that psycho-sociologic thought holds a place of first rank in the field of sociology. It bids fair to become the central force in social thinking and to lead the social sciences. It deals with the most vital social concepts, namely, groups, personality, behavior, conflict, co-operation, and process. Of all the main approaches to an understanding of societary problems, it promises most.

CHAPTER XXIV

THE TREND OF APPLIED SOCIOLOGY

In the preceding chapters the discussions have dealt primarily with the philosophic and psychologic phases of social thought. Another important phase of our field is applied sociology. The hosts of individuals who have been engaged in dealing directly with societal problems have learned valuable lessons from their personal experiences. Sometimes they have labored according to false theories; often they have scorned theories entirely. At the other extreme, the world has often accepted fine theories, but made a pitiable spectacle of itself in falling away from its idealistic professions.

As the term implies, applied sociology treats of techniques for improving the quality of human living. The best techniques have been developed experimentally, but by persons who have combined a high estimate of social theory with practical programs of activity. The useful concept of social technology, a more accurate term perhaps than applied sociology, was given to society by Charles R. Henderson, whose balanced thinking, sane judgment, and important ameliorative activities made him the founder of this branch of sociological science. Dr. Henderson's name is synonymous with a practical interpretation of both democracy and Christianity, with the spirit of vigorous yet kindly reformation in penology, with the concept of prevention in philanthropic endeavors, and with justice and love in all the fields of human achievement. There are many other important names in the list of those persons who helped to found applied sociology; for example, such individuals as Canon Barnett, Arnold Toynbee, Jacob Riis, Jane Addams, and many other social welfare saints.

Poverty and crime have been the two chief phenomena with which welfare work has been concerned. Until the present century the attempts to meet the problems of poverty have been largely remedial. Jesus said that the poor are always present in any age of society. St. Francis of Assisi, tiring of monastery life, sought out the poor in the natural walks of life, and dedicated himself in their behalf.

For centuries England has experimented with solutions for the problems of poverty and pauperism. She has learned that when she cares too assiduously for the poor she encourages the spirit of pauperism and increases the numbers of dependents. When she provided liberal aid for illegitimate children, she found that illegitimacy was furthered.

England has had a series of important literary leaders who have interested themselves in behalf of the poor and outcast. Dickens drew minute word pictures of poverty. Carlyle, the iconoclast and individualist, pierced repeatedly the shams of society which are partly responsible for the perpetual existence of social misery. In beautiful diction Ruskin spoke in behalf of social justice. In similar fields, France has her Hugo and Balzac; Germany, her Hauptmann; Russia, her Tolstoi and Gorky; Scandinavia, her Bjornson, Ibsen, and Strindberg. Individuals of this type, however, cannot be considered social technologists. They have directed public opinion to specific social problems, but rarely offered technological programs of practical value.

Since 1900, the leaders in social technology, such as C. R. Henderson,[1] Sidney and Beatrice Webb,[2] and E. T. Devine,[3] have made clear the specific conditions under which the poor may be permanently aided.[4] Remedial care will always be necessary, but it must be offered in ways that will not encourage anyone to make a living by begging. The prevailing thought today regarding poverty is in preventive terms. The individual should be shown how to help himself up the economic pathway. Education will make the individual efficient and safeguard him against falling into a chronic state of pauperism.

Above all else, social technology urges the establishment of justice in economic conditions. As shown in Chapter XIV, Henry George, in his *Progress and Poverty,* made a fundamental analysis of one set of causes of poverty, which he found in the unjust factors in the economic system. He showed how ownership in land may be traced back to force. Shall the first person who acquires a section of land be allowed to fence it in and to keep out all other persons unless they pay him a price that rises rapidly as the number of other persons increases?[6] Why is there increasing misery amid advancing wealth? The larger the city the greater the degree of squalor—this was George's perplexing observation. Material progress does not improve the condition of the lowest classes. Prosperity under the present economic system appears to be a heavy wedge driven into society. The individuals who are below the line of cleavage are crushed down; those who are above this line are hoisted upward into positions of luxury and affluence.

Henry George, despite the large number of followers which his ideas have today, was probably in error in believing that to take the ownership of land out of the hands of individuals, through the method of the single tax, would prevent poverty. However, no one should be blind to the fact that increasing land values result from mere increase in population. Either the birth rate or immigration increases population and sends up land values, which in turn is accompanied by a rising scale of rents with an elevated cost of living and increased poverty.

The history of human thought concerning crime has run a vicissitudinous career. It was not until the days of John Howard and Beccaria that a truly scientific approach was made to the problem. John Howard (1726-1790), sheriff of Bedford, became interested in criminals. He visited jails throughout England. He traveled widely in Europe, usually at his own expense, studying the causes of typhus fever and endeavoring to effect a more humane treatment of offenders.

Beccaria (1735-1794), an Italian criminologist, published in 1764 a remarkable book, *Crimes and Punishment.* Beccaria protested against attempting to repress crime by the use of fear. Retaliation is an entirely inadequate motive for administering punishment. Torture is inhuman. Neither retaliation nor repression meets the problem. Reformation was the concept with which Beccaria startled Europe. Punishment should be administered so as to reform.

In modern days the names of Cesare Lombroso (1836-1909) stands out prominently in the field of criminology.[6] Lombroso was a determinist, finding in heredity and environment all the causes of crime, and relieving the individual of moral responsibility. The mental defective, the alcoholic, the frantically angry are irresponsible for the crimes they commit. By defining one irresponsible group after another the Lombrosan school has practically included all individuals in this classification, leaving no one responsible for his conduct.

The remedy for crime, according to Lombroso

and his followers, is found in society. Society is responsible for the criminal acts of its members. If society should surround all individuals from infancy with a favorable environment, then crime would end. In the writings of Garofalo, Ferri, de Quiros, Gross and other Continental criminologists, a broader point of view is usually taken, making the responsibility for crime to rest on three factors, heredity, environment, and individual morality. The margin of choice, and therefore of individual responsibility, is usually made very slender. European criminological experts, and even American writers, such as Parmelee, have commonly minimized the importance of moral character and the accountability of the individual.

In the United States the trend of interest has been penological. Since the days of William Penn, who had been a prisoner in England, American thought has centered on the problem of prison reform. Barrows and Brockway devoted their lives to the reorganization of prison procedure. Wines and Lane show lucidly the trend in penological thought, paying splendid tribute to the achievements of Z. R. Brockway in establishing the Elmira Reformatory (New York).[7]

The fundamental principles of the Elmira procedure are as follows: (1) The average prisoner can be reformed. (2) Reformation of the prisoner is the duty of the state. (3) Prisoners must be considered as individuals and accorded the treatment which each needs in order to bring him to a normal attitude of life. (4) The prisoner's reformation requires his own co-operation in the process. (5) The prison must have the power to lengthen or shorten the sentence according to the offender's stage of reformation. (6) The entire process of reformation is educational, giving the offender opportunity for psychical, mental, and moral growth. (7) Punishment for crime is administered in the discipline and labor, which are unremitting and exacting.

In recent years Thomas M. Osborne has been developing the honor system and self-government among prisoners.[8] The idea is dramatised by Burleigh and Bierstadt in *Punishment*.[9] The conception is that kindly administration and the personal touch of love will win the offender's heart and mind, and effect a reformation.

The last twenty years have seen a remarkable development of the concept of prevention of crime. This theory, however, takes the problem back to pre-adult years, to the adolescent, to childhood, and even to the pre-natal years of the specific individual. The establishment of the juvenile court, with the success of Judge Ben B. Lindsey, has served to call attention to the fact that criminals are made as a rule before they reach the age of twenty-one.

The contributors to recent thought about delinquency, such as Jane Addams, Breckinridge and

Abbott, W. R. George, Ben B. Lindsey, Mrs. Louise de Koven Bowen, Flexner and Baldwin, are pretty largely agreed that the causes of delinquency, and hence of criminality, are as follows: (1) The defective home—made defective by illness, poverty, shiftlessness, ignorance, immorality, desertion, divorce, death—is the leading single causal element. Nearly all criminals begin their careers as disobedient sons. The law of obedience and self-discipline, if not observed in the home, is learned later only at the expense of anti-social and criminal acts. (2) Mental defectiveness often causes delinquency. The mentally defective child, if energetic, has great difficulty in withstanding the evil temptations of life. He or she has bodily passions that are further developed than his mental inhibitions. In this connection the public school has an important function to perform in detecting mental defectives and in segregating them under special educational care. They should be segregated also by sexes, so that they may not reproduce their kind, and they should be kept under educational and institutional direction throughout their lives. They can be made useful and happy under a guarded environment. (3) Civic neglect is a third cause of delinquency and crime. Young people are released from the public schools, often without proper home training and supervision, and drift about in a highly complex urban environment, full of commercialized and vicious devices for preying upon the curious and the unsuspecting. (4) Social injustice, for example in industry, arouses feelings of hatred of class against class, and leads to criminal acts. (5) Moral thoughtlessness and religious indifference are common causes. A moral and religious attitude gives a balanced expression to personality, wholesomeness and obedience in the home; and a deep, constant, and abiding interest in public welfare is an invaluable preventive of sin, vice, and crime.

A growing conception relative to juvenile courts is that a considerable portion of the work that such courts are now called on to perform belongs to the public schools. The compulsory attendance, child welfare, and continuation school departments may well assume responsibility for and direction of many youth who now become court charges. It is urged that a fully organized procedure of constructive work and play activity under the supervision of the schools will greatly reduce juvenile delinquency.

Another cause of juvenile delinquency is parental negligence. It is believed by many authorities that problems of this character should be taken care of through the domestic relations court rather than in the juvenile court. Another causal factor is the growing disrespect for parents on the part of children, that is, the increasing degree of failure of children to appreciate the significance of the concept of obedience.

In regard to labor problems, social technology has made notable contributions. Child labor is a term which refers to the employment of adolescent children for wages, when such children are thereby deprived from normal opportunities of mental and physical growth. Children should learn to work, even at unpleasant tasks, but when at an early age they are taken out of or quit school and become gainfully employed, they are deprived of a normal adolescence; they and society both lose.[10]

The problem of women in industry is due to the migration of millions of women from the home into industry. While women are entitled to equality of opportunity with men, they are often unmindful that constitutionally they are not fitted to perform all the tasks that men are doing; that if they fail in the bearing and rearing of children rationally, the race dies; and that, if they neglect to make the home attractive, the family as an essential social institution is undermined.

The labor problem, when applied to men, brings forth a multiplicity of contradictory opinions. The idea of industrial democracy is the storm center. While praising modern capitalism for its stimulus to initiative and for its large-scale enterprises that have been highly beneficial in many ways, the social technologist pronounces modern capitalism undemocratic. He declares that it must purge itself or be supplanted by another industrial order; it must take cognizance of social changes and adjust itself accordingly or be routed.

The injustice in modern capitalism is often stressed in social technologic thought. Only one factor, wealth, is represented in the management of business. The skilled or unskilled laborers, often "the hardest working partners" in the business, are not represented. Applied sociology, unlike socialism, would keep industry in the hands of individuals. The idea has been best developed, perhaps, by a social theorist, Professor A. W. Small. Labor and capital must both have representation on boards of directors, if capitalism is to prove that it is not undemocratic.[11]

Tripartite management of industry is a current phase of industrial thought. Where employers and employees have reached a common ground of co-operation, they have often joined forces in collusion against the public and the consumer. The employer agrees to a rise in wages for the employee, and the employee to an increase in dividends, providing he receives a portion of the added returns—meanwhile the public is apathetic or rages impotently. The best thought today is urging that on boards of directors and managers all three interested parties shall have representation, namely, labor, capital, and the public.

It is a current opinion that the failure of capitalism to democratize itself will result in the rise of socialism by revolutionary means. If capital with its one-sided control of industry is supplanted by labor with another type of control, it is doubtful how much will be gained. The labor standard is manifesting itself as a class standard, and at times arbitrarily. To have society controlled by labor standards, no matter under what form of socialism they may appear, will not guarantee progress. The labor classes, the capitalist classes, the professional classes—all must rule, and unselfishly for the welfare of society.

The current socialist thought ranges from a radical bolshevist theme of a dictatorship of the proletariat to a conservative state socialism, like that advocated by John Spargo. Bolshevism has the earmarks of class autocracy. Progress cannot be secured by a social order in which the least educated and trained are in control. On the other hand, it is not clear that state socialism, with its governmental control of interest-producing capital and rent-producing land, will best guarantee progress. The socialization of individuals will probably be more effective than the socialization of industries.

The tendency is toward the elimination of profitism. This negative thought, it is claimed, will relieve capitalism of its worst evils, and allow the educational process of socializing individuals to go forward.

The concept of social insurance has been given a remarkable reception since 1882. Social insurance was introduced as a means of pacifying labor and of making it contented under the rule of capitalism. It was admitted into governmental economy by Bismarck as an agency of forestalling socialism. It spread rapidly. It has met with two setbacks. (1) In the first place it has acquired such momentum that capitalism sees it as the entering wedge of a genuine socialism. (2) In the second place social insurance is guaranteeing so much security to the workingman that he is constrained at times to sacrifice his initiative and even to become shiftless, saying in effect to himself, "I'll be taken care of anyway." It is this second type of antagonistic thought that indicates the real weakness in social insurance. It would be better to have a society in which the workingmen as a class would have an ample opportunity of caring for, and be stimulated to care for, their old age and for periods of disability. For the individual exceptions, special provisions could be made.

The unemployment problem has produced many reform theories. Unemployment insurance, now being made the subject of experiment, is probably not reaching the main causes. The causal factors are many and deep-seated; they range from individual shiftlessness and mental defectiveness on one hand, to economic injustice and social callousness on the other.[12] The prevailing thought urges a more efficient training of the individual; the increasing of the workman's opportunity to enlarge his personality through each day's work; the development of industrial democracy and justice; and a complete socialization program.

Another set of problems concerning which applied sociology is endeavoring to find solutions relates to the family, feminism, marriage, divorce, and housing. Professor George Elliott Howard[13] and Dr. Edward Westermarck[14] have traced the development of the family and marriage throughout human history. The primitive relationships between sexes have been described by many anthropological writers. A history of the American family has been written by A. W. Calhoun.[15] Single volume treatments of the family as a social institution have been made by Bosanquet[16] and Goodsell.[17] These works essentially agree that the family is an evolutionary product, that the primitive family centered about the mother and child, that patriarchalism introduced a high degree of masculine arbitrariness, and that the family is at present undergoing marked changes whereby the spirit of democracy is gaining ground.

In the new found spirit of freedom, woman has sometimes been captivated by the desire to follow man into all the man-made occupations. Sex nature predestines woman to the chief occupation or profession of all, that of motherhood. For woman to rush headlong after men into industry may turn out to be not liberty, but license and deterioration. Current social thought protests vigorously against the idea of women being household drudges, and also against women wasting their time in pluming themselves or in idling away their days in dolls' houses, supported dependents of men. Women are entitled to learn vocations and to live constructive lives, in an atmosphere of the largest possible freedom consistent with the development of themselves and the race. On the other hand, any movement which weakens the home as a societary training institution apparently defies the laws of social advance.

The housing problem is provoking urgent thought. With the rise of large cities the economic order favors exorbitant land values and extraordinarily high rents. The social increment goes into the hands of the few. The flat and apartment house life often favors pet bulldogs rather than children, and decreases the efficiency of the home as a social institution. These untoward tendencies, furthermore, are being supplemented by an attitude of more or less helpless apathy on the part of the public.

Another field of applied sociologic thought is represented by the terms, race problems, immigration, and naturalization. These concepts are all outgrowths of the population concept which has been treated in an earlier chapter. The human race with its common origin has subdivided and wandered into all the inhabitable parts of the globe. Climate, geography, and social environment have operated to make the race subdivisions distinct and discriminatory. Race pride and prejudice have raised impassable race barriers.

In the United States the leading race problem involves the Negroes. Booker T. Washington[18] urged that if the Negro shows himself industrially efficient and morally worthy, the prejudice against him will disappear. W. E. B. DuBois[19] asks that the prejudice against the colored race by the white race be removed in order that the Negro may have a fair chance to show himself capable. The Southern white people declare that the colored people must be segregated on a lower plane than that occupied by the white race. Northern people assert that the trouble lies chiefly in an undemocratic attitude of Southern white people toward the colored race. Thus the currents of thought concerning the Negro come into conflict, but without forming a common current of action.

Another phase of the race problem is conveyed by the concept of hyphenated interests. The Americanization movement has assumed momentum because of the need for a more unified spirit within the nation. Although some of the promoters of Americanization have used autocratic means, the opinion is gaining ground that the transference of the loyalty of the immigrant from his home country to his adopted country can best be effected by treating the immigrant sympathetically and democratically in all his contacts—industrial, social, political—with the people of our land.[20]

The public health movement has acquired force

because of the belief that only public and widespread action can remove many of the causes of disease. Tuberculosis, for example, is a disease that is caused by a microscopic germ which thrives and multiplies in the tissues of susceptible and weakened organisms. Tuberculosis and unsanitary housing conditions flourish together. The individual is often helpless, but the thought is now well grounded that public action can stamp out the breeding places of the tubercle bacilli and relieve the country of the white plague. An improved economic and educational status for the unskilled laborer and his family would also help to improve the health level of the country. Current social thought supports the contention that the real work of a physician is to keep people well rather than to cure them after they have fallen seriously ill. Preventive medicine and the public health movement are strongly urged by social technology.

Another phase of applied sociology of current significance is indicated by the term, community organization.[21] The idea of this movement originated in the failure of people to develop a democratic consciousness. Community organization refers to attempts of communities to organize themselves for neighborhood efficiency. When a community organizes its own recreations and amusements, it functions in two important directions. (1) It supplants commercialized amusements, operated for profit and often on a socially destructive basis, by community recreation, maintained by the people themselves in socially constructive ways and at a minimum of expense. (2) In participating in and building up community enterprises such as community recreation, the people of the community develop a co-operative democratic consciousness. The problem of the use of leisure time is growing in proportion to the extent that the laboring classes are winning a shorter work day. In addition to community recreation, community health movements, community newspapers, community co-operative stores, community committees for securing needed legislation and for breaking the force of economic monopoly, are attracting widespread attention. The social unit and the block system of community service, are terms which indicate variations of the community organization concept, originally a product of the need of meeting the leisure time problem constructively with the very important result of re-creating democracy.

Social technology has produced the survey.[22] The social survey, being related in its origin to the census, is an accurate method of gathering social facts, not merely facts about the numbers of people, the acreage, and the amount of wealth, but the facts about the societary assets and liabilities of a city or community, and concerning the constructive and the destructive forces. By making surveys at regular intervals of five or ten year periods, a community can determine the amount and direction of its own progress. The idea of a survey is similar to that of an inventory of a business house—to find out the gains and losses, and to plan for the future according to the verdict of the inventory.

In recent years social case work has acquired an important rank in the field of applied sociology. Social reform deals with methods for improving the whole mass of individuals and for raising the level of the entire group; social case work on the other hand stimulates individuals to improve the quality of their lives, to adjust themselves more adequately to their environment, and to transform their environments. Social case work insists that sound social reforms can be effected only on the basis of first-hand experiences with the needs of individuals who are the victims of social imperfections or their own shortcomings. Social work with individuals has provided a body of specific facts of first magnitude as a foundation for measures of social amelioration and progress; it has mirrored life which is under the harrow of circumstances; it has portrayed life where living conditions are harshest.

Applied sociology represents methods of social attack. It furthers progress by planning for society on the basis of past societal experiences and current facts and tendencies. It fulfils the demands of social telesis.

Chapter XXV

The Rise of Educational Sociology

In recent decades educational leaders have been thinking in sociological terms. In its experimental phases educational sociology constitutes a phase of applied sociology. The principles of modern educational sociology have a thousand sources.

Pestalozzi (1746-1827) may be considered a forerunner of current social theories of education. He was interested in humanity for humanity's sake. Like St. Francis of Assisi, he lived with the poor in order that he might teach them to be thrifty and worthy citizens. In his *Leonard and Gertrude,* he described the life of the poor, and formulated an educational procedure for educating the poor. He was a lover of little children, of poor people, of anyone in trouble, of all humanity. He spoke in dignified terms of the function of a good woman, no matter how humble her station in life. Her first duty is to educate her children and to meet the needs of her family. She has, also, obligations to her neighbors and community. Others, seeing her constructive work, will be inspired and motivated to do likewise.

In opening an industrial school for the poor, Pestalozzi recognized that the poor have the least opportunities for development and the largest numbers of problems to solve,—therefore they are in the greatest need of educational advantages. He held that all the phases of human personality should be trained, and that there should be "a harmonious development of all human powers." Hence, education is the greatest gift that anyone, rich or poor, can receive. In urging that the child should be educated in company with other children, that is, in groups, he took an attitude superior to that of Rousseau, but presaging that of Froebel.

Froebel (1782-1852), the founder of the kindergarten, considered little children "as plants in a garden." He recognized the educative importance of the early years of life. He perceived the possibilities of teaching through the use of plays and games. He understood the "interests" of little children. His most important conception, perhaps, was his recognition of the gregarious impulses as an effective setting for the educative processes. While neo-Froebelians have sometimes turned all work into play and have neglected to train the child in doing some things in which he is not interested at the particular time, the utilization of the gregarious and play impulses as vital backgrounds for education is not unworthy. The evils in this connection are no greater than when the Montessori method is followed, with its emphasis upon a maximum of individual choice.

In Horace Mann (1796-1859), American education found a new social emphasis. Education in a democracy, according to Mann, should be public and open equally to all classes of people. Moreover, in a democracy, education is not a mere acquisition of knowledge; it is not concealed in college degrees as such; it is not aristocratic. It was Mann's contention that education should be an actual training for rearing worthy families, for living an unsefish social life, for being a public spirited citizen in one's daily activities.

Mann asserted that the common school is the bulwark of the nation. He believed that education should encourage true religion. He inaugurated the normal training school,—in support of his theory of specially trained teachers. His social philosophy is contained in a statement from his last public address: "Be ashamed to die until you have won a victory for humanity."

During the intervening decades since the days of Horace Mann, the social conception of education has been assuming new practical phases. Professor John Dewey has pointed out that all communication is education; that the terms, common, community, and communication, possess more than a verbal relationship.[1] Anything is educative which produces similar emotional and intellectual dispositions, that is, like ways of responding to stimuli. Societal life, hence, is unusually educative. Education consists of processes of self-development, of self-continuation, of social continuation. These processes are possible only on bases of common means of communication. It is these means, as Professor C. H. Cooley has indicated, which make even the powerful factors of suggestion and imitation so universal.

It is not the environment which directly implants certain desires in individuals.[2] The environment sets up conditions which stimulate certain ways of acting. The child gets a real idea of a hat, not by seeing a hat, or by being told of its uses, but by actually using a hat. The social environment, in other words, forms "the mental and emotional disposition of behavior in individuals by engaging them in activities" that arouse various impulses, purposes, and produces certain consequences.[3]

As society becomes exceedingly complex, it is essential that society provide a simplified social environment through which the child may pass, in order that he may adjust himself the more quickly and easily to the complex societal environment. To this end the school serves a valuable purpose. However, in order to function best, the school must be a replica in as many ways as possible of real society.[4]

The special social environment, namely, the school, must simplify and arrange in an orderly way the dispositional factors it wishes to develop in children. It must present the existing social customs in purified and idealized forms. It must create a wider and better balanced environment for the young than they would have if they were not in school.

Imitation, to Dr. Dewey, is a less useful term than many social psychologists believe. What objectively is a process of imitation is subjectively a process of like response to like stimuli. The term imitation does not explain; it simply describes—objectively. The fundamental fact that the sociological student needs to keep in mind is that "persons being alike in structure respond in the same way to like stimuli."[5] This conception is similar to ideas that Professors Giddings and Cooley have elaborated. The societal significance of this interpretation can be stated best in terms of social control. The highest type of social control is that which plans for a common mental disposition, a common way of understanding objects, events, and acts, common sets of socially constructive stimuli.

Professor Dewey argues for a school life which fully connects theory and practice. While pragmatic, he emphasizes the necessity for a correct theory, but more particularly the combining of theory and practice—in the school life itself. In other words, anything which sets school life apart from actual life is a disutility; it is educationally harmful. Hence school life must include the actual occupations, nature study, and the like. It must relegate formal education to a secondary position. The moral atmosphere of the schoolroom must change from one primarily of discipline, even formal discipline, to one of co-operation.

School life, in other terms, is properly an embryonic community life. It is the business of the school to train each child into membership of a little community that is a counterpart of society at large, "saturating him with the spirit of service, and providing him with the instruments of effective self-direction."[6] Professor Dewey would make the school a miniature society, fitting its members by their daily activities in the schools for normal membership in "a larger society which is worthy, lovely, and harmonious."

The literature on educational sociology is growing rapidly. Within recent years several books on educational sociology have appeared. In the list of the authors of these works are the names of O'Shea, Snedden, Smith, King, Clow, Betts, Dutton, and others of equal importance.[7] Professor Walter R. Smith, for example, in applying sociological principles to educational work, contends that normal school graduates have been taught to look to psychology alone for the key to sound pedagogy, whereas sociology is perhaps an equally important key to effective teaching. Education is not entirely a matter of training the mind of the individual; it is also a process of acquainting the individual with the needs of society and of helping him to participate in improving the quality of societary life. Dr. Smith urges training not *for* citizenship, but training *into* citizenship.[8]

Inasmuch as men and women live and develop and work as members of groups, it is vital, according to Dr. Snedden, that children be taught as integral units of group life. It is sociology that must determine the aims of education.[9] By sociological standards it has been proved that existing curricula in the United States are excessively individualistic in aim as well as in method. Their purpose has been to encourage the individual to win against, rather than with, his fellows. Our curricula provide self-culture studies and self-development studies, but few social culture and social development studies. The former are indispensable, but if not properly balanced by the latter they are positively dangerous.

The responsibilities of individuals for collective thinking and acting have never been taught to any degree in the schools, and yet these responsibilities, not only in time of war, but increasingly so in time of peace, must be assumed widely, else democracy itself will collapse. By training pupils in the principles of individual success primarily, the schools have turned out a generation of persons who are unready to meet the new world problems that are at hand, and who are unable to promote "constructive programs making for international co-operation and friendliness."[10]

Custom, not social needs, has too often controlled school curricula. The *Anabasis* and Caesar's *Commentaries,* although splendid bits of literary composition, "are about as significant to the realities of a nineteenth or twentieth century as bows and arrows would be in modern warfare, or Roman galleys in the naval contests of tomorrow.[11] The study of forgotten tongues and antiquated fragments of literature falls far short of training twentieth century youths for the conscious co-operative direction of the social forces of the future.

Vocational education is not all-sufficient. Youth must be taught to be socially and morally efficient—no less than physically and vocationally.[12] In addition to the current emphasis upon vocational education, attention must be given to a moral education in the schools that can produce in individuals the moral character required to meet the needs of a highly developed democracy.

Educational sociology has viewed with alarm certain recent tendencies in vocational guidance. It has supported heartily the plans for giving every child an occupational training and of enabling him to earn his own living. On the other hand, it has deplored the idea that a vocation or earning a living is an end in itself. It has insisted that the main reason for teaching a boy a trade is that the boy may have a larger opportunity for developing his personality and for serving society.

Likewise, educational sociology has often looked askance at scientific management, or the movement for educating all workingmen to the point of highest productive efficiency. Such a training has frequently produced a maximum increase in profits for those who have promoted it and a minimum of increase in wages for the workers, besides tending to turn the latter into mere machines, instead of into human leaders with increased capacities for enjoyment and spiritual service.

The studies in all school curricula must be evaluated in terms of social worth. For example, what is the purpose of teaching history? Is it to give the pupil a chronology of dates and a catalogue of ignoble kings and bloody battles, or is it to give the pupil the meaning of social evolution, social progress, social inheritances, the rise of social needs?[14]

Educational sociology holds the theory that training for unselfish social living is as important as training for individual pecuniary success. It is engaged at the present time in working out techniques for introducing every member of the public schools to the sociological viewpoint. The names under which such techniques appear is immaterial, whether as community civics, American history studies, elementary social science, or elementary sociology. The next few decades will undoubtedly be marked by the rapid spread of educational sociology.

Chapter XXVI

The Sociology of Modern Christianity

In a foregoing chapter the invaluable contribution of the Hebrews to social thought was presented; the attack of the prophets on social injustice was the outstanding feature. In another chapter the emphasis by Jesus upon love as a dynamic societal principle was described. In the centuries which followed the beginning of the Christian era, the Church apotheosized beliefs, creeds, dogmas. Near the close of the nineteenth century a renaissance of the social teachings of Jesus occurred.

The trio of writers who brought forward the social ideals of Christianity in a new, positive, and stimulating way in the closing decades of the last century were Washington Gladden, Josiah Strong, and Richard T. Ely. All three of these men began about 1885 to discuss in print the social content of Christianity. These men had been aroused by the apparent impotence of the Christian Church in face of the increasing power of capitalism. While many church leaders allowed themselves to be carried along in the powerful arms of capitalism, there were a few who perceived the wreck of human lives that was often left in the wake of the capitalistic movement. These individuals, while not blind to the social values of capitalism, were in touch with the laboring man, and by these contacts caught the social need of the hour. In this social crisis they heard the still, small voice coming down through the centuries, even the voice of Jesus as he spoke in behalf of the poor and outcast.

It was Washington Gladden who startled and even angered the world of religious and economic thought by protesting against the acceptance of "tainted money." By this term he referred to money which had been made under a capitalistic system at the expense of the lives of men, women, and little children in the industrial processes. Dr. Gladden weathered the storm of protest and gave the capitalistic world a new concept which, while it aroused anger, also brought introspection and a new type of social conscience into the lives of many Christians.

It was Dr. Gladden's contention that employer and employee ought to be friends, because they are so closely associated. It is a very large part of the business of the employer to maintain sympathetic relations between himself and his employees.[1] If the business man will not let his fellowmen share in his prosperity, he will become in spite of himself a sharer in their adversity.

The attitude of Dr. Gladden toward the acceptance of railway passes by the clergy attracted widespread attention. He came to the conclusion that a railroad company is bound to render an equal service to all the people; its business is not to show special favors to the representatives of either religion or charity.[2] "What it has no right to give me, I have no right to take, and for several years I have not taken it; I pay the regular fare as all my neighbors do or ought."

Dr. Gladden urged the abolition of city slums by governmental action. Inasmuch as slums are rife with moral miasmas and are breeding-places of pauperism and crime, the city has the same right to abate such curses as to drain a morass. Moreover, individuals ought to have no property rights "in premises which breed death and engender vice. When they have proved that they lack the power to keep their property from falling into such conditions, their property must be summarily taken away from them."[3]

Without minimizing the importance of conflict as a principle of social progress, Dr. Gladden stressed the concept of co-operation. For example, in industrial matters he advocated the idea of a true trades union—"the union of employers and employed—of guiding brains and willing hands—all watchful of each other's interests, seeking each other's welfare, working for the common good."[4]

In his well-known treatise on *Social Salvation,* Dr. Gladden asserts that, in order to be soundly converted, an individual must comprehend his social relationships and strive to fulfil them, as well as set up right relationships with God.[5] Sanctification consists in fulfilling one's social as well as one's divine privileges, and in living according to the needs of human society as well as according to the needs of the human soul. An individual can no more be a Christian by himself than he can sing an oratorio alone.[6]

It is no purely social gospel that Dr. Gladden taught. He was correct in protesting against the attitude of certain reformers who hold that changing the environment is all-sufficient. It is possible to go too far in removing temptations from the pathway of men; it would be unwise to neglect the problem of equipping men to resist temptation, and hence to weaken the sense of moral responsibility.[7]

In the field of practical social reform Dr. Josiah Strong did effective work. He also re-interpreted the social principles of Jesus, and boldly proclaimed the spirit of love as the cardinal principle for the organization of human society.[8] He indicated that people have stressed properly the importance of *believing* the truth, but underestimated the importance of *living* the truth.[9] He protested against the tendency to separate the sacred and the secular, and to divorce doctrine from conduct. He believed that the prevailing religious tendency to neglect the sacred commandment, of loving one's neighbor as one's self, has led to a selfish individualism on the part of many religious people.

The contributions to social thought by Gladden and Strong were ably supported by the social ideas of Richard T. Ely. Professor Ely remonstrated against the tendency of many church people to think that they can serve God without devoting their lives to their fellowmen.[10] He made vivid the complaint of American workingmen that church membership on the part of employers and landlords does not necessarily insure just and considerate treatment of employees and tenants.[11] Professor Ely insisted that it is as holy a work "to lead a crusade against filth, vice, and disease in slums of cities, and to seek the abolition of the disgraceful tenement houses of American cities, as it is to send missionaries to the heathen."[12]

The pioneer work of Gladden, Strong, Ely, and others in rejuvenating the social meaning of Christianity in the closing years of the nineteenth century has been carried forward in the present century by a host of able writers. The list includes the names of well known socio-religious thinkers such as Peabody,[13] Mathews,[14] Rauschenbusch,[15] Batten,[16] Ward,[17] Atkinson,[18] Ryan,[19] Stelzle,[20] and Taylor.[21] Special attention will be given to the contributions of Rauschenbusch and Ward, because each has been a storm-center in socio-religious matters.

In his *Christianity and the Social Crisis,* Professor Rauschenbusch gave a brief history of Christianity and its Hebrew antecedents, showing first that "the essential purpose of Christianity was to transform human society into the Kingdom of God by regenerating all human relations and reconstituting them in accordance with the will of God."[22] He then raised the question, why has Christianity not undertaken the work of social reconstruction? He believed that if the Church were to direct its full available force against any social wrong, probably nothing could withstand it.[23] Despite the fact that Christianity has played a leading part in lifting woman to equality and companionship with men, in changing parental despotism to parental service, in eliminating unnatural vice, in abolishing slavery, in covering all lands with a network of charities, in fostering institutions of learning, in aiding the progress of civil liberty and social justice, in diffusing a softening tenderness throughout human life, in taming selfishness, and in creating a resolute sense of duty, it has not yet undertaken a reconstruction of society on a Christian basis.[24] It has been engaged in suppressing some of the most glaring evils in the social system of the time.[25]

Dr. Rauschenbusch pointed out several historical factors which have prevented Christianity from entering upon a program of reconstructing society, many of which no longer obtain.[26] These hindering factors have been: (1) the moral resentment of the classes whose interests are endangered by a moral campaign; (2) the belief in the immediate return of Christ, which precluded a long outlook; (3) the primitive attitude of fear and distrust toward the state; (4) the other-worldliness of Christian desire; (5) the ascetic and monastic ideals; (6) ceremonialism; (7) dogmatism; (8) the monarchial organization of the church; (9) an absence of the intellectual prerequisites for social reconstruction. To the extent that Christianity is no longer hampered by these characteristics it is ready to undertake the task of making over society.

The main danger in the present crisis which demands the attention of social Christianity was found by Professor Rauschenbusch in the autocratic, unjust phases of capitalism, with its somewhat undemocratic wage system. To this expression of autocracy there is a three-fold class reaction.[27] First, there are those classes which are in practical control of wealth; they have no reformatory program; they are anxious to maintain the present social order intact. Second, there are the middle social classes, which, sharing partially in the advantages of the present social adjustment, are also chafing under social grievances which their ideals do not allow them to attack vigorously; they want reform work by peaceful and gradual methods. Third, there are the disinherited classes, which see a widening chasm between themselves and the wealthy, a chasm that "only a revolutionary lift can carry them across." It is around the condition and attitudes of the masses that the social crisis revolves. This social attitude is like a tank of gasoline, which by a single explosion will blow a car sky-high, or which, by a series of little explosions will push a car to the top of a mountain.[28] Which process does Christianity wish to further? If the latter, then Christianity must socialize first the attitude of the classes of wealth and social power. Unfortunately, wealth often grows stronger than the man who owns it; it may own him and rob him of his moral and spiritual freedom.[29] Can Christianity dissolve this dilemma?

The principle that a Christian should seek an ascetic departure from the world of life and work is no longer acceptable. He has two other possibilities. He can either condemn the world and try to improve it, or tolerate it and gradually be conformed to it.[30] By these sharply drawn alternatives, Professor Rauschenbusch awoke the Christian world. While many Christians did not believe that the situation was as crucial as thus depicted, they nevertheless were jarred from a state of moral lethargy.

As a pastor for eleven years among the working people of New York City, Dr. Rauschenbusch learned to understand the heart throbs and yearnings of the masses, and dedicated his life through Christian service to easing the pressure upon the working classes and to increasing the forces that bear them up. He saw the solution of the social problem in a Christian socialism that would destroy the autocracy of wealth and establish a democratic form of industrial relationships. He believed in the social or public ownership of the natural resources of the earth. "It is preposterous to think that an individual or a corporation can have absolute ownership in a vein of coal or copper. A mining company owns the holes in the ground, for it made the holes; it does not own the coal; for it did not make the coal. The coal is the gift of God and belongs to the people."[31]

Another difficulty is found in the fact that business methods and the principles of Christianity have always been at strife.[32] Individuals are struggling to get the better of their fellows. This tendency has been institutionalized in the form of business enterprise. Private persons have been permitted "to put their thumbs where they can constrict the life blood of the nation at will."[33] Christianity, on the other hand, lauds the principle of unselfish service, and of ranking the individual as the greatest who gives most. Christianity is awakening to its gigantic task of stopping the nation on "its headlong ride on the road of covetousness."

It is in this connection that Professor Rauschenbusch has made famous the phrase, "Christianizing the social order." This term means "bringing the social order into harmony with the ethical convictions which are identified with Christ."[35] Such a program involves attacking "the last intrenchment of autocracy," namely, in business,—and Christianizing business. The struggle is already on. In many of the phases of the conflict, capitalism is swallowing up Christianity. The church becomes traditional, narrowly ecclesiastical, dogmatic, opposing science and democracy. Where capitalism is strongest, the churches as virile social forces are weakest.[34]

In reply to the often repeated charge that socialized Christianity is no Christianity at all, Professor Rauschenbusch shows that personal religion, instead of being defeated by a socialized religion, will gain strength and be able to present a much stronger appeal than it now does. The advocate of the social teachings of Jesus is not attacking personal religion, but rather endeavoring to give personal religion a new dynamic, especially in those phases of modern life where personal religion has lost most of its appeal. The opponents of social Christianity cannot afford to neglect the fact that the often one-sided, mechanical, and superficial gospel and methods of evangelism have created a religious apathy, if not a definite reaction against religion.[37] It is blind foolishness to try to fence out the new social spirit from Christianity instead of letting it fuse with the older religious faith and "create a new total that will be completer and more Christian than the old religious individualism at its best."[37]

Dr. Rauschenbusch insisted that there must be a Christianizing of international relations, that individuals must be taught to see the sinfulness of the present social order, and that the popular conception of God must be democratized.[39] He reinterpreted the organic unity of human society,—asserting that when one man sins, other men suffer; and that when one class sins, other classes bear a part of the suffering.

In 1908, the Federal Council of the Churches of Christ in America was organized at Philadelphia. The Council adopted with slight modifications the resolutions which some months earlier had been accepted by the General Conference of the Methodist Episcopal Church (North), and which Rev. Harry F. Ward and others had drawn up.

This Bill of Rights, as the Resolutions have been called, imposed upon the members of the more than thirty Protestant denominations the duty of obtaining industrial justice for the cause of labor. It spoke for (1) the principle of arbitration in industrial dissensions, (2) the adequate protection of workers in hazardous trades, (3) the abolition of child labor, (4) the safeguarding of physical and moral health of women in industry, (5) the suppression of the "sweating system," (6) the reduction of the hours of labor to the lowest practicable point, (7) a living wage in all industries, (8) one day of rest in seven for all workers, (9) the most equitable division of the products of industry that can ultimately be devised, (10) suitable provisions for old age or disability of workers, and (11) the abatement of poverty.

At the meeting of the Federal Council of the

Churches of Christ in America at a special meeting held at Cleveland, Ohio, May 6-8, 1919, the foregoing platform was re-affirmed; and in addition, as a means of meeting the needs of the reconstruction days following the World War, the following notable resolutions were adopted. The Council declared not only that labor is entitled to an equitable share in the profits of industry, but took the new step of expressing the belief that labor is entitled also to an equitable share in the management of industry. "The sharing of shop control and management is an inevitable step" in the attainment of an ordered and constructive democracy in industry. The Council asserted that the first charge upon industry should be wages sufficient to support an American standard of living.

In 1919, the Committee on Special War Activities of the National Catholic War Council published a brief but important document on social reconstruction. In this pamphlet the defects of the capitalistic system of industry are declared to be: "Enormous inefficiency and waste in the production and distribution of commodities; insufficient incomes for the great majority of wage-earners; and unnecessarily large incomes for a small minority of privileged capitalists."[50] The Committee urged that employees shall exercise a reasonable share in the management of industrial enterprises, and that the State should inaugurate comprehensive provisions for health insurance and old age insurance.

It recognized that the true line of progress is in the direction of co-operative production and of co-partnership arrangements. "In the former, the workers own and manage the industries themselves; in the latter, they own a substantial part of the corporate stock and exercise a reasonable share in the management."[41] The Catholic pronunciamento demands that the spirit of both labor and capital be reformed. The laborer must give up the desire of a maximum of return for a minimum of service; he must remember that he owes society an honest day's work for a fair wage. On the other hand the capitalist must learn that wealth is not possession but stewardship, and that "profit-making is not the basic justification of business enterprise."[42]

Inasmuch as the Rev. Harry F. Ward has written more extensively on social Christianity than any other person, save Rauschenbusch, and has created widespread and heart-searching discussions, his contributions to socio-religious thought will be considered next. Dr. Ward does not believe in social service as a bait for drawing people into the church. He objects to bribing people in order to get them into an evangelistic meeting. To him social service is a natural phase of religion, expressing itself freely and without sinuous designs. In his estimation, soup kitchens are not to be established as a means of enticing the laboring man inside the church walls, but as an unselfish expression of the Christian's desire to be true to the Christ spirit. Social service is not a selfish program, on the part of the church, for increasing its membership. It is as natural to Christianity as personal evangelism, and equally intrinsic and vital. It has won more than national recognition. While it is radical in the eyes of the conservative, it contains an analysis of social conditions that many of its critics have not appreciated. It breathes a sincerity and a straightforwardness that compels the fair-minded reader to give heed.

Slavery was rejected as the economic basis of civilization, and monarchy has recently been rejected as the political basis. In each instance the world came to a junction where idealistic impulse overthrew entrenched power. It is Dr. Ward's contention that the world is now reaching a similar junction point, a point where idealistic impulse will dethrone the autocracy in capitalism. The idealistic impulse, to which reference has been made in the foregoing lines, is germinal in the teachings of Jesus.

With prophetic vision, more organized than the vision of Amos, Hosea, Isaiah, but equally sincere, and fearless, Dr. Ward points out the principles of the new social order which he believes are almost upon the world. He then describes the various factors which are struggling each in its own way to inaugurate the new order.

The five principles of the new social order are equality, universal service, efficiency, the supremacy of personality, and solidarity. (1) Equality is the old word which won attention in the American and French Revolutions. It grew out of the theory of natural rights which was discussed in Chapter XI. The American emphasis on the principle of equality is shown in the admiration that is accorded the achievements of energy and toil, in the common struggle for more wealth and luxury, in foreign missionary activities, in the rise of the democratic conscience and the idealistic impulses of the people.

On the other hand, the principle of equality is being violated when, instead of trying to remove the natural inequalities among folks, "we increase them by giving special privileges to the strong as the reward of their strength." The United States is at the crossroads. One highway is characterized by luxury and extravagance on one side, and by poverty and slavery on the other; it leads to revolutionary attempts on the part of the masses to overthrow the privileged classes. It ends in national decadence. The second highway is characterized by justice. Those in economic authority are willing to grant representation to labor in the management of industry and to further the rise of the co-operative spirit. They are willing to sacrifice their own special privileges for the sake of the welfare of the disinherited.

The intellectuals of the middle class hold vast power. In crises, they usually join the privileged classes rather than the masses; and hence, their influence often swings to the side of injustice.[43]

(2) Universal service is the principle of equal obligation. Equal rights, by itself, may mean equal rights to cheat, to exploit. It needs to be checked by its complement of equal obligation. During the World War there was a frequent demonstration of the principle of universal service. "We are engaged in helping the boys at the front" became the slogan. At the front as well as in the home towns and cities, wealthy and poor, capital and labor served together. The end of the War gave prominence to this question: Will the universal service idea spread or will it be discarded? Will industry go back to the unashamed pursuit of private gain?[44]

Dr. Ward makes a careful distinction between the service of democratic mutual helpfulness and the service of a governing class, no matter how excellent.[45] It is a low type of service which grants Christmas dinners to the poor with the result that the poor are thereby made contented with their lot in life.

(3) Efficiency is a term which is the product of the mechanical era, which originated in the business world, and which is now being applied to all phases of social organization.[46] Its aim is perfection in social mechanics. Social efficiency includes not only social engineering but social knowledge, social philosophy, social ethics, and social religion. Evidences of social inefficiency are common; for example, the failure to use and apply the social knowledge that

we have, and the loss of energy through an overemphasis on competition. Democracy will never be able to succeed merely because of its splendid ethical ideals.[47] The need is for an efficiency in government that is scientific and not simply a business efficiency.[48] Scientific efficiency includes "the spirit of service to the common interest by which alone democracy can live."[49]

(4) The supremacy of personality is a principle of life that conflicts today with the current emphasis on economic efficiency. It is because the latter is so often reckless of human values that the new social order will stress the development of things of the spirit rather than material goods; even business must practice this ideal. The World War raised the estimate which the common people put on their own lives; but the ultimate result will depend on whether or not people took part in the war voluntarily and conscious of high moral purposes, and whether or not the peace which follows shall bring a new world organization that conserves all the advances in human living that have thus far been made.

Institutions possess an inherent fallibility. They tend to become mechanical and repressive, even those dedicated to high purposes, such as institutions of democracy, of education, and of religion. The supreme object of any social institution and organization, no matter in what field it may exist, should be the increase of personality.[50]

(5) The new social order will be governed by a sense of solidarity, that is, by a community of feeling and thought which arises when individuals associate together in working for a common end. World solidarity will come when all peoples learn to work together for public welfare, and subordinate all selfish desires to this end. Christianity is moving in this direction when it advances the concept of "comradeship of all men with each other and with the Great Companion," when it gradually unfolds the idea of a unified world life, when it applies its doctrines of brotherhood of man to the relations of the employer and employee or to the relations of white and black races, when it seeks the democratic solidarity of the human race rather than the imperialistic solidarity of an overhead religious control, when it endeavors to spread love and faith, rather than to spread dogmas and promote organizations.[51] Class cleavage, nationalism as distinct from nationality, race prejudice, ignorance, and selfishness are the main opponents of the world brotherhood principle.

Dr. Ward, having defined what he considers the chief principles that will govern the new social order, proceeds to measure current movements by certain standards. He reviews the declarations of the British Labor Party, the Russian Soviet Republic, the League of Nations, and the labor movements in the United States. These tendencies are all expressions of a more or less blind desire for justice. In all countries of the world the masses are restless, stirring, and experiencing a keen sense of injustice. Their leaders are struggling, unscientifically as a rule, toward the light of a new day of democracy. The trend which this struggle takes depends on the given social environment and the attitude of the persons in authority. If undue repression and autocracy are exercised for a long period of time, as in Russia under the Czars, revolution is the only means of escape open to the masses. Schooled for a long time under the lash of autocracy, when they themselves come into control, they will use the only means of control that they know, the lash of autocracy.

The British Labor Party is moving in the direction of guild socialism, which includes the organization of industry into large units, in charge of the workers and relatively free from the rule of the politicians. The national government is to have a general oversight over the large industrial units. As immediate steps in this direction, the Labor Party demands the nationalization of the railroads, mines, and of the production of electric power. Municipalities participate in the common ownership program. The method of transformation is to be gradual, largely based on political action.

In regard to the League of Nations Covenant, which was agreed upon in Paris in 1919, Dr. Ward takes a negative attitude. Although he believes firmly in an organization of good will, in international friendship and in world solidarity upon democratic bases, he asserts stoutly that the Paris Covenant is "a symbol of the sacred right of private property,"[52] that it provided for an international organization of capitalism with all the force of powerful national governments behind it, that it represented a series of compromises between nationally selfish units, that it was an expression of the wishes of the rulers of the democratic states who are essentially of "the same moral caliber as the ruling class of imperialistic militarism, and bear a similar sinister relationship to the future welfare of the common folk."[53]

The weakness of Dr. Ward's treatment of the programs for the new social order is that it discusses almost entirely programs, platforms, ideals, without considerating the relations between the progams and the actual practices of the various organizations. In contrasting the best phases, for example, of the British Labor Party with the worst phases of capitalism, an incomplete picture is given. However, this weakness in method need not obscure the strength of thought which Dr. Ward displays. Some of the most thought-provoking deductions are:

1. That individualistic Christianity is losing ground.

2. That the middle class is becoming a class of privilege.

3. That the intellectuals of the middle class,

while keenly aware of the evils in the capitalistic system, are so much indebted to that system that they would consider themselves ingrates if they spoke out against it, or they are simply afraid to speak out.

4. That jails and machine guns will not stop the laboring classes in appealing for a democratic reorganization of industry, but will rather hasten revolutions, with resultant dictatorships of the proletariat.

5. That capitalism is passing, as it is bound to do, because it is organized selfishness—its fundamental principle is wrong.

6. That political democracy is fighting for its life today, being attacked on the one flank by economic imperialism and on the other by the dictatorship of the proletariat.[54]

7. That unless the struggle can be ended by a process of reason and orderly progress, the world is doomed to devastation by universal conflict.

8. That the goal of social development is, in broad terms, "a fraternal world community, the great loving family of mankind, knit together by common needs but most of all by loyalty to common ideals, and by the power of its common love efficiently directing and controlling its common life."[55]

An important question arises: How shall the social teachings of Jesus become widely taught? Evangelistic Christianity, with its personal emphasis, cannot be expected adequately to carry the social message. Preachers, theologically trained, are bound to give the social phases of Christianity a secondary place. In recent years, however, a movement known as religious education has been acquiring momentum. Moreover, a social theory of religious education has been formulated. In this connection, Dr. George Albert Coe has perhaps done the most significant work. Our life, Dr. Coe believes, gets its largest meaning not from the fact of individual self-consciousness alone, but from the equally important fact that life is social.[56] Without a belief in social consciousness, an endless existence after death, in terms of self-consciousness primarily, would be meaningless and probably valueless. Religion must solve the problem of establishing a Kingdom of Heaven on earth, and also train its votaries for a societal life in Heaven. The latter problem will be met easily when the former is solved. It is well illustrated by the young Christian lady from Virginia who asked: Won't there have to be a separate Heaven for Negroes, since we hate them so here? In other words, will there not have to be a thousand or a million Heavens in order to accommodate happily all the antagonistic Christian groups now on earth? How can the Protestant Ulstermen and Catholic Irishmen live together lovingly in Heaven? The problem goes back to solving the social implications of Christianity in earthly relationships.

The social aims of Christian education, according

to Dr. Coe, are as follows: (1) Social welfare, or the control of the non-human environment in the interest of human life. (2) Social justice, or the inauguration of fair play in all the dealings of every individual, no matter how strong and shrewd, with every other individual, no matter how weak and ignorant. (3) A world society or the promotion of a code of conduct that leads to "the integration of all peoples into a single, democratically governed mankind." Nationalism must melt into a larger regard for human beings; and that which is "a climactic expression of the selfishness, that is to say the injustice that is organized in our legal systems and our national sovereignties," must be revealed to all, even in the Sunday schools.[57]

The implications of a sound social theory of religious education are met by the religious doctrine of personal fellowship between God and man, and between man and man; by a reorganization of the church as a religious institution in a way which shall put religious education on as scientific a basis as the ordinary day school education; and by training the church school pupils in the principles of social justice, co-operation, and love, as well as in matters pertaining to personal salvation.

Another current development is the religious social service director. For some time the religious education director has been a recognized force in church work. The social service director in church life is coming into the foreground, bearing the responsibility of working out social welfare programs for the church services, directing the training of the membership in volunteer social work, inaugurating religious social surveys, in fact, carrying the social message of the church into all the church activities.

The social service activities of the church have often been used as a net for catching the churchless. Social service as a bribe, however, will fail. Genuine religious social service is that which emanates naturally and easily from the lives of the church members and of the church itself, asking no pay and possessing no sinuous ends. The church that inaugurates a social program for building up the family life, the play life, the moral life, the economic life, as well as the religious life, in the community in which it is located, most truly represents a socialized church. The church, however, that uses its social welfare program merely in order to build itself up, fails to understand the social calling as a religious institution.

The social thought of the Hebrews revolved about the idea of social justice; of Jesus, about the concept of active love; and of modern Christianity, at its best, about an unselfish social program for bringing about a just, co-operative, and harmonious life, ranging in its operation from the individual in his family and local community life to the individual as a functioning unit in a new world society.

Chapter XXVII

Methods of Sociological Investigation

In any line of thought or endeavor a correct method of procedure is all-important. Inaccurate theories of procedure have wrecked nations, hindered civilization for centuries at a time, and flooded the world with negative and harmful ideas. It will be worth while, therefore, to consider the methods by which sociology has advanced.

The ancient makers of social proverbs crystallized what they had individually observed many times to be true, or what they had heard repeated on many occasions as being true. Such methods were based on observation and generalization, carelessly used. Moreover, the data at the command of the makers of social proverbs were very limited.

The Hebrew prophets, fired by exalted ideas concerning the nature of Jehovah, insisted upon a practical application of these ideas to the daily life of the people of their time. When they perceived that the actions and living conditions of the people fell far below the implications of the pattern-ideas for which the name of Jehovah stood, they vehemently proclaimed definite social ideals, and condemned all who hindered the realization of these ideals. This method of creating social thought is noteworthy because of the religious dynamic behind it, and because of the social pattern-ideas which it produced.

Plato and Aristotle were pioneer social philosophers who took cosmic views of life. One followed the method of abstract reasoning and centered his thought in a world of Ideas; the other viewed life pragmatically, employing a method of empirical tests. While sociology will always have a place for methods which interpret the daily facts of individual and social experience in their relationships to the whole human society and to the universe, it will insist that as large a body of societary data as possible be gathered together before philosophic sociology speaks positively.

In the teachings of Jesus a rare insight to human nature is manifested. Jesus studied individuals as individuals and, perceiving their selfish natures, proclaimed a remedy in an inner transformation through consecration to objective factors, such as persons and ideals. Jesus was peculiarly happy in his method of moving among all classes of people, of studying their needs, and of testing in practice his social principles. While his acquaintance with human life was limited to small groups of one race, he sought universal as well as particular human tendencies. His method included an absolutely unselfish spirit, a search for the truth, a broad viewpoint—all of which are thoroughly scientific.

The *Utopia* of Sir Thomas More, preceded to be sure by Plato's *Republic,* introduced another social thought method. The utopian formula consists in setting forth a set of ideals which presumably are distinctly in advance of current standards. The method of arriving at utopian ideas is largely through the use of the imagination. Standards are postulated so far in advance of current conditions as to make them of little value. Utopian social thought, however, does have some scientific merit. The imagination may be used in revealing reality to otherwise blind individuals. A utopian thought may startle a selfish individual out of a part of his selfishness. A utopian idea possesses the power which is inherent in indirect suggestion; it may arouse without antagonizing.

In the approach to the social question through an analysis of the natural rights of the individual, the seventeenth and eighteenth social writers fell into a deductive and a priori procedure which led them far astray. Like the theory of individual rights, the correlative doctrine of the social contract contained more error than truth.

The method of positivism, ordinarily connected with the writings of Comte, essayed a scientific approach to the social question. It insisted upon accuracy, induction, and a right emphasis upon sequence and co-existence. But positivism, even in the hands of its exponents, became deductive and philosophic. It promised well scientifically, but fell into nearly all the errors which it condemned. It was, however, a factor in producing the nineteenth century humanitarianism.

The organic analogy method of studying human society attracted widespread attention, appealed strongly to the imagination even of scholars, but resulted in findings of negligible value. The parallelisms between an organism and society proved to be scientifically valueless, except as they revealed some of the connections between organic volution and social evolution. They created a considerable vocabulary of bio-social terminology which has been more of a hindrance than a help in social thinking.

The psychical approach to the study of societary life, introduced by Lester F. Ward, and made scientific by the findings of inductive and behavioristic psychology, has proved thus far to be the best method of understanding the social process and of arriving at a statement of sociological laws. This method has revealed human life as a series of social conflicts and co-operations, and of forms of social control designed to regulate individuals for selfish and unselfish group purposes. An explanation of the more important phases of the psychical methodology has been presented in several chapters of this volume.

The individual rights doctrine, the social contract theories, the concept of positivism, and the organic analogies belong to the unscientific age in sociological methodology. In the main these sets of social theories were philosophic, deductive, a priori, and argumentative. They were based chiefly on opinions, positivism alone leaning to observation and induction but failing to live up to its promises. On the other hand, recent decades have been marked by the rise of scientific methods in sociology, attention has been centered on the social process, and particularly on the psychical processes of which the social process is an elaboration. Although he possessed an entirely inadequate knowledge of psychology, Lester F. Ward laid the foundations of modern sociology when he insisted that society is a psychical affair, capable of mastering itself. As a result of this contribution to method, not by a psychologist but by a paleontologist, social thought moved forward into the field of scientific sociology.

There are many writers who would class Ward with the pre-scientific contributors to sociological thought. His methods, it is true, were largely deductive; his psychology was seriously faulty; his philosophy was inefficient. Nevertheless, he pointed the way for sociologists so clearly that in this treatise his work has been considered as giving the trend to recent sociology, rather than as being the last word of discredited types of social thought.

Then there are other types of sociological methodology of which mention should be made, notably, the statistical, and the classificatory procedures. The statistical approach had its origin in the early census. There are evidences that rulers and kings, at least two or three millenniums before Christ, had enumerations of their subjects made. In connection with poor-law administration, people as early as the Roman Era were counted. But it was not until the eighteenth century that statistics became scientific, with statistical laws drawn from a study of tabulated facts. Quetelet gives 1820 as the birth year of statistical science. It was Frederick William I of Prussia who is reported to have had an enumeration made of occupational facts; and Frederick the Great, with having established a system for making regular statistical studies of population. It is said that early in the eighteenth century the University of Jena began to offer courses in statistics.

In England, in the latter part of the seventeenth century, Captain John Graunt is credited with applying methods of counting, measurement, and induction to the births and deaths in London. His studies were referred to as political arithmetic, and were a forerunner of the current investigations in vital statistics. Malthus made use of statistical methods in his work (1798) on population changes.

Quetelet (1796-1874) is usually considered the founder of statistical science. He not only applied the method of counting to the study of the members of human society (the census method in its common form), but he tried to get at the problem of causation, and to indicate rules of procedure for making causal studies in statistics. Although this celebrated Belgian statistician tabulated and analyzed facts ranging from the astronomical to the societary fields, his ideas can be mentioned here only so far as they contribute to the subject of social thought. Quetelet pointed out certain of the pitfalls in the way of gathering accurate data. He improved the methods of census taking, and undertook the difficult tasks that are involved in qualitative human studies.

Among the results of Quetelet's work, the concept of "the average man" is well known. Quetelet defined the law of averages and described types, especially the average individual. Although it is very important and useful to know about the "average man," the term is practically fictitious, since no one even in a large group exactly fits the description. All individuals are either "above" or "below" the average.

The contributions of Quetelet in the field of social statistics were admirably supplemented by the achievements of Le Play (1806-1882). This French sociologist and mining engineer applied the methods of physical science to social science. He insisted upon observation of data and the use of induction in making generalizations. His method is illustrated by his studies in family budgets. In order to secure accurate data he lived with individual families, studying at first-hand the conditions by which they made a livelihood. Le Play opposed *laissez-faire* theories and urged programs of reform through the journal which he founded, namely, *La Reforme Sociale.* He rejected socialism, and advocated the method of conciliation and sympathy for effecting agreements among employers and employees.

Similar methods were evolved by Engels and Bücher, German investigators. Engels' studies of family budgets led him to draw certain average observations. These "averages" are known as Engels' laws, for example: (1) The smaller the income, the larger the percentage of expenditure for food. (2) The percentage of expenditure for clothing, and for lodging or rent, varies directly with the income. (3) The larger the income, the larger the percentage of expenditures for sundries (including luxuries).

The statistical method has been carried forward by a large number of social investigators. With averages, modes, and medians, it is now possible to make accurate quantitative studies. Current statistical methods include the use of index numbers, frequency tables, discrete series, deviations, skewness, correlations. Statistics has thrown a flood of light upon important phases of societary life, such as the economic, where wage scales and price levels are significant concepts. Statistics has been widely utilized in the study of crime and poverty. The various methods of graphic presentations are valuable in interpreting tables of statistical data to the lay mind.

Statistical methods can be used, however, to prove almost anything. The ordinary individual is helpless when statistical methods are treated unscrupulously. On the other hand, it is probably true that social thought will become increasingly accurate by the judicious use of statistical studies.

A recent development, closely related to statistical science, is the social survey. Beginning with the Pittsburg Survey in 1907-1908, the social survey method has been widely adopted in the United States. Its use has been applied to inventories of a specific community, such as a rural district or a small number of city blocks. There is the specific survey of a given social problem, such as housing or poverty. Then there is the survey of an entire industry or a school system.

The social survey is one of the most important sources today of sound social thinking. By it, large quantities of social facts are being collected. Urban and rural surveys, specific and general surveys alike, are affording the best bases at the present time for inductive social thinking. Some of these results have been indicated in a preceding chapter upon the contributions of applied sociology.

The nature of the classificatory method has already been indicated in this treatise. The Greeks classified the various fields of knowledge under three heads: physics, ethics, and politics. Francis Bacon classified knowledge according to his understanding of mental operations. He divided mental processes into three, namely, feeling, memory, reasoning; and made a corresponding division of knowledge into art, history, and science. Auguste Comte classified the social elements into four groups: the industrial, the esthetic, the scientific, and the philosophical (previsional). His hierarchal classification of the sciences into mathematics, astronomy, physics, chemistry, biology, and sociology has been discussed in an earlier chapter.

Guillaume de Greef may be considered the best exponent of the classificatory method. De Greef accepted Comte's hierarchy of the sciences with its basic principles of decreasing generality and increasing dependence of parts, assented to Spencer's evolutionary dictum of increasing coherence and heterogeneity, and added his own concept of volitional contractualism.

De Greef argued that social progress is characterized by an increasing degree of volitional activity and freedom. This volitionalism is the basis of rational social control. The telic factors, however, are not well developed by de Greef. His social thought rests upon a certain logical but inaccurate classification of the social elements.

The basis of this classification is increasing volitionalism and particularism. De Greef gives the following classification: economic, industrial, genetic, artistic, scientific, moral, juridical, and political. In holding that the economic elements in society represent the least volitionalism, and the political the most volitional activity, with graded degrees of volitional activities represented by the intermediate factors, the weakness of de Greef's analysis becomes evident. While an improvement over Comte's classification and superior to Spencer's mechanistic order, de Greef's contribution possesses only a relative degree of logical merit. It is far from being objectively correct, and is indicative of the difficulties in the way of classifying social elements in an evolutionary or filial order. There is no doubt but that any classification of merit would have to be arranged according to some correlative plan, which would serve the purposes of an exhibit but would not be of much scientific value. Moreover, the classifications that are most useful are those classifications of societary forces; these are psychical in nature and have been treated in foregoing chapters.

De Greef perceived the importance of the principle of socialization. He emphasized the importance of a "we" feeling in societary life. His social unit is the primitive family. In the evolution from the primitive family and state, the evidence of progress is the degree of "togetherness" that has been developed. De Greef advanced the idea that there is an increasing degree of contractualism and hence of freedom in society. De Greef's work may be taken as the best attempt to carry Comte's classification of the sciences to a logical conclusion by furnishing a classification of the elements which function in the field of the "highest" science of all, namely, sociology.

At this point and in concluding, the methodology of Albion W. Small will be considered. Professor Small's other contributions to sociological thought have been indicated at the proper places in earlier chapters. The correct method for pursuing sociological analyses is to treat human society in terms of process. The main current in all sound sociological study is the social process. The significant test of progress in this social process is achievement.[2] According to Professor Small's classification, there are six main phases of social progress, namely:

1. Achievement in promoting health,
2. Achievement in harmonizing human relations,
3. Achievement in producing wealth,
4. Achievement in discovery and spread of knowledge,
5. Achievement in the fine arts,
6. Achievement in religion.

These grand divisions are the expressions of certain interests[3] that human beings possess: (1) health interests, (2) wealth interests, (3) sociability interests, (4) knowledge interests, (5) esthetic interests, and (6) rightness interests. As a result of the operation of these interests, social problems are produced. Sociology is "the science of human interests and their workings under all conditions."

In this classification human interests serve as the main key forces to an understanding of the social process. Upon psychological examination, however, the interests are found to be bafflingly complex. The psychologist has not given a satisfactory description of interests. And yet it is clear that what people are interested in is a fair criterion of the direction which their evolution will take. Furthermore, the changes in the interests of people are fundamental in telic social progress. With a correlation of interests as a subjective criterion, and of achievement as an objetcive test, Professor Small has shown the dualistic nature of the social process. Those methodologists who would measure all things human in purely objective terms are scientifically negligent of important human elements. Mind is not simply matter; the social process is not entirely behavior.

Professor Small has sharpened three important tools for the use of the sociological investigator. These are: the social process, personal interests, and the group. His analyses are sound, except as he does not show how "interests" usually possess social origins. Otherwise he speaks consistently and helpfully in terms of groups and group processes.

With concepts such as have been favorably presented in the forcgoing paragraphs—and chapters—the sociologist of the future will be able to make contributions to thought that will help to determine educational, religious, economic, political, and other important human aims.

Chapter XXVIII

The Dissemination of Sociological Thought

Despite its youth, inchoateness, and naïveté, sociological thought is exerting a vital influence in the world. It is giving a new rating to all the established values of life, undermining some, strengthening others, and creating still others.

The chief values in sociological thought are that it constitutes the center of all worth while thought; it gives balance and proportion to thinking in any field; it defies race prejudice and social intolerance; it smites selfish living; it rivets attention to the essentially human values; it stimulates personal development in harmony with group and societary welfare. At the same time, it postulates group advancement, not upon paternalistic or autocratic grounds, but upon a constructive projection of personalities that harmonizes with unselfish group service.

For centuries genuine social thinking was confined largely to a few of the intellectually élite. These few lived, and did even their social thinking, in a more or less isolated way. It was not until the first decades of the last centuries that social thought began to be scientific in character, that is, became sociological. Sociological thinking, however, was isolated and uncorrelated for many years. In the last decade of the nineteenth century, sociology began to develop a considerable body of thinkers and to create a new morale. There were many disagreements that tended to break the new science asunder. The opening decades, however, of the twentieth century witnessed a development of sociological thought that was followed by the establishment of the teaching of sociology as a profession.

With the rise of professional sociologists, the dissemination of socialized thought became noteworthy. For a long time sociology was considered only as a post-graduate study. In the last few years, however, sociology has been making its way downward in college and university curricula, until it is being widely taught to college freshmen and sophomores. In this connection there is a variety of textbooks that have been written to meet the needs of beginning students. There are some teachers who would introduce sociology through anthropological studies, beginning with the origin of man. Others would give a survey or prospectus of social institutions, processes, and problems.[1] Still others would deal only with social problems. Then there are those persons who would build a text-book around a central theme, tracing it through social relationships. For advanced work in sociological thought there is a variety of treatises dealing with systems at once profound, complex, and fundamental.

For high schools, the technique of sociological teaching is in the beginning stages. The importance in high schools of social science teaching is generally recognized, but there has been great difficulty in effecting an agreement among the various social science branches. Some high school teachers prefer a "social problems" course, although the demand is growing for a "social science" course, extending throughout the year, dividing the time more or less evenly between economics, sociology, and civics. There are other high school teachers who contend that sociology can be taught best in a general "citizenship" course. One of the specific difficulties is that the high school curriculum is full, and that the representatives of none of the established courses are willing to see the subjects in which they are interested crowded out. Another difficulty is the power which the self-culture and self-development concepts possess. The equal importance of the social culture and social development concepts is being recognized, but with amazing slowness.

In the grades the teaching of sociology is gaining ground. In the sense that there is an advanced group of mathematical studies for university men and women and an elemental mathematics for the grades, so there is advanced sociology, and also an elemental sociology centering around the activities of the primary groups, such as the family, play, neighborhood, and school groups. A child who is old enough to learn to obey is old enough to begin elemental sociology, in fact, when he learns to obey, he is already beginning to experience the meaning of a social, if not a sociological concept. Simple social studies are being prepared for the grades, even beginning with the first grade.

The dissemination of sociological thought is a practical question to which in the last score of years special attention has been given. The universities and colleges began to establish chairs of sociology in the closing decade of the last century. The movement has acquired a remarkable momentum in the United States. Normal schools and high schools have adopted the movement. Many churches are promulgating a socialized gospel. Literature is gradually assuming an appreciation of the sociological viewpoint.

From the social proverbs of primitive man to a treatise such as Ross' *Principles of Sociology,* with its admirable analysis of significant societal processes, such as equalization, domination, individuation, socialization—this is the main span of social thought. Social thought began in the simplest form of observations about social relationships between individual and individual, between chieftain and tribal member, between master and servant. It experienced various stages of denunciation of social wrongs. It produced perspectives of perfect societies. It moved profoundly forward in the form of social philosophies. Now it is proceeding either as the investigator of new social facts, or the psychological interpreter of these facts in terms of social processes. It is assuming a scientific procedure, although a portion of the results of its undertakings finds expression in social philosophy. It is beginning to formulate sociological laws. It is inaugurating a technique for preventing the maladjustments that produce social evils; it is establishing a teaching technique. Although the masses of the human race are beginning to feel blindly the meaning of social values, they have not yet been able to make their highest social aspirations rationally articulate. Until that time comes, democracy will remain an experiment, and world progress a toy of autocratic forces.

A history of social thought is essentially a review of an irregular but positive acceptance of social values. Individual after individual, leader after leader, profession after profession, group after group, have felt and accepted the challenge of the sociological viewpoint. They have changed from living selfishly to living socially. They have even given up the ideal of service for self advancement, setting up in its place the ideal of service for the welfare of others. In so doing and living they have found expansion of personality and contributed to the advancement of society. Since the days of Comte in particular, the social sciences have been increasing in variety and scope until they number a score or more, and sociological influence has been widening until the related sciences are inviting sociology, which is the scientific study of group phenomena, to define their objectives for them. In fact, sociological concepts are permeating the farthermost reaches of personal living and societal control. A history of social thought is a history of the socializing of human attitudes and interests, presaging a human society in which personal achievement and group progress are equally and supremely sought.

FOOTNOTES

CHAPTER II

1. W. I. Thomas, *Source Book for Social Origins,* University of Chicago Press, 1909, p. 161.
2. Daniel Crawford, *Thinking Black,* Doran, 1913.
3. E. M. Curr, *The Australian Race,* Melbourne, 1883, 1:339.
4. A. M. Howitt, *The Organization of Australian Tribes,* p. 452.

CHAPTER III

1. *Boulak Papyrus,* trans. by Griffith, p. 5340, *La Moral Egyptienne.*
2. *"The Instruction of Ptah-Hotep,"* trans. by Gunn, Wisdom of the East Series.
3. Code of Hammurapi, Sect. 196.
4. Ibid., Sect. 198.
5. Ibid., Sect. 229.
6. *Shoo King,* 27:3.

CHAPTER IV

1. C. F. Kent, *The Social Teachings of the Prophets and Jesus,* Scribner, 1917, p. 4.
2. Exodus, 3:7, 8.
3. Amos, 2:6, 7, 8; 3:10; 4:1, 2; 5:7, 15; 6:4.
4. Isaiah, 1:23.
5. Isaiah, 3:14, 15.
6. Micah, 3:2, 3.
7. Jeremiah, 22:13, 15, 17 (Modern Reader's Bible).
8. Louis Wallis, *Sociological Study of the Bible,* University of Chicago Press, 1912, Ch. VII.
9. Hosea, 4:11; 9:11, 16.
10. Exodus, 20:12.
11. Proverbs, 20:20.
12. Proverbs, 12:4.
13. Proverbs, 29:15.
14. Isaiah, 5:11.
15. Proverbs, 20:1.
16. Proverbs, 31:7.
17. Exodus, 21:13; I Kings, 1:50; 2:28.
18. Job, 31.
19. Amos, 9:7.
20. Isaiah, 9:5; cf., Kent, *The Social Teachings of the Prophets and Jesus,* p. 112.

CHAPTER V

1. Hesiod, *Work and Days,* trans. by A. W. Mains, Oxford, 1908.
2. *The Works of Hesiod, Callimachus and Theognis,* trans. by Banks, Bohn's Classical Library, p. 227.
3. Botsford and Sihler, *Hellenic Civilization,* p. 64.
4. George Rawlinson, translator, *History of Herodotus,* 4 vols.
5. Plutarch's Pericles, revised by Clough, 1:234 ff.
6. Botsford and Sihler, op. cit., p. 340.
7. *On Air, Water and Places* in the Genuine Works of Hippocrates, trans. by Adams, Vol. I.
8. Plato I, 338 C. All references to Plato's *Dialogues* in this chapter or in later chapters are to Jowett's translation.
9. Adela M. Adam, Plato, *Moral and Political Ideals,* p. 10.
10. The reader will find in Will Durant's *Philosophy and the Social Problem,* Ch. I, a unique although ideocentric interpretation of Socrates.
11. *Laws,* 738.
12. The beginning student of Plato's social thought should first read the *Republic,* especially V 472 A to VII 541 B.
13. *Republic,* 369 B.
14. Ibid., 370 B.
15. Ibid., 373.
16. Laws, 803.
17. *Statesman,* 308.
18. Ibid., 307.
19. Ibid., 297.
20. *Republic,* 398 E, 412.
21. *Laws,* 731, 732.
22. *Republic,* 412.
23. *Statesman,* 303.
24. *Republic,* 525; cf. *Laws,* 818.
25. Ibid., 537, 539, 540.
26. Ibid., 413.
27. Ibid., 416.
28. Ibid., 416, 417.
29. Ibid., 457C, 464C.
30. Ibid., 414, 415.
31. Ibid., 415.
32. Loc. cit.
33. Ibid., 460 C, 461 C.

34. *Statesman*, 310.
35. *Laws*, 773.
36. *Statesman*, 310.
37. *Republic*, 422 A; *Laws*, 744, 745.
38. *Republic*, 421.
39. Ibid., 550 D. E; *Laws*, 742, 791.
40. *Republic*, 550.
41. Ibid., 550 C.
42. Ibid., 556.
43. Loc. cit.
44. Ibid., 552 D.
45. Ibid., 552 E.
46. *Laws*, 744, 745.
47. Ibid., 729.
48. Loc. cit.
49. *Republic*, 377, 401.
50. *Laws*, 772.
51. *Statesman*, 294.
52. Ibid., 300.
53. In books, IX-XII.
54. *Laws*, 934.
55. Ibid., 862 ff.
56. Ibid., 936.
57. Ibid., 955.
58. *Republic*, 455, 456; *Laws*, 805.
59. *Republic*, 451
60. Ibid., 475A; *Laws*, 814.
61. *Laws*, 759.
62. Ibid., 929, 930.
63. *Republic*, 457A; *Laws*, 795 ff, 813 ff, 830 ff.
64. Ibid., 410.
65. Ibid., 441.
66. Ibid., 498 B.
67. Ibid., 518.
68. Ibid., 536.
69. Ibid., 425; *Laws*, 643.
70. *Republic*, 537.
71. *Laws*, 729.
72. *Republic*, 435 ff.
73. *Laws*, 903.
74. *Republic*, 545-549.
75. Ibid., 550, 551.
76. Loc. cit.
77. Ibid., 555.
78. Ibid., 564.
79. Ibid., 339; *Laws*, 714.

CHAPTER VI

1. *Ethics*, trans. by Welldon, II, 2.
2. *Politics*, trans. by Jowett, I, 2.
3. Loc. cit.
4. Ibid., II, 3.
5. Ibid., II, 5.
6. Loc. cit.
7. Ibid., II, 7; VII, 10.
8. Ibid., II, 4.
9. Ibid., I, 4.
10. Ibid., III, 7.
11. Ibid., III, 15.
12. Ibid., V, 8; VII, 2.
13. Ibid., II, 8.
14. Ibid., V, 8.
15. Ibid., IV, 11.
16. Ibid., V, 7.
17. Ibid., IV, 11.
18. Ibid., II, 6.
19. Loc. cit.
20. Ibid., II, 9.
21. Ibid., II, 12.
22. Ibid., V, 1.
23. Ibid., VII, 14.
24. Loc. cit.
25. Ibid., VII, 4.
26. Ibid., VII, 11.
27. Ibid., VII, 15.
28. Ibid., VII, 16.
29. Ibid., I, 12.
30. Ibid., VII, 16.
31. Ibid., VIII, 2.
32. Ibid., VIII, 3.
33. Ibid., VIII, 4.
34. Ibid., VIII, 5.

CHAPTER VII

1. Lucretius, *Dererum natura*, trans. by Muno, in Bohn's Libraries, V. 335 ff., 778 ff.
2. *De officiis*, trans. by Edmonds, Bohn's Libraries, I, XVII, XIV; *De republica*, trans. by Younge, Bohn's Libraries, I, XXV-XXVI, XIV.
3. *Dialogues*, VII, 9.
4. *Thoughts*, trans. by Long, VII, 31.
5. Ibid., VI, 7.
6. Ibid., VIII, 59.
7. Ibid., IX, 23.
8. Ibid., VI, 42.
9. Ibid., XII, 36.
10. Seneca, *Dial*, IX, 4.
11. Ibid., VII, 20.
12. *On Anger*.
13. Loc. cit.
14. Epictetus, *Discourses*, Book I, Ch. XVIII.
15. Matthew, V, 44.
16. *Thoughts*, VII, 22.
17. Romans, XII, 17.
18. *Thoughts*, VII, 26; III, 7.
19. Seneca, *On a Happy Life*.
20. Loc. cit.

CHAPTER VIII

1. Luke 17:20, 21.
2. Luke 13:34.
3. Matt. 12:48; Mark 3:34.
4. Matt. 13:31, 32; Mark 4:30; Luke 13:18, 19.
5. Luke 6:36.
6. Matt. 5:23; Matt. 18:15; Luke 6:41, 42.
7. Matt. 5:44, 46; Luke 6:20, 35.
8. Matt. 28:20; 24:14.
9. John 12:43; Matt. 6:5.
10. Matt. 4:8.
11. Luke 9:48; Mark 10:14; Matt. 18:1.
12. Matt. 25:31-46.

13. Mark 9:41; Matt. 10:42.
14. Luke 6:30; 3:11.
15. Matt. 23:23-33.
17. John 2:13-17; Matt. 21:12, 13; Mark 11:15-17; Luke 19:45, 46.
18. Mark 11:18; Luke 19:47.
19. Matt. 15:4; 19:19.
20. Mark 10:7, 8; Matt. 19:5.
21. Mark 9:42.
22. Matt. 19:21.
23. John 12:8; Mark 14:7; Matt. 26:11.
24. Luke 12:16-21.
25. Luke 13:14; Matt. 12:2, 10-13.
26. Mark 2:27; 3:4.
27. Matt. 10:34-39.
28. Luke 12:49-53.
29. John 18:10; Matt. 26:50-56.
30. Matt. 5:39.
31. Luke 2:13, 14.
32. Acts 15:9; 10:28; Galatians, 3:28.
33. Romans 8:16; 32.
34. I. Corinthians, Ch. 13.
35. Galatians 5:13; Romans 12:10.
36. Galatians 6:2; 6:10; Acts 20:35.
37. Romans 8:35-39; 12:17; Ephesians 1:21; 2:4; 3:17, 18.
38. Romans 12:4-8; cf. I. Corinthians 12:12.
39. Romans 14:7.
40. Ephesians 5:22-23; Colossians 3:18, 19; I. Corinthians 11:9. 19; I Corinthians 11:9.
41. I. Timothy 6:7-10; 17, 18.
42. James 1:26, 27.
43. Revelation, Ch. 21.

CHAPTER IX

1. B text, Passus VIII. The manuscripts of *Pier's Ploughman* number over forty and fall into three sets: A, B, and C.

CHAPTER X

1. *The Utopia of Sir Thomas More*, Bell and Sons, London, edited by George Simpson in Bohn's Classical Libraries, 1910, p. 75.
2. Ibid., p. 104.
3. Ibid., p. 111.
4. Ibid., p. 153.
5. Ibid., pp. 84, 93.
6. Ibid., pp. 135, 84.
7. Ibid., p. 93.
8. Ibid., p. 97.
9. Ibid., p. 92.
10. Ibid., p. 88.
11. Ibid., p. 90.
12. Ibid., p. 96.
13. Ibid., p. 110, cf. Bacon, *The New Atlantis* in Ideal Commonwealths, Collier, 1901, p. 125.
14. Ibid., p. 131.
15. Ibid., p. 93.
16. Ibid., p. 115.
17. Ibid., p. 117, cf. Campanella, *The City of the Sun*, in Ideal Commonwealths, Collier, 1901, p. 157.
18. Ibid., p. 174.
19. Ibid., p. 95.
20. Ibid., p. 101.
21. Ibid., p. 175.
22. Ibid., p. 174.
23. Ibid., pp. 153 ff.
24. Ibid., p. 154.
25. Ibid., p. 103.
26. Ibid., pp. 140, 141.
27. Ibid., p. 67.
28. Bacon, *The New Atlantis* in Ideal Commonwealths, Collier, 1901, pp. 135 ff.
29. Bellamy, *Looking Backward*, Grosset and Dunlap, 1898, p. 57.
30. Ibid., p. 88.
31. Ibid., p. 89.
32. Ibid., p. 67.
33. Ibid., p. 192.
34. Ibid., pp. 220 ff.
35. Ibid., pp. 287 ff.
36. H. G. Wells, *Anticipations*, *Mankind in the Making*, and *A Modern Utopia*. See *A Modern Utopia*, Scribner, 1905, pp. 5, 11.

CHAPTER XI

1. Machiavelli, *The Prince*, Routledge, London, n.d., p. 53.
2. Ibid., pp. 104, 105.
3. Ibid., p. 71.
4. Ibid., p. 77.
5. Hobbes, *Leviathan*, Putnam, 1904, Ch. XIII.
6. Locke, *Two Treatises on Government*, Routledge, n.d., p. 18.
7. Ibid., p. 193.
8. Ibid., p. 199.
9. Ibid., p. 315.
10. Rousseau, *Contrat social*, Garnier, Paris, p. 240.
11. Ibid., p. 246.
12. Ibid., p. 249.
13. John Winthrop in *Selections from Early American Writers, 1607-1800*, edit. by W. B. Cairns, Macmillan, 1910, p. 52.
14. *A Treatise of Human Nature*, edit. by Selby-Bigge, Oxford, 1896, II:777, 114, 140, 150.
15. Ibid., p. 534.
16. Ibid., p. 546.
17. Adam Smith, *The Wealth of Nations*, Putnam, 1904, II:114.
18. Ibid., II:83.
19. Ibid., II:143.
20. Ibid., II:203.
21. Ibid., I:80.

22. Ibid., I:81.
23. Ibid., II:203-207.
24. Ibid., I:11.
25. Kant, *Theory of Ethics*, trans. by Abbott, p. 9.
26. H e g e l, *Philosophy of Right*, trans. by Dyde, Part III, p. 150.
27. W. G. Sumner, *What Social Classes Owe to Each Other*, Harper, 1920, p. 12.
28. Ibid., p. 25.
29. Publications of the American Sociological Society, Vol. XV.

CHAPTER XII

1. Adam Smith, *Wealth of Nations*, Putnam, 1901, I:81.
2. Ibid., p. 147.
3. *An Essay on the Principle of Population*, eighth edit., Reeves and Turner, 1878, p. 1; cf. W. S. Thompson, *Population: A Study in Malthusianism*, Columbia University, 1915, Ch. I.
4. Ibid., p. 2.
5. Ibid., p. 8.
6. Ibid., p. 9.
7. Ibid., p. 13.
8. Ibid., p. 371.
9. Ibid., p. 402.
10. Ibid., p. 416.
11. Ibid., p. 437.
12. Ibid., p. 481.
13. T. N. Carver, *Essays in Social Justice*, Harvard University Press, 1915, Ch. XIV.
14. Cf. W. S. Thompson, *Population: A Study in Malthusianism*, Columbia University Studies. 1915.

CHAPTER XIII

1. Auguste Comte, *Positive Philosophy*, trans. by Martineau, Vol I. pp. x, xi.
2. Ibid., p. xi.
3. Ibid., p. xv.
4. Ibid., Vol. III, p. 13.
5. Ibid., Vol. I, p. 26.
6. Ibid., p. 27.
7. Ibid., p. 34.
8. Ibid., p. 35.
9. Ibid., p. 36.
10. Ibid., p. 41.
11. Ibid., pp. 27 ff.
12. Ibid., p. 149.
13. Ibid., p. 153, 154.
14. Ibid., Vol. II, p. 30.
14. Ibid., p. 219.
16. Ibid., p. 175.
17. Ibid., p. 176.
18. Ibid., p. 180.
19. Ibid., p. 193.
20. Ibid., p. 234.
21. Ibid., p. 292.
22. Ibid., p. 287.
23. Ibid., p. 286.
24. Ibid., p. 300.
25. Ibid., Vol. III, p. 320.
26. Comte, *Positive Polity*, London, 1871, I:1.

CHAPTER XIV

1. Proudhon, *What Is Property?* Twentieth Century Press, 1908.
2. Rodbertus, *Overproduction and Crises*. Scribner, 1906.
3. Lassalle, *Science and the Workingman*, Kerr, 1903.
4. Marx and Engels, *Manifesto of the Communist Party*, Kerr, 1902.
5. Marx, *Capital*, trans. by Moore and Aveling, Kerr, 1909, I:673 ff., 834 ff.
6. Kropotkin, *Mutual Aid; a Factor of Evolution*, Doubleday, Page, 1902.
7. Henry George, *Progress and Poverty*, Doubleday, Page, 1916, p. 9.
8. Ibid.
9. Ibid., pp. 286, 287.
10. Ibid., p. 342.
11. Ibid., p. 339.

CHAPTER XV

1. Jean Bodin, *The Six Bookes of A Commonwealth*, trans. by R. Knoles, London.
2. H. T. Buckle, *History of Civilization in England*, Appleton, 1874, 2 vols., I:14.
3. Ibid., p. 29.
4. Ibid., p. 31.
5. Ibid., p. 32.
6. Ibid., p. 33.
7. Ibid., p. 36.
8. Ibid., pp. 44 ff.
9. Ibid., p. 52.
10. Ibid., p. 85.
11. Ibid., p. 95.
12. Ibid., p. 96.
13. Ibid., p. 99.
14. Ellen Semple, *Influences of Geographic Environment*, Holt, 1911, p. 635.
15. See Ellsworth Huntington, *Civilization and Climate*, Yale University Press, 1915.
16. W. Z. Ripley, *Races in Europe*, Appleton, 1899, p. 571.

CHAPTER XVI

1. Charles Darwin, *The Descent of Man*, Appleton, 1904, pp. 229 ff.

2. Herbert Spencer, *First Principles*, Appleton, 1900, Section III-145.
3. Spencer, *Principles of Sociology*, Appleton, 1914, I:596, 597.
4. Ibid., p. 84.
5. Ibid., Part II, Ch. II.
6. Ibid., pp. 457 ff.
7. Ibid., Part II, Ch. VI-IX.
8. Ibid., p. 592.
9. John Fiske, *Destiny of Man*, Houghton Mifflin, 1904, p 12.
10. John Fiske, *Outlines of Cosmic Philosophy*, Houghton Mifflin, 1874, Part II, pp. 340 ff.
11. Ibid., pp. 360 ff.
12. Ibid., pp. 303 ff.
13. Paul von Lilienfeld, *Gedanken über die Socialwissenschaft der Zukunft*, II, pp, viii ff.
14. Lilienfeld, *Pathologie S o c i a l e*, 1904.
15. J. S. Mackensie, *Outlines of Social Philosophy*, Macmillan, 1918, p. 14.
16. Ibid., p. 65.
16. Ibid., p. 243 ff.

CHAPTER XVII

1. Lester F. Ward, *Dynamic Sociology*, Appleton, 1911, Vol. I, pp. XXV ff.
2. Ibid., p. 22.
3. Ibid., pp. 22, 23.
4. Ibid., pp. 56, 57.
5. Ibid., p. 60; Ward, *Pure Sociology*, Macmillan, 1914, p. 4.
6. Lester F. Ward, *Applied Sociology*, Ginn, 1906, pp. 5 ff.
7. *Dynamic Sociology*, Vol. I, p. 72.
8. Ibid., p. 143.
9. Ibid., p. 320.
10. Ibid., pp. 408, 409.
11. Ibid., p. 464.
12. Ibid., p. 452.
13. Ibid., p. 467.
14. Ibid., p. 474.
15. Ibid., p. 486.
16. Ibid., p. 497.
17. Ibid., p. 516.
18. Ibid., pp. 518 ff.
19. Ibid., p. 520.
20. Ibid., Vol. II, p. 341.
21. Ibid., Vol. I, p. 520.
22. Ibid., p. 522.
23. Ibid., p. 541.
24. Ibid., p. 583.
25. Ibid., p. 579.
26. Ibid., p. 594.
27. Ibid., pp. 606 ff.
28. Ibid., p. 615.
29. *Pure Sociology*, p. 403.
30. *Dynamic Sociology*, Vol. I, p. 641.
31. *Pure Sociology*, Ch. XV.
32. Ibid., p. 420.
33. Lester F. Ward, *Psychic Factors of Civilization*, Ginn, 1906, Ch. XXXIV.
34. *Dynamic Sociology*, Vol. I, pp. 669, 670.
35. Ibid., pp. 473, 474.
36. *Pure Sociology*, p. 438.
37. Ibid., pp. 457 ff.
38. Ibid., p. 469.
39. Ibid., pp. 231 ff.
40. Ibid., p. 237.
41. Ibid., pp. 79 ff.
42. Lester F. Ward, "Eugenics, Euthenics, and Eudemics," *Amer. Jour. of Sociology*, 18; 737-54.

CHAPTER XVIII

1. H. F. Osborn, *Men of the Old Stone Age*, Scribner, 1918, Ch. I.
2. W. G. Sumner, *Folkways*, Ginn, 1907, p. 43.
3. Ibid., p. 13.
4. Ibid., p. 266.
5. Ibid., pp. 343, 362.
6. Ibid., p. 378.
7. W. I. Thomas, *Sex and Society*, p. 51.
8. Ibid., p. 182.
9. Ibid., p. 41.
10. Ibid., p. 40.
11. Ibid., p. 41.
12. Ibid., p. 54.
13. Ibid., p. 61.
14. Ibid., p. 65.
15. Ibid., Ch. II.
16. Ibid., p. 76.
17. Ibid., p. 201.
18. Ibid., p. 418; cf. W. I. Thomas, *Sex and Society*, University of Chicago Press, 1907, pp. 201-220.
19. Ibid., p. 629.
20. A. G. Kellor, *Societal Evolution*, Macmillan, 1915.
21. Edward Westermarck, *The Origin and Development of the Moral Ideas*, Macmillan, 1906, I:159.
22. Ibid.
23. Ibid., p. 160.
24. Ibid., Vol. II. p. 740.
25. Ibid., II:745.
26. L. T. Hobhouse, *Morals in Evolution*, Holt, 1919, p. 1.
27. Ibid., p. 2.
28. Ibid.
29. Ibid., p. 43; cf. Hobhouse, *Social Evolution and Political Theory*, Lemcke, 1911, pp. 128 ff.
30. Ibid., p. 60.
31. Ibid., p. 64.
32. *Social Evolution and Political Theory*, p. 148.
33. *Morals in Evolution*, pp. 130, 71.
34. William Wundt, *Elements of Folk Psychology*, trans. by Schaub, Macmillan, 1916, p. 1.

35. Ibid., p. 478.
36. Ibid., p. 514.
37. Ibid., p. 515.
38. Ibid., p. 516.
39. Franz Boas, *The Mind of Primitive Man,* Macmillan, 1911, p. 102.
40. Hobhouse, *Social Evolution and Political Theory,* p. 39.
41. W. I. Thomas, *Source Book for Social Origins,* University of Chicago Press, 1909, p. 18.
42. Ibid., p. 20.
43. Ibid., p. 14.
44. Thomas, *Sex and Society,* p. 51.
45. Thomas and Znaniecki, *The Polish Peasant in Europe and America,* University of Chicago Press, 1918, I:22.

CHAPTER XIX

1. Francis Galton, *Hereditary Genius,* Macmillan, 1914.
2. *Inquiries into the Human Faculty,* Dutton, 1908.
3. See C. W. Saleeby, *The Progress of Eugenics,* Funk and Wagnalls, 1914, pp. 1 ff.
4. Karl Pearson, *The Grammar of Science,* Black, 1911, p. 1.
5. Ibid., p. 6.
6. See Saleeby, *The Progress of Eugenics,* Ch. II.
7. See C. B. Davenport, *Heredity in Relation to Eugenics,* Holt, 1911.
8. See Popenoe and Johnson, *Applied Eugenics,* Macmillan, 1918.
9. Ibid., p. 213.
10 Ibid., pp. 218, 231.
11. Ibid., Ch. XVI.
12. Ibid., p. 381.
13. Ibid., p. 380.
14. Saleeby, *The Progress of Eugenics,* p. 65.
15. Popenoe and Johnson, op. cit., p. 387.
16. Hobhouse, *Social Evolution and Political Theory,* Lemcke, 1911, p. 45.
17. Popenoe and Johnson, op. cit., p. 292.

CHAPTER XX

1. Ludwig Gumplowicz, *Der Rassenkampf,* Innsbruck, 1883, p. 64
2. Gumplowicz, *Grundriss der Sociologie,* tr. by Moore, 1885, p. 134.
3. Gumplowicz, *Sociologie und Politik,* p. 94.
4. Friedrich Nietzsche, *Genealogy of Morals,* New York, 1897, p. 46.
5. Nietzsche, *The Will to Power,* 1889, pp. 90, 269, 660 ff.
6. S. N. Patten, *A Theory of Social Forces,* 1896, Ch. IV.
7. T. N. Carver, *Essays in Social Justice,* Harvard University Press, 1915, pp. 30, 34.
8. Ibid., p. 46.
9. Ibid., pp. 49, 50.
10. Ibid., p. 56.
11. Ibid., p. 77.
12. Op. cit.
13. T. N. Carver, *Principles of Political Economy,* Ginn, 1919, pp. 37 ff. Also see *Essays in Social Justice,* p. 86.
14. *Essays in Social Justicc,* p. 86.
15. Ibid., p. 108.
16. *Principles of Political Economy,* p. 43.
17. J. Novicow, *War and its Alleged Benefits,* trans. by Seltzer, Holt, 1911.
18. E. A. Ross, *Principles of Sociology,* Century, 1920, p. 167.
19. Ibid., p. 183.
20. Ibid., pp. 207, 206.

CHAPTER XXI

1. Cf. S. H. Swinny, "Giambatista Vico," *Sociological Review,* Jan. 1914, pp. 50-57.
2. Peter Kropotkin, *Mutual Aid; a Factor in Evolution,* Doubleday, Page, 1902, p. 3.
3. Ibid., p. VII; cf. Kropotkin, *Fields, Factories and Workshops,* Putnam, 1901, Ch. 1.
4. *"The State; Its Historic Role,"* London, 1898 — reproduced in *Man or the State* by W. R. Browne, Huebsch, 1919, p. 21.
5. Gustav Ratzenhofer, *Die sociologische Erkenntniss,* Leipzig, 1898, Sect. 22; see A. W. Small. *General Sociology,* University of Chicago Press, 1905, Ch. XIII.
6. *Soziologie,* Leipzig, 1907, pp. 13-17.
7. *Die sociologische Erkenntniss,* p. 233.
8. Albion W. Small, *General Sociology,* ibid., p. 196.
9. Ibid., pp. 433 ff.
10. Ibid., pp. 201 ff.
11. Ibid., p. 217.
12. Ibid., p. 325.
13. Ibid., pp. 389, 390.
14. *Between Eras, From Capitalism to Democracy,* Inter-Collegiate Press, 1913, Ch. XXIII.
15. E. A. Ross, *Principles of Sociology,* Century, 1920, p. 121.
16. Ibid., p. 135.
17. *The Function of Socialization in Social Evolution,* Univ. of Chicago Press, 1916.
18. Ross, op. cit., pp. 257 ff.
19. Ibid., p. 395.

20. Ibid., p. 405.
21. L. T. Hobhouse, *Social Evolution and Political Theory*, Lemcke, 1911, p. 127.
22. C. H. Cooley, *Social Process*, Scribners, 1918, p. 38.

CHAPTER XXII

1. David Hume, *A Treatise of Human Nature*, edit. by Selby-Bigge, Oxford, 1896, p. 363.
2. Ibid., p. 362.
3. Ibid., pp. 499, 500.
4. Ibid., p. 521.
5. Ibid., pp. 575 ff.
6. Ibid., p 535.
7. Gabriel Tarde, *The Laws of Imitation*, tr. by Parsons, Holt, 1903, p. XVII.
8. Ibid., p. 59.
9. Ibid., p. 146.
10. Ibid., p. 74.
11. Ibid., p. 78.
12. Ibid., p. 87.
13. Ibid., p. 114.
14. Ibid , p. 39.
15. Ibid , p. 141 ff.
16. Ibid., p. 213; cf. Tarde, *Social Laws*, trans. by Warren, Macmillan, 1907, p. 65.
17. *The Laws of Imitation*, p. 225.
18. Ibid., p. 111.
19. Ibid., p. 14.
20. Ibid., p. 288.
21. Ibid., pp. 341 ff.
22. Ibid., p. 369.
23. Ibid., p. 30.
24. *Social Laws*, p. 132.
25. *Laws of Imitation*, p. 169.
26. *Social Laws*, p. 195.
27. Ibid., p. 204.
28. Ibid , p. 171; cf. Tarde, *La logique sociale*, Paris, 1898, Ch. IV.
29. *Laws of Imitation*, p. 87.
30. Ibid., p. 138.
31. Ibid., p. 344.
32. Ibid.,
33. Ibid., p. 387.
34. E. A. Ross, *Social Psychology*, Macmillan, 1908, p. viii.
35. M. M. Davis, Jr., *Psychological Interpretations of Society*, Longmans, Green, 1909.
36. Tarde, *L'opinion et la foule*, Paris, 1901, pp. 177 ff. Cf. Sighele, *Psychologie des sectes*, Paris, 1898, pp. 45 ff.
37. F. H. Giddings, *Principles of Sociology*, Macmillan, 1896, p. 17.
38. Ibid , pp. 71, 126 ff.
39. Ibid., pp. 101 ff. Cf. Giddings, *Descriptive and Historical Sociology*, Macmillan, 1911, Ch. III.
40. *Principles of Sociology*, p. 109; *Descriptive and Historical Sociology*, pp. 157 ff.
41. *Principles of Sociology*, p. 138.
42. Ibid., pp. 141 ff.
43. Ibid., pp. 147 ff.
44. *Descriptive and Historical Sociology*, p. 541. Cf. Giddings, *Inductive Sociology*, Macmillan, 1914, Part III.
45. *American Journal of Sociology*, Vol. XXV, p. 387.
46. Ibid., p 388.
47. J. M. Baldwin, *Social and Ethical Interpretations*, Macmillan, 1906, p. 15.
48. Ibid., p. 18.
49. Ibid., pp. 529 ff.

CHAPTER XXIII

1. C. H. Cooley, *Social Organization*, Scribner, 1909, p. 5.
2. C. H. Cooley, *Human Nature and the Social Order*, Scribner, 1902, p. 3.
3. Ibid., p. 5.
4. Ibid., pp. 152 ff.
5. *Social Organization*, ibid., p. 11.
6. Ibid., p. 12.
7. Ibid., p. 26.
8. Ibid., p. 28.
9. Ibid., p. 37.
10. Ibid., p. 61.
11. Ibid., p. 63.
12. Ibid., p. 80.
13. Ibid., p. 103.
14. Ibid., p. 121.
15. Cooley, *Social Process*, Scribner, 1918, pp. 68 ff.
16. *Social Organization*, ibid., Chs. XVIII, XXV-XXVII.
17. Ibid., p. 320; cf. *Social Process*, 297 ff.
18. *Introduction to Social Psychology*, Luce, 1914, pp. 23 ff.
19. Ibid., pp. 268, 322, 279.
20. E. A. Ross, *Principles of Sociology*, Century, 1920, Chs. XXXIV XXXV. Cf. Ross, *Social Control*, Macmillan, 1910, Chs. VII, VIII.
21. *Social Control*, ibid., pp. 49 ff.
22. Ibid., Chs. X ff.
23. Ibid., pp. 257 ff.
24. Ibid., pp. 411 ff.
25. Ibid., Ch. XXXI.
26. Ross, *Social Psychology*, Macmillan, 1908, Ch. II.
27. Ibid., p. 70. Cf. McDougall, *Introduction to Social Psychology*, ibid., Ch. IV.
28. Ross, *Social Psychology*, Ch. XVIII.
29. See Chapter XVIII of this book.
30. Ross, *Principles of Sociology*, Ch. XLII.
31. Ibid., Ch. XXXVI.
32. Ibid., Ch. XXXVIII.
33. Ibid., pp. 549 ff.
34. Ibid., p. 564.

35. Ibid., p. 590.
36. Ibid., p. 626.
37. Ibid.
38. Ibid., p. 632.
39. Ibid., p. 652.
40. Ibid., p. 653.
41. Ibid., p. 693.
42. Graham Wallas, *The Great Society*, Macmillan, 1914, p. 11.
43. Ibid., p. 276.
44. Ibid., p. 319.
45. Ibid., p. 368.
46. C. A. Ellwood, *Sociology in its Psychological Aspects*, Appleton, 1912, Ch. IX.
47. Ibid., p. 100.
48. Ibid., p. 117.
49. G. H. Mead, "Social Consciousness and the Consciousness of Meaning," *Psychological Bulletin*, VII: 405.
50. Ellwood, *Sociology in its Psychological Aspects*, p. 153. Cf. *Introduction to Social Psychology*,, p. 149.
51. Ellwood, *Sociology in its Psychological Aspects*, p. 138.
52. Ellwood. *Introduction to Social Psychology*, p. 149.
53. Ibid., p. 147.
54. Ibid., p. 151.
55. Ibid., p. 170.
56. Ellwood, *The Social Problem*, Macmillan, 1919, p. 2.
57. Ibid., p. 4.
58. E. C. Hayes, *Introduction to the Study of Sociology*, Appleton, 1915, p. 586.
59. Ibid.
60. Ibid., pp. 586 ff.
61. Ibid., pp. 664 ff.
62. Ibid., p. 669.
63. T. Veblen, *The Theory of the Leisure Class*, Macmillan, 1912, p. 31.
64. Ibid., p. 169.
65. Ibid., p. 68.
66. Ibid., p. 38.
67. Veblen, *The Instinct of Workmanship*, Macmillan, 1914, p. 349.
68. *The Theory of the Leisure Class*, p. 15.
69. Ibid., p. 17.
70. Publications of the American Sociological Society, Vol. XII, p. 2.
71. Ibid., p. 27.
72. Ibid., p. 59.
73. Ibid., p. 68.
74. Ibid., p. 3.
75. Ibid., p. 6.
76. Ibid., p. 10.

CHAPTER XXIV

1. For example, see C. R. Henderson, *Modern Methods of Charity*, Macmillan, 1904.
2. See Webb, *The Prevention of Destitution*, Longmans, Green, 1912.
3. See Devine, *Misery and its Causes*, Macmillan, 1913; also Devine, *The Principles of Relief*, Macmillan, 1904.
4. Also, see Amos G. Warner, *American Charities*, Crowell, 1919, 3rd. edit.
5. Henry George, *Progress and Poverty*, Doubleday, Page, 1916.
6. Lombroso, *Crime, Its Causes and Remedies*, Little, Brown, 1911.
7. Wines and Lane, *Punishment and Reformation*, Crowell, 1919, Ch. X.
8. T. M. Osborne, *Society and Prisons*, Yale University Press, 1916.
9. Burleigh and Bierstadt, *Punishment*, Holt, 1916.
10. See G. B. Mangold, *Problems of Child Welfare*, Macmillan, 1914.
11. A. W. Small, *Between Eras, From Capitalism to Democracy*, Inter-Collegiate Press, 1913.
12. See W. H. Beveridge, *Unemployment*, Longmans, Green, 1912.
13. George Elliott Howard, *A History of Matrimonial Institutions*, University of Chicago Press, 1904.
14. Edward Westermarck, *History of Human Marriage*, Macmillan, 1902.
15. A. W. Calhoun, *A Social History of the American Family*. Clark, 1917-1919.
16. Helen Bosanquet, *The Family*, Macmillan, 1915.
17. Willystine Goodsell, *A History of the Family as a Social and Educational Institution*, Macmillan, 1915.
18. Booker T. Washington, *Up from Slavery*, Doubleday, Page, 1901.
19. W. E. B. DuBois, *Darkwater*, Harcourt, Brace and Howe, 1920.
20. Peter Roberts, *The Problem of Americanization*, Macmillan, 1920.
21. J. K. Hart, *Community Organization*, Macmillan, 1920.
22. M. C. Elmer, *Technique of Social Surveys*, World Co., Lawrence, Kansas, 1917.

CHAPTER XXV

1. *Democracy and Education*, Macmillan, 1916, p. 6.
2. Ibid., p. 16.
3. Ibid., p. 19.
4. Ibid., pp. 26, 27.
5. Ibid., p. 41.
6. Cf. ibid., p. 416.

7. See M. V. O'Shea, *Social Development and Education,* Houghton Mifflin, 1909; David Snedden, *Sociological Determination of Objectives in Education,* Lippincott, 1921; W. R. Smith, *Educational Sociology,* Macmillan, 1917; Irving King, *Social Aspects of Education,* Macmillan, 1912; also King, *Education for Social Efficiency,* Appleton, 1913; F. R. Clow, *Principles of Sociology with Educational Applications,* Macmillan, 1920; G. H. Betts, *Social Principles of Education,* Scribner, 1913; S. T. Dutton, *Social Phases of Education,* Macmillan, 1907.
8. Smith, *Educational Sociology,* p. 669.
9. Snedden, *American Journal of Sociology,* 25:132 ff.; see also, Snedden, *Sociological Determination of Objectives in Education,* Lippincott, 1921, p. 15.
10. Snedden, *Sociological Determination of Objectives in Education,* p. 94.
11. Ibid., pp. 97, 107.
12. Ibid., pp. 109, 267.
13. Ibid., p. 228.

CHAPTER XXVI

1. Gladden, *Social Facts and Forces,* Putnam, 1897, p. 37.
2. Ibid., p. 152.
3. Ibid., p. 81.
4. Ibid.
5. Gladden, *Social Salvation,* Houghton Mifflin, 1902, p. 14.
6. Ibid., p. 7.
7. Ibid., p. 136; cf. Rauschenbusch, *A Theology for the Social Gospel,* Macmillan, 1918, pp. 8, 91.
8. Strong, *The New Era,* Baker and Taylor, 1893, p. 121.
9. Ibid., p. 124.
10. Ely, *Social Aspects of Christianity,* Crowell, 1889, p. 17.
11. Ibid., p. 65.
12. Ibid., p. 73.
13. See Peabody, *Jesus Christ and the Social Question,* Macmillan, 1900.
14. See Mathews, *The Social Teachings of Jesus,* Macmillan, 1897; *The Church and the Changing Order,* Macmillan, 1907; *The Gospel and the Modern Man,* Macmillan, 1910.
16. See Rauschenbusch, *Christianity and the Social Crisis,* Macmillan, 1913; *Christianizing the Social Order,* Macmillan, 1912; *A Theology for the Social Gospel,* Macmillan, 1918.
16. See Batten, *The Social Task of Christianity,* Revell, 1911.
17. See Ward, *The New Social Order,* Macmillan, 1919.
18. See H. A. Atkinson, *The Church and the People's Play,* Pilgrim Press, 1915.
19. See John Ryan, *Distributive Justice,* Macmillan, 1910; and *Social Reconstruction,* Macmillan, 1920.
20. See Charles Stelzle, *The Workingman and Social Problems,* Revell, 1903.
21. See *Religion in Social Action,* Dodd, Mead, 1913.
22. *Christianity and the Social Crisis,* supra, p. xiii.
23. Ibid., p. 145.
24. Ibid., p. 147.
25. Ibid., p. 149.
26. Ibid., pp. 201 ff.
27. Ibid., p. 33.
28. Ibid., p. 91.
29. Ibid., p. 74.
30. Ibid., p. 342.
31. Ibid., p. 386.
32. *Christianizing the Social Order,* p. 1.
33. Ibid., p. 2.
34. Ibid., p. 125.
35. Ibid., p. 320.
36. Ibid., pp. 113, 114.
37. Ibid., pp. 121, 122.
38. *A Theology for a Social Gospel,* pp. 4, 5, 48.
39. Ibid., p. 182.
40. "Social Reconstruction," Nat'l Catholic War Council, Washington, 1919, p. 22.
41. Loc. cit.
42. Ibid., p. 24.
43. Ward, *The New Social Order,* p. 74.
44. Ibid., p. 112.
45. Ibid., p. 114.
46. Ibid., p. 121.
47. Ibid., p. 125.
48. Loc. cit.
49. Ibid.
50. Ibid., p. 143.
51. Ibid., p. 159.
52. Ibid., p. 287.
53. Ibid., p. 363.
54. Ibid., p. 21.
55. Ibid., p. 25.
56. Coe, *Psychology of Religion,* University of Chicago Press, 1916, p. xiv.
57. Coe, *A Social Theory of Religious Education,* Scribner, 1917, pp. 59, 58.

CHAPTER XXVII

1. De Greef, *Introduction a la Sociologie,* Paris, 1911, T. I., pp. 189, 202.
2. *General Sociology,* pp. 718 ff.
3. Ibid., p. 442.

CHAPTER XXVIII

1. Blackmar and Gillin's *Outlines of Sociology* is one of the best textbooks in sociology.

INDEX